One of my continuing frustrations has been trying to persuade Bible-believing Christians that not only do they not need psychotherapy, it is in fact a religion destructive to the teachings of the Word of God. I grew up in the psychiatric community, my father having been a psychiatrist and a director of mental hospitals through all of my formative years. My understanding of psychotherapy, therefore, came by osmosis, as well as later by academic and personal study. From that exposure, and after becoming an evangelical Christian, it was easy to recognize the corruptive synthesis of psychology with biblical teachings which continues to flood the church. Convincing most evangelicals as to the harm of such an amalgamation regarding their life in Christ, however, too often seems like trying to hold back a riptide. Therefore, I welcome this book written by the Bazlers. From Lisa's education and background as a psychotherapist and Ryan's understanding of the Scriptures for ministering, *Psychology Debunked* presents "been there, done that" clinical experience in sharp contrast with the truth of how God would have us minister to one another in dealing with the problems of life. I would encourage anyone who thinks there is any hope whatsoever in psychotherapy to read this very informative book.

–T. A. McMahon
Executive Director of The Berean Call
and co-author of *The Seduction of Christianity*

I commend this excellent book to all believers in Jesus Christ— especially those who are involved in church leadership and those who desire to be greatly used of the Lord. The instruction on how to live a victorious and fruitful Christian life reflects the primary themes of Scripture: exaltation of Christ, confidence in His fully sufficient word and reliance upon the work of the Holy Spirit. The warnings about the worldly, self-centered wisdom of man take serious the biblical injunction to "contend earnestly for the faith which was once for all delivered to the saints" (Jude 3). May God greatly bless you, Ryan and Lisa, and every hungry disciple who reads your book!

–Bob Hoekstra
Director of Living in Christ Ministries
and author of *How to Counsel God's Way*

ACKNOWLEDGEMENTS

While God used many people along the way to help us navigate the journey of writing this book, we want to specifically thank:

Martin and Deidre Bobgan for your helpful books and materials on "psychoheresy." Your thorough understanding of the biblical care of souls has proven invaluable.

David Kopp for your guidance and encouragement during the initial writing stages. Thank you for believing that God could use us.

T.A. McMahon for your extensive and painstaking editing to ensure biblical accuracy. We admire your passion for biblical truth.

Dr. Allen Quain and the rest of the Creation House book team for your hard work, patience and servant attitude in bringing this book to fruition. May God bless all of you for taking a biblical stand on this controversial issue.

Jesus, our Wonderful Counselor and Helper, for calling us to write this book and giving us the ability to do it.

PSYCHOLOGY DEBUNKED

Lisa & Ryan Bazler

CREATION
HOUSE
PRESS

PSYCHOLOGY DEBUNKED
by Lisa and Ryan Bazler
Published by Creation House Press
A part of Strang Communications Company
600 Rinehart Road
Lake Mary, Florida 32746
www.creationhouse.com

Unless otherwise noted, all Scripture quotations are from the Holy Bible, New International Version. Copyright © 1973, 1978, 1984, International Bible Society. Used by permission.

Scripture quotations marked NKJV are from the New King James Version of the Bible. Copyright © 1979, 1980, 1982 by Thomas Nelson, Inc., publishers. Used by permission.

Case examples are composites of a number of clients who share similar issues and are protected with name and information changes to remain confidential (other than cases that are a matter of public record). Any similarity between the names and stories of individuals in this book and individuals known to readers is coincidental and not intentioned.

Readers are advised to consult their own doctors or qualified health professionals regarding the treatment of their medical problems. Neither the publisher nor the author takes any responsibility for any possible consequences to any person reading or following the information in this book. If readers are taking prescription medications, they should consult with their physicians and not take themselves off of medicines without the proper supervision of a physician.

Cover design by Terry Clifton

Library of Congress Catalog Card Number: 2002103144
International Standard Book Number: 0-88419-886-3

02 03 04 05 — 87654321
Printed in the United States of America

CONTENTS

Foreword vi
Introduction vii

PART I
CAN PSYCHOLOGY HELP YOU?

1. Meet Karen and Keith. 1
2. Can You Trust Psychology As a Science? 9
3. Does Psychology Deliver on Its Promises? 19
4. Answering the *Why* of Life 29

PART II
PSYCHOLOGY AND CHRISTIANITY: WHAT'S THE DIFFERENCE?

5. Two Opposing Faiths. 43
6. Who Is at Fault? 55
7. Which Figurehead Do You Follow? 63
8. Where Is Your Focus? 71

PART III
PSYCHOLOGY IN THE CHURCH

9. My Disorder Made Me Do It 89
10. Should I Take Psychiatric Medication? 101
11. What About "Christian" Psychology? 119
12. A Royal Priesthood 141
13. Choose This Day Whom You Will Serve 151

PART IV
THE OVERCOMING LIFE

14. Do You Meet the Qualifications of the
    Overcoming Life? 157
15. Overcoming Your Sinful Nature 171
16. Overcoming the World. 179
17. Overcoming Your Circumstances 187
18. Overcoming Satan. 195
19. Suffering With a Purpose 205
20. Treatment That Works! 219
21. Victory in Jesus 241

Notes 251

FOREWORD

Lisa and Ryan Bazler, the authors of *Psychology Debunked*, have done a bold and courageous thing—they have taken on the entire field of modern psychology! In so doing, they have made a tremendous contribution to the world in general and to the Christian community in particular. Armed with biblical truth, they strip bare the claims of psychology, exposing harmful deceptions and empty promises. With careful research and documentation, they reveal that the theories and answers offered by psychology are actually the antithesis of God's Word. And they clarify why psychology and the Bible are totally incompatible:

- Psychology is man centered; the Bible is God centered.
- Psychology says that man is a victim; the Bible says that man is a sinner.
- Psychology teaches that man is discontent because of his environment; the Bible teaches that man is discontent because of his rebellion against God.
- Psychology says that man's problems can be cured through therapy; the Bible says that man's problems can only be cured through "repentance toward God and faith toward our Lord Jesus Christ" (Acts 20:21, NKJV).

The Bazlers demonstrate that there is no common ground between the practice of secular or Christian psychology and the practice of biblical principles. In short, they debunk the claims of modern psychology and point readers to the only true source for overcoming life—the person of Jesus Christ.

–Dr. Max F. Morris
Inventor of the Kwickscan™
Reading System and Kwickscan Bible™

INTRODUCTION

Who, me? Live an overcoming life? Although it sounds unthinkable, living an overcoming life that pleases God and satisfies your soul lies well within your reach. With God's power working in and through you, your search for answers from therapists, psychiatrists, support groups and twelve-step programs can finally end. Whether you have already received this type of help or are still considering it, this book will show you a more effective way to understand and treat the problems of living that we all experience.

I do not promise the next breakthrough in psychology or self-help, I do not promise you will feel better about yourself, and I do not promise a life free of problems and pain. I do promise, however, a more abundant, purposeful, fulfilling life gained not by our power, nor by our might, but by God's Spirit. I promise the power of God to help you overcome and find victory in every area of your life. I promise a personal God who wants to walk and talk with you in every moment of every day. By the end of this book, you will no longer see God as an impersonal force, a Sunday morning ritual or an impractical belief system—you will see Him as your all in all, the One in whom you live and move and have your being. Whether you are a long-time Christian, a new Christian or just searching for meaning and fulfillment in your life, reading and living this book will reveal a God who wants to fill your sails with power, comfort you in your storms and direct you into the peaceful harbors where He dwells.

SEARCHING FOR A BETTER WAY?

Perhaps you opened this book because you have visited a therapist or psychiatrist and didn't get what you expected. You have been undergoing therapy; maybe you have been diagnosed with a disorder and possibly have even taken medication, but your problems seem just as bad or even worse than when you first began. This book will open your spiritual eyes to God's accurate diagnoses and heavenly prescription for you—a prescription no therapist or psychiatrist can give. This prescription will improve your relationship with God, your relationship with others and ultimately your personal contentment.

If you've never visited a therapist or psychiatrist, you may fall into a much larger category of the millions of people suffering from mental-emotional-behavioral problems who go unreported. Perhaps you experience emotional stress or anxiety; family conflict or tension; unexplained fatigue; difficulty coping with changes; unusual eating patterns; feelings of loneliness, isolation, depression or moodiness; sexual disturbances; child behavior problems; divorce or separation; fear, anger or guilt; or grief or emotional pain.[1] You may wonder, "Do I need to get help from a therapist, psychiatrist, support group, or twelve-step program for my problem?" This book will help you answer that question.

On the other hand, you may have already ruled out these options completely, but you wish to learn how to handle your problems and live your life in a biblical and practical way. This book will help you understand the nature and treatment of your problems in light of God's Word *alone*. In a few words, this book is a clearly written guidebook for anyone who wants to live an overcoming life . . . without psychology.

Losing My Faith in Psychology

Ironically, I used to be a therapist myself. Ever since my childhood, I've always wanted to help people in some capacity. That childhood dream became my motivation to enter the field of psychology. After earning a bachelor's degree in psychology, I hoped to make a real difference in people's lives. But little did I know of the harsh realities that awaited me.

Working as a youth care worker in a youth shelter, I noticed no changes in the kids receiving psychotherapy from other therapists. Later I worked in hospital psychiatric wards as a mental health worker while earning my master's degree in counseling psychology. Sadly, the vast majority of patients undergoing psychiatric treatment in these hospitals never experienced improvement in the years that I knew them. After completing graduate school, I finally had an opportunity to make a difference as a marriage and family therapist intern by providing psychotherapy at two counseling centers. I thought I could do what the other therapists couldn't. But I soon realized the theories and treatments that didn't work for other therapists didn't work for me either. My clients still struggled with the same problems they had at the first session. Needless to say, I started to lose my faith in the field of psychology.

A THERAPIST TRANSFORMED

Enter Ryan, the man who would become my future husband. After dating for five months, Ryan and I began thinking that there just had to be more to life—more than career, more than money, more than pleasure. We experienced an emptiness in our hearts and a lonely searching that would not cease. We couldn't understand why we felt this way. At this point Ryan brought up the most ludicrous thing I had ever heard. He said to me, "I think we need to read the Bible." Neither one of us had ever talked about God before this.

I replied in disbelief, "Go ahead, but I don't see how that's going to help." So he dug out a Bible from the garage that someone had given him as a gift, and we started reading the Gospel of Matthew in the New Testament. For the next month we read the Bible together almost every night.

Then on November 27, 1995, God made Himself real to us. We read a pamphlet together that we were using as a Bible bookmark titled *Would You Like to Know God Personally?* At the end of the pamphlet Ryan looked at me and asked me if I wanted to pray a prayer along with him to receive God's forgiveness through Jesus Christ, and I said yes. That night, in Ryan's bedroom, we got down on our knees, took hold of each other's hands, bowed our heads and prayed the prayer. Immediately we experienced a change—a feeling of peace and cleansing—and began to weep in each other's arms in the wonder of God's perfect love. That day was the happiest day of my life. We knew even then that our lives had been completely changed by the grace and mercy of God. No church, no preacher, no therapist—just the Word of God and the Holy Spirit transforming our hearts.

We had so much excitement about our new lives in Christ that we shared our experience with everyone we knew. To our surprise, people weren't happy for us; some even became annoyed with us. But we didn't care. We had a joy that no one could touch. Life as new Christians proved difficult, though, as we experienced some of the most traumatic events of our lives. But the power of God inside of us helped us overcome them all. God gave us an inner joy even in the midst of our painful trials. God had made Himself very real in our lives.

GOD'S PURPOSE AND MINE

God's purpose began to unfold for me as He gently dealt with my career. At this point I had accumulated over three thousand hours of work experience as a psychotherapist in hospitals, skilled nursing facilities, secular and Christian private practices, group homes and outpatient services—on top of graduate and undergraduate degrees in psychology. But God had a purpose different from my own. He opened my eyes to the truth as I began to see the true nature of psychology. God's Spirit began working in my heart, and I just knew psychology wasn't the way to live. As I continued to read the Bible, I would find passages of Scripture that would say the exact opposite of what a therapist would say. I began to notice that the psychotherapeutic methods I used in therapy sessions contradicted the teachings of Scripture.

I found myself, however, resisting God's will on this issue because I had such a hard time giving it all up. "After all, look at how hard I worked! I even put myself through school! What a waste of effort and money that would be!" I would say to God. While I worried about my career, He worried about my eternity. I knew in my heart that psychology was wrong, but I began to justify it by disguising it in Christian terms. "I will just be a 'Christian psychotherapist,'" I thought. So I got a job as an intern psychotherapist at a Christian counseling center, thinking it would get better...but it didn't. Unbelievably, I never used the Bible, or even the word *God* for that matter, in therapy sessions. I merely performed secular psychotherapy with a Christian label. Even at this Christian counseling center, most of our clients were not Christians and therefore did not request biblical counseling. It seemed Christian psychology wasn't the answer either.

If going against God's Word and feeling no peace inside my heart weren't enough to drive me to leave the field of psychology, God even put two godly women in my path during that time on two separate occasions who asked me how I would go about being a Christian psychotherapist. Needless to say, neither of them accepted the answers I gave them. No matter what those women said, I still wanted my way over God's way. I couldn't understand why other Christian psychotherapists had no concerns with the inconsistencies of Christian psychology. After all, these Christian psychotherapists had been Christians for many years. Was I missing something?

I finally heeded the voice of God after hearing a pastor on my car radio talk about sitting on the fence, so to speak. He said, "If you need to give in to the things of this world and do a little of this or a little of that in order to obtain what you're striving for, it isn't right. There is no gray area with God. It's as clear as black and white." I felt as if God spoke directly to me. I could no longer resist His loving nudges. Now I knew what I had to do! I had to leave my professional counseling career for good.

Of course, I received a lot of opposition and alternative suggestions from others after making this drastic decision. Many suggested I open a purely biblical Christian counseling practice, without any psychological influence. After some consideration, I realized I could not biblically or realistically pursue this alternative. Even if I opened my own Christian counseling center using only the Bible, I would still have to run the center like a business and charge hurting people for spiritual help that should be free (more about this later in the book). With my own Christian practice, I would still have to earn continuing education units and attend workshops that teach the anti-Christian theories of psychology to remain licensed. Even worse, the law would require me to use psychological theories and treatments for clients who prefer psychology to the Bible. Thus with a purely biblical practice, I would still live a compromised Christian life. I could no longer ignore God's Word, God's Spirit and God's people crying out in unison, "You are living a lie!" So I left the field of psychology, and I haven't looked back since.

EVERYTHING WE NEED FOR LIFE

Psychology has infiltrated our American culture and the Christian church with its false theories and false treatments of the problems of man. With its self-focused, pleasure-seeking mentality, psychology cheats countless Christians out of the overcoming life that God desires for them. I believe that God wants to use my "before-and-after" experiences in the psychology field to reveal His unchanging truth about the overcoming life to you. I firmly believe that God can make Himself real in *your* life. This book centers around the idea that God—not psychology—has given us *everything* we need for life just as the apostle Peter said in 2 Peter 1:3:

> *His divine power has given us everything we need for life and godliness through our knowledge of him who called us by his own glory and goodness.*

Are you ready to overcome?

PART I

CAN PSYCHOLOGY HELP YOU?

Can psychology help you? Many of us have asked this question at one time or another in this therapeutic, healing age in which we live. The psychology industry has experienced phenomenal growth over the past half century, with more than 40,000 psychiatrists, 65,000 family therapists, 125,000 psychologists, 10,000 psychoanalysts, and 150,000 social workers in the United States alone.[1] The number of psychologists in America has almost doubled just in the last five years. It seems that the more people there are in the psychology field, the more people need to see them. What lies behind this modern-day phenomenon called psychology? In the following chapters we will take a brief look at psychology's basic theories and beliefs, its claim as a science and its effectiveness in solving personal problems.

Before we begin, a few terms I use in this book deserve clarification:

- *Psychology* refers to the overall study of the soul and mind.
- *Psychotherapy* refers to the practice of conversation between counselor and client regarding the client's problems.
- *Psychiatry* refers to the medical practice of prescribing medication to clients.
- A *psychiatrist* refers to a medical doctor who prescribes medication.
- A *psychologist* refers to a doctorate-level professional who performs client testing and psychotherapy.
- A *psychotherapist* refers to a professional with a master's degree who performs psychotherapy (I write from the perspective of the psychotherapist).
- A *therapist* refers in a general sense to either a psychologist or a psychotherapist.

Now let's take a peek into the lives of Karen and Keith, a frustrated couple seeking help from a therapist.

CHAPTER 1

MEET
KAREN AND
KEITH

Therapist: Tell me about the last fight you had.

Karen: Well, I spent all afternoon last Sunday preparing a full-course meal for Keith's parents. Keith sat on the couch watching football while I slaved over the stove and his parents talked my ear off. Keith's mom watched my every move. She was always quick to point out faults in my cooking techniques. When she wasn't criticizing my cooking, she would wait until she thought I wasn't looking, and then wipe her finger across the top of every conceivable cabinet and countertop she could find. Then, if that wasn't enough to push me over the edge, Keith's dad reprimanded me for taking away the kids' dessert when they wouldn't eat their dinner.

Keith: *[To Karen]* C'mon, Karen, they were just being kids!

Karen: *[To Keith]* Kids need discipline, and I don't appreciate your parents telling me how to raise my kids!

Therapist: How does that make you feel, Karen?

Karen: I am sick and tired of Keith's parents never accepting me and never treating me with respect. I'll never be good enough for them.

Keith: *[To Karen]* How can you be good enough when you never see them? It took two years for you to finally have them over for dinner. But you can see your parents every weekend.

Therapist: Tell me more about that, Keith.

Keith: She's never around! I work all week to put food on the table, and when the weekend comes I expect some quality time together. But off she goes with the two kids to grandma's house, to "shop 'til they drop" as they always say. Then the credit card bills come rolling in, and who has to pay them? Me! In fact, we're maxed out on nothing short of nine credit cards right now. I see her bills more than I see her. And it's not like the bills are for things we need. No, she always has to have the latest everything—clothes, shoes, jewelry—and it piles up in the closet. Then she buys our kids everything they ask for. But when it comes to me, it's socks and underwear, socks and underwear.

Therapist: *[After a long, pensive pause]* I can see that both of you are feeling neglected. You feel that the other doesn't care about your needs and doesn't think you're important. You want your needs to be taken seriously, and you want to be viewed as valuable. The resentment and hurt you are feeling are nothing new for either of you. Keith, did you ever feel neglected as a child?

Keith: *[Awkwardly]* Uh, I don't remember my childhood too well.

Therapist: Did your parents buy you nice things as a child?

Keith: *[Resentfully]* Nope, just the necessities.

Therapist: OK, can you remember times when your parents took time out to spend with you, to play a game or go to the park? Did they ever let you know how special and important you were to them?

2

Keith: No, not really. They were pretty busy.

Therapist: Keith, you seem to have had a self-sufficient childhood. Did your parents have anything to do with this?

Keith: Well, my dad left my mom when I was nine years old, and my mom had to raise the four of us alone.

Therapist: How did she handle that?

Keith: She had to go to work full time to make ends meet, but I think she handled it well. She didn't have much time to spend with us—she was always working, cooking or cleaning. So the four of us entertained ourselves, and it worked out all right, I guess.

Therapist: It sounds like your mother needed you to be in the background, and you respected that need.

Keith: *[Solemnly]* Yeah, that's probably true.

Therapist: Keith, it sounds like you've reached a point in your life when you just won't be in the background anymore. You want more attention, more quality time. I think that when you see Karen spending all her time with her mother, you get very frustrated—especially when you work so hard to provide for her. You've decided that it's time to stop putting your own needs aside in order to take care of others.

Keith: I'd agree with that.

Karen: I know I spend a lot of time with my mom, but *[to Keith]* at least she accepts me as I am—unlike your parents.

Therapist: Karen, does it make you happy to feel accepted?

Karen: Of course!

Therapist: I wonder if there are other people in your life who don't accept you the way your mother does. Can you think of anyone close to you who, for example, puts you down or doesn't praise you frequently?

Karen: Sure, my husband and my kids. They always seem to whine and complain. I feel very unappreciated in my home.

Therapist: OK, let's go with that...

Karen: Well, I'm always trying to please them, but they never seem to want to please me. Some days I feel like a complete failure as a wife and a mom—especially when Keith's parents visit. I just don't measure up with any of them.

Therapist: I understand. It sounds like Keith and your kids are simply not fulfilling your need for greater self-esteem and value. So, you turn to your mother to restore your self-worth. She makes you feel valuable. Would you say this is true?

Karen: Yes, I would.

Every day, marriage problems like those between Karen and Keith echo in therapist offices throughout the country. The United States of America boasts the most technically advanced and economically prosperous nation in recorded history. From the outside looking in, you would think that Americans would be the happiest, most content people on earth. But a closer look reveals a surprisingly different story. Stress, domestic violence, child abuse, divorce, violent crimes and alcohol and drug abuse represent just a sampling of the problems facing Americans. Why is the most prosperous nation on earth also the most miserable?

The field of psychology has risen to the occasion to give us the answers to our chronic misery. Ever since psychology's birth in the 1850s, Americans have flocked to the therapists with questions like, "Why am I unhappy?" "How can I improve my life?" We have gone from 14 percent of the U.S. population who had ever received psychological services in the early 1960s to an estimated *80 percent* of the population at the start of the twenty-first century.[1] Each year in America more than 15 percent of adults and 21 percent of children visit mental health professionals.[2] Americans pay more than $17 billion annually for psychological therapies,[3] contributing to a staggering $69 billion mental health industry growing at an annual rate of 7 percent.[4] Americans can't seem to get enough of psychology.

PICK A THEORY

Much of psychology's popularity stems from its promises of fulfillment and meaning made by therapists proffering the latest theories and treatments. Therapists use these theories to attempt to explain human nature—why people act, think and feel the way they do—

in order to treat psychological problems. Although more than four hundred kinds of psychotherapy exist today,[5] you could group them into four basic categories for simplicity's sake. If you were to walk into a therapist's office and explain your problems, the therapist would treat you based on one or more of these four categories that attempt to explain human nature:

Psychoanalytic theories

You are determined by your instinctual drives and your unconscious, formed early in life; you can overcome your problems with a therapist to help you discover and repair your unconscious (developed by Freud and others).

Behavioristic theories

You are determined by your biology, genetics and environment; you can overcome your problems with a therapist to help you work through and heal from your past experiences (developed by Watson, Skinner and others).

Humanistic theories

You can overcome your problems yourself by self-effort (developed by Allport, Maslow, Rogers and others).

Transpersonal theories

You can overcome your problems yourself by faith in your inner spirituality and goodness (developed by Maslow, Fromm, May, Rogers and others).

PSYCHOLOGY'S MAJOR BELIEFS

These four categories of theories can be summarized into three major beliefs that permeate most psychological thinking:

- People are basically good, and through extensive introspection and self-effort they can improve themselves without God in order to achieve more pleasure in life.
- Our current problems result from environments and people from the past who have negatively influenced our inherently good unconscious, which controls our present behavior; we are victims of our past.

- To fix our current problems, we must gain insight into our unconscious to reveal and deal with past hurts using a trained therapist as our helper.

In other words, psychology tells me that I experience problems in my life because of past experiences in my environment that determine how I live my life in the here and now. I should not blame myself for my problems, for I am inherently a good person. To overcome my problems I must see a therapist who uses techniques to help me analyze my unconscious and my past. Through extensive self-analysis with a therapist and much self-effort, I can recover from my problems, regain my happiness and experience pleasure once again.

A typical therapist like the one treating Karen and Keith will apply these three psychological beliefs to questions clients ask about their problems of living.

Client: Why am I unhappy?

Therapist: You are unhappy because of past environments or people who have hurt you in some way. You are a victim of your past.

Client: What is wrong with me?

Therapist: Your unconscious is influencing your present behavior without your knowledge or control.

Client: How can I solve my problems and be happier?

Therapist: You've come to the right place. I can help you analyze yourself and your past, and help you heal and be happier.[6]

Although therapists and their clients rarely express these questions and answers directly, these underlying themes run throughout most therapy sessions.

THERAPY FOR ALL

Therapists view themselves as the experts on who we are and how we should live life. From the therapist's viewpoint, every occurrence in life could use a good dose of psychotherapy:

- Birth
- Child development

- Teenage years
- Young adulthood
- Marriage
- Children
- Career
- Sex
- Midlife crisis
- Job loss
- Divorce
- Grief
- Emotional stress
- Fear
- Anger
- Guilt
- Depression
- Fatigue
- Injuries
- Obesity
- Eating disorders
- Alcohol and drug use
- Elderly care
- Death and dying

Therapists have countless theories, diagnoses and treatments ranging from the normal to the bizarre. Some of the most humorous treatments include:

- Certified Shamanic counseling
- Call-in TV counseling
- Licensed volunteer therapy dogs
- Llama therapy
- Phone counseling for hotel guests
- Commuting stress intervention
- Horticultural therapy
- Juror stress therapy
- Compassion fatigue therapy
- Genetic sexual attraction therapy
- Tickle healing
- Internet chat therapy
- Personal cognitive therapy
- Art therapy
- Aromatherapy
- Recovery network TV
- Legal abuse therapy[7]

As a culture, we view the therapist as a kind of all-knowing deity that we consult to understand and deal with the unseen forces in our souls. Although modern psychology has existed for just one hundred fifty years, it has had a profound impact on our Western culture and the Christian church. While other developed nations of the world live seemingly normal lives without psychology—China, Israel and Korea have fewer psychological professionals than America has sex and art therapists[8]—Americans incessantly look to psychology for good feelings and happiness. Under the guise of science, psychology promises to answer the big questions of life: "Who am I?" "Why am I here?" "How can I achieve fulfillment?" But has this lucrative industry proven its scientific claims, and has it delivered on its lofty promises?

CHAPTER 2

CAN YOU TRUST PSYCHOLOGY AS A SCIENCE?

The way our culture has embraced the principles and practices of psychology, you would think psychology was the biggest scientific discovery since the light bulb. But can we trust the claims of many that psychology is a science as credible as any other? If psychology is in fact a science, then we can trust its theories and treatments just as we trust that when we hit the switch, the light turns on. But if psychology is less than a science, we must reconsider entrusting our problems to the pundits of this field. Let's take a closer look at what lies behind the powerful image of psychology to test the accuracy of the public's perception of psychology as science.

SCIENCE OR SUBJECTIVITY?

What criteria would classify psychology as an objective science and not a subjective art? To consider psychology an objective science, we must verify psychology's assumptions, observations, theories, diagnoses, treatments and outcomes by empirical (measurable) evidence. These rules would apply to any scientific discipline, from biology to engineering to medicine. Let's see if we can classify medicine as a science, where a woman sees a doctor because she hurt her ankle hiking. Here is the step-by-step process the doctor would take:

1. **Assumption:** First the doctor makes certain objective, factual assumptions about the patient, such as age and weight.
2. **Observation:** Then the doctor looks for symptoms. The doctor asks the patient a series of questions like, "How did you injure it?" "How long has it been since you've injured it?" "Where does it hurt?" "Can you walk?"
3. **Theory:** Based on these objective, measurable answers, the doctor forms the theory that the patient may have a broken ankle.
4. **Diagnosis:** After taking X-rays and analyzing the film, the doctor confirms that the patient does in fact have a broken ankle.
5. **Treatment:** The doctor then treats the injury by wrapping a cast around the foot, ankle and calf because this technique has been proven effective in healing the ankle quickly in other patients.
6. **Outcome:** The doctor encourages the patient that other patients with similar injuries have healed completely in six to eight weeks, and she should expect a similar outcome.

Since we can verify the assumption, observation, theory, diagnosis, treatment and outcome by empirical evidence, we can consider medicine (at least medicine dealing with broken ankles) a scientific discipline.

Now let's apply this scientific approach to psychology to see if we can classify psychology as a science. A woman sees a therapist because she continually feels anxious, which affects her work and family life. Let's follow the step-by-step process the therapist would take:

1. **Assumption:** First, the therapist makes certain subjective assumptions about the client, such as demeanor and overall appearance.
2. **Observation:** Then the therapist looks for symptoms. The therapist asks the client a series of questions like, "When do you become anxious?" "Did your parents expect a lot from you when you were younger?" "Was there ever abuse in your home?" "How did your teachers treat you?"

3. **Theory**: Based on these subjective, qualitative answers, the therapist forms the theory that the client may have an anxiety disorder.
4. **Diagnosis**: After discussing the past with the client and asking subjective, qualitative questions that would uncover reasons for anxiety, the therapist confirms that the client does in fact have an anxiety disorder.
5. **Treatment**: The therapist then refers the client to a psychiatrist, who then treats the disorder by prescribing anti-anxiety medication, even though this technique has not always proven reliable in curbing anxiety in other clients.
6. **Outcome**: The psychiatrist encourages the client to continue taking the medication, even if anxiety symptoms persist or the client experiences harmful side effects, regardless of the fact that other clients with similar disorders have been permanently damaged by this medication.

Since we *cannot* verify the assumption, observation, theory, diagnosis, treatment and outcome by empirical evidence, we *cannot* consider psychology (at least psychology dealing with disorders that have not been medically proven) a scientific discipline. In this example the therapist and psychiatrist could not objectively measure and analyze the causes and cures of anxiety with statistical repeatability as the doctor and patient could measure and analyze the causes and cures of a broken ankle.

Psychology amounts to subjectively interpreting the reasons behind behaviors and subjectively developing ways to change these behaviors. Since the theories of psychology have never been proven true by objective empirical evidence, we cannot consider psychology a science. Psychologist Robert Rosenthal says, "There is no compelling evidence to convince us that we do understand human behavior very well."[1]

SHIFTING SAND

We can also consider a discipline a true science when the body of knowledge upon which it rests never changes and only builds upon

11

itself with time. For example, two plus two will always equal four. In a few years we won't see a mathematician stand up and say, "I've discovered a new mathematical theory! Two plus two now equals five." That would be absurd! The fact that two plus two equals four has been tested and proven over and over again. That fact forms the basis of higher mathematical formulas. In a true science, scientists suggest, test and prove theories with predictable and measurable results. These theories form a body of knowledge that grows with time to form a knowledge base.

Psychology, however, does not contain a knowledge base that has remained unchanged over time. The theories and treatments of psychology change continuously with the times. Like shifting sand, psychology provides a weak foundation on which to build a body of knowledge. Psychology icons like Freud, Jung, Adler, Maslow, Fromm, Rogers, Ellis, Glasser, Harris, Janov, Watson, Skinner, Allport and May have over the years created a hodgepodge of conflicting theories and therapies. The psychology field continues to grow, and theories and treatments continue to multiply and contradict each other.

Psychological theories are quickly replaced by the next "theoretical breakthrough" once therapists realize their ineffectiveness in everyday practice. Since 1889 when the term *psychotherapy* became known, countless psychological theories have been publicized, rallied behind and used in treatment, with not one—yes, not one—theory gaining universal acceptance and withstanding the test of time in the psychology field.[2] You could fill bookshelves with once-promising psychological treatments that have now become virtually obsolete. True science knows no bounds of time and culture; it transcends them.

Psychological theories resemble fad diets: People jump on the bandwagon of the latest diet plan, try it for awhile with little success and then quit, hoping the next one will work better. With hundreds of fad diets in the past, should not one have worked by now? Since past fad diets have not delivered on their promises, we can safely assume future ones will give similar, sub-standard results. The same applies to

12

psychological theories—over-promised and under-delivered.

GUT TREATMENTS

It may surprise you that the treatment you receive from a typical therapist comes from the gut, grounded in intuition rather than science. Many therapists now adopt a "melting pot" approach in treating their clients, using whatever theory seems right at the time and even throwing in some of their own ad hoc techniques. Some therapists adhering to a certain theoretical persuasion even seek personal help from other therapists who use completely opposing theories![3]

As you can imagine, a licensed, professional therapist taking a "what feels right" approach in treating the client's problems leaves much to chance. No longer does the therapist progress toward a proven, methodical solution. Instead, the therapist must fill the time with questions about the client's life, empathetic responses and an occasional comment, all the while hoping their client will improve. I can relate to a group of professional therapists who painted this beautifully honest picture of the mind-set of a typical therapist over his or her career:

> We recall when we ourselves were students. We kept waiting to be admitted to that inner circle where the secrets of the profession would be laid bare. We floundered through sessions with clients, but we were certain that sooner or later we would learn important tricks of the trade that would decrease the frequency of such occurrences. It was hard to imagine that seasoned professionals could be experiencing as much uncertainty as we were.
>
> Yet each course we took seemed to survey much but provide few operational details. We held onto whatever specifics we could get our hands on, becoming overly infatuated with approaches that seemed to offer concrete techniques. When we saw clients, we used a number of ploys to cover our lack of confidence in our role. For example, we frequently lapsed into a non-directive "reflective" mode, not because we were Rogerians, but because we were not sure what to say next to the client. "Reflecting" was an easy out. For similar reasons, we sometimes affected a posture of psychoanalytic silence, even though we had

no particular affinity for analytic tenets. Most of all we asked questions. We relentlessly explored the history of the client's symptoms and the background of the problem: "When did you first notice that?" "Is it the same when you are at work?" And so on. Of course, such information can have legitimate treatment planning uses, but for us these question-and-answer series were mainly a stall. They successfully postponed that awful moment of truth when actual treatment would need to begin.

We found that clients were usually cooperative with these efforts, at least at first. They assumed that information-gathering was a necessary preliminary to the start of treatment and appreciated the sense of "being understood" that our attempts at reflection provided. They rarely realized at the outset that we had little idea what was coming next or where the therapy was headed. As novice therapists, we kept our "safe" procedures going as long as humanly possible.

When clients appeared to be demanding more immediate or concrete help than we had been offering, we tended to launch into lecturettes on the principles of good living. We doled out tidbits of practical advice on this subject or that. The advice we gave was usually invented on the spot, derived loosely from a combination of common sense and personal experience, having little relation to theoretical postulates, professional training, or scientifically validated information. We were plagued by the nagging concern that "real therapists" don't do this. Indeed, we had been warned by supervisors to scrupulously avoid lecturing or advising. We were also vaguely aware that the advice we gave was not necessarily different from what the client had already heard a million times before from friends and relatives. Nevertheless, the desperation to offer something substantive induced us to traffic in cheap homilies and to invent instant prescriptions for problem solving. Again, the clients were pretty good sports about all this. They generally listened appreciatively to what we had to offer, nodding in agreement from time to time and even promising to try out our suggestions. Naturally, they didn't always do what they had promised.

In later years, we discovered to our surprise that students were

14

not the only ones experiencing distress about playing the role of therapist. Even seasoned therapists report finding themselves in an agonizingly ambiguous role, feeling somehow obliged to offer solutions they do not think they possess. We have noted that in these circumstances such professionals tend to use exactly the same time-filling and structuring devices that we thought we had invented as students, but with a degree of polish and panache we would have envied.

Evidently, history repeats itself. Today's students report the same role confusions we endured, and they continue to grasp at straws. Trainees we have spoken to confess that, despite extensive classroom training, they still feel at a loss when confronted with a live client. Moreover, practicum and internship supervisors often fail to provide them with the basic "how-to" information they feel they need. Supervisors often act as if these basics are simply too obvious to discuss. However, the central tenets of practice are never obvious to trainees, and their befuddlement about how they are supposed to "cure" anyone by just talking to them may last for years. They, too, feel as if there is a conspiracy of silence about the fundamental underpinnings of psychotherapeutic practice.[4]

Psychology's "conspiracy of silence" results from the absence of any established knowledge base in the field. Ten different therapists will diagnose and treat one problem ten different ways. Therapists base your treatment on their view of reality instead of on a proven psychological theory. Theories that are short-lived, conflicting and for the most part ignored add up to bad science.

THE WHAT VS. THE WHY AND THE HOW

Although we sometimes see truth in a psychological observation, this does not make psychology a science. We can see many truths in the portions of psychology that deal with observable behaviors such as anger and grief displayed in different situations. These behavioral truths are scientific in that we can test and observe these behaviors with repeatable accuracy. If someone in the family dies, you grieve. If someone steals your purse, you get angry. It doesn't take a trained therapist to identify these "what" behaviors. The problem arises when therapists attempt to peer into the heart, explain the motivations or the "why" of behaviors, and then claim to know the "how" of treating these behaviors with psychological treatments. The psychology field has failed to produce any real evidence that their theories (the why) and treatments (the how) of their observations (the what) are scientifically sound.

THE HIDDEN TRUTH

Other professionals in the psychology field now admit that we cannot view psychology as a hard science based on facts, but as an art form defined and practiced as the therapist sees fit. After studying the theory and practice of psychology and publishing a seven-volume work called *Psychology: A Study of a Science*, Dr. Sigmund Koch from the American Psychological Association (APA) concluded, "I think it by this time utterly and finally clear that *psychology cannot be a coherent science*..."[5] In 1985, over seven thousand psychology professionals attended a convention billed as "the Woodstock of psychotherapy." At the convention, "criticisms by the speakers themselves included reports that most of the present distinct schools of psychotherapy are doomed to fizzle, that psychiatry is not a science, and that nothing new in human relations has surfaced from a century of psychotherapy."[6]

R. Christopher Barden, a psychologist, lawyer and president of the National Association for Consumer Protection in Mental Health Practices, says, "It is indeed shocking that many, if not most forms of psychotherapy currently offered to consumers are not supported by credible scientific evidence... Too many Americans do not realize that much of the mental health industry is little more than a national consumer fraud."[7] As if these aren't heavy enough words, in 1984, the former president of the Association for Humanistic Psychology, Dr. Lawrence LeShan, boldly admitted, "Psychotherapy may be known in the future as the greatest hoax of the twentieth century."[8]

However, as other psychology professionals join me in admitting psychology's unscientific ways, the American public in general still

16

believes the lies of psychology. Psychological "experts" coax us into believing their so-called insight expressed in professional-sounding terminology. From the professional therapist to the church psychologist to the talk-show host, everyone is an expert when it comes to human behavior, even though these "expert" opinions consist of little research, manipulated data and special interest hype.

Then why isn't the truth being told about the unscientific, go-with-your-gut nature of the psychology field? Much of it has to do with the sheer number of people this profession employs. The multibillion-dollar psychology industry would crumble if the truth were told. Psychology also has an attractive component for the client, in that psychology provides excuses and labels for behavior—an appropriate service for our "everybody's-a-victim" culture.

Despite this age of medical discovery in which we live, you cannot trust psychology as a science. Therapists have admitted it's a fraud and a hoax. They perform psychotherapy by going with their gut. In fact, any therapist can develop a theory (no matter how unscientific and weird it might sound), market it as their specialty and attract unsuspecting clients. It's done all the time. Therapists require no elite qualifications to develop a new theory. No standards organization exists to test the theory's validity. Instead, innocent clients expecting proven theories from professional therapists become pawns in the therapist's quest to make a name and a career out of people's problems.

STUDY OF THE SOUL

The psychology industry has failed to realize that no person can measure the soul and mind and classify them into categories. Science cannot study individuality. God made each person unique. Any attempt at explaining and treating mental, emotional or behavioral activity will ultimately fail, because only God is the expert on the soul. Only God can see the condition of the heart.

But the psychology industry would have us think otherwise. Psychology takes us on a journey through the steps and process of the psychological machine, treating the emotions and behaviors of human beings like products on an assembly line. But as hard as they try to make it into a science, they have not succeeded. So often you hear professional-sounding terms that make psychology appear as a science, when in reality they are conjectures based on subjective notions. Don't get fooled by the big words that therapists use to describe psychological disorders. Although we look like we know what we are talking about, we really don't.

CHAPTER 3

DOES PSYCHOLOGY DELIVER ON ITS PROMISES?

The field of psychology overflows with promises of understanding and curing common human problems such as those listed in the advertisement to follow. But does psychology deliver on its lofty promises? In this chapter we will take an honest look at the effectiveness, or lack thereof, of the treatments of psychology.

WE OFFER SPECIALIZED PSYCHOTHERAPY
TO HELP YOU OVERCOME:

- Anxiety
- Depression
- Addictions
- Eating Disorders
- Childhood Abuse
- Marriage/Family Problems
- Ministry Issues

SEARCHING FOR A CURE

My typical day as a therapist for seventeen psychiatric outpatients, each diagnosed with some form of mental illness, looked something like this:

8:30 A.M.	All clients arrive at facility
8:30 A.M.	One-to-one therapy session with a client
8:45 A.M.	One-to-one therapy session with a client
9:00 A.M.	Group therapy session with multiple clients
10:00 A.M.	Group therapy session with multiple clients
11:00 A.M.	Group therapy session with multiple clients
12:00 P.M.	One-to-one therapy session with a client
12:15 P.M.	One-to-one therapy session with a client
12:30 P.M.	Eat lunch while doing paperwork on each client's progress
1:00 P.M.	Group therapy session with multiple clients
2:00 P.M.	Group therapy session with multiple clients
3:00 P.M.	All clients go home
3:00 P.M.	More paperwork into the evening on each client's progress

My clients received so much therapy each day that they could probably become therapists themselves. This daily schedule continued for six straight months. But with all of the individual and group therapy each of these seventeen clients underwent, not a single client's mental condition improved. The same held true for clients treated by the other therapists with whom I worked—not one client was cured of their mental illness.

WHAT DO THE EXPERTS REALLY KNOW?

To date, no one has been able to generate real evidence that professional psychology works. Psychology's own American Psychiatric Association (APA) has even admitted that research fails to prove psychology's effectiveness.[1] The APA publishes the *Diagnostic and Statistical Manual of Mental Disorders*, psychology's bible of mental disorders, yet they admit they cannot effectively treat the disorders they identify!

Despite psychology's failures, the psychology field still leads us to believe that therapists have a secret, hidden knowledge that the rest of us don't have and that this knowledge will assist us in curing our ills. Therapists claim to have "expert" knowledge in dealing with those really difficult cases—those that the intern or layperson cannot handle. Many church pastors have bought into this philosophy of turning over the difficult cases to the "experts," for fear that their knowledge of God's Word will only go so far.

Fortunately, one study blows the myth of "expert" knowledge to pieces. Psychologist D. L. Rosenhan, professor of psychology and law at Stanford University, conducted an experiment where he and seven other normal people (that is, people with no perceived mental illness) feigned mental illness by complaining of hearing voices. They asked for psychiatric help and got it. After expressing truthful past experiences, the psychiatrists diagnosed them with schizophrenia and manic depression and admitted them to mental hospitals. During their stays they acted completely normal, but despite their normal behavior they received medication and extended stays—some as long as fifty-two days. After telling one hospital the truth about their experiment, Rosenhan threatened to send more "pseudopatients" their way within the next three months. In response, the hospital's psychiatrist labeled over twenty patients as "pseudopatients," although Rosenhan never actually followed through with his threat.[2] If this is the kind of accuracy the professionals can muster, should pastors, or anyone for that matter, become intimidated by psychology's "experts"?

After extensive schooling and years of real-world experience in the psychology field, I can honestly say that I was no more of an expert on people's problems than the average person on the street. I just knew all of the psychological jargon.

GOOD LISTENING

Research confirms this lack of expert knowledge in the psychology field, showing that psychotherapy proves no more effective than a good listener who shows empathy. The client simply pays for someone who has credentials and experience, but he or she does not receive anything more than he or she would receive from a close friend. In fact, psychology studies have shown that sympathetic college professors, bartenders, taxicab drivers and hairdressers make great therapists because they show effective listening techniques.[3] The professionals just cost more! My therapy sessions never went much beyond listening, caring and asking psychological questions. I charged clients sixty to ninety dollars per hour to provide this service.

Numerous studies have shown that the type, length and intensity of the therapy and the training and experience of the therapist *have no effect on improving the client's symptoms*.[4] Research shows that the only contributing factors to improvement include the interpersonal qualities of the therapist, along with the client's expectations, perceived progress, the time factor (life changes over time that help someone improve, independent of therapy) and similarity between the client's view of life and that of the therapist.[5] This sounds remarkably like a good friendship. It's no wonder many refer to a therapist as a paid friend.

A SELF-FULLFILLING CURE

To those readers who claim that psychology has helped them, I challenge you with these questions: Did you find temporary relief of your problem, or did you truly change? In other words, was your treatment simply satisfying, or was it effective? Did the therapist seek more to empathize with you and reaffirm your established position or to reveal the truth about the situation and confront any responsibility you might have in order to induce change? Sometimes we think therapy works because we have opinions about a situation, and we find a therapist who reaffirms these opinions. If a therapist does not see things the way we do, we go to another therapist and another and another until we find one that does. Psychotherapy provides a great way to pay another "professional" to listen to us and justify our behavior. Of course we feel better after psychotherapy—we now have someone else on our side! But did the problem really get resolved? Was the treatment effective?

I do know of one person who was "cured" by psychology. Just

when her insurance money ran out at her last therapy session, her therapist told her she was cured of her problem. My friend didn't feel any different and her problem seemed just as insurmountable as before, but the therapist declared her problem officially over.

MORE HARM THAN GOOD?

Psychology also has a dark side that most people do not realize. Not only is psychology ineffective, but also it has many times unnecessarily inflicted severe damage in people's lives. On the surface, psychology appears caring and compassionate. But when you look behind the facade, psychology actually degrades morality, causes idolatry, promotes selfishness, damages families and encourages victimization, all in the name of feeling happy.

BELIEVING LIES

Take, for example, Recovered Memory Therapy, or RMT. In RMT, the therapist attempts to uncover events from the client's childhood that lie buried in the client's unconscious. This treatment method has undergone severe criticism inside and outside of the psychology industry because people have "remembered" traumatic events that never truly happened to them. The therapist succeeds in influencing the client to believe, for instance, that his parents sexually abused him, beat him, deserted him or in some way harmed him, in order to "advance in the healing process"—healing of an event that never happened. The therapist assumes the client is in denial until he comes up with some horrific event. You can imagine the unnecessary pain and destruction of relationships that could result from these therapist-infused lies.

But lying doesn't seem to bother some therapists. They believe that the end justifies the means. If they can satisfy the client by lying, they will do so. According to one psychology author:

> Telling clients that we can help them is assuredly helpful even if it is not strictly true ... By communicating confidence, however false it might feel, we establish hope and motivation in the client ... We would never get a client to come back if we were completely honest with them ... The client may need to believe in this lie ... in

order to get better.[6]

He concludes, "Certain lies may therefore be necessary, if not therapeutic. If lying to a client, deliberately or unintentionally, is unethical since it promotes deceit and deception, perhaps it is just as unethical to be completely truthful."[7] Now there's a new concept. Telling the truth would be unethical. But to many psychologists, it doesn't matter if past memories are true or not; it only matters if the client believes them. It doesn't matter if you see the truth in a person's situation; it only matters that you make them happy so they will return for another session. Other professions would call this way of thinking unethical and even illegal. Psychology, however, endorses it.

PSYCHOLOGICAL IDOLATRY

Truth can get quite blurred in the psychology field. A client can experience the "Jehovah effect" or "God effect," where the therapist becomes the center, or god, of the client's life. Clients become so "victimized" and dependent on their therapists for every need and discomfort that they lose their very identity. They no longer feel confident to take care of themselves; instead, they become like helpless little children. Their god becomes the therapist, who defines their identity, their abilities and inabilities and their future. Instead of understanding their problems and improving their lives, clients lose their identity and become disciples of the therapist supposedly there to help them.

SELFISHNESS AND THE FAMILY

Psychology can also damage the family unit. Instead of improving marriage relationships, many therapists focus on the individual's selfish desires at the expense of fulfilling the marriage vows. Therapists would recommend divorce much more often than sticking it out for better or for worse.

Instead of promoting discipline of children, many therapists would rather you pamper a child at the expense of developing the child's character. Many psychological child development theories from the early 1900s have now been proven ineffective and even harmful.

Louise Ames, co-director of the Gesell Institute for Child Development, admitted, "Most of the damage we have seen in child rearing is the fault of the Freudian and neo-Freudians who have dominated the field. They have frightened parents and kept the truth from them. In child care I would say that Freudianism has been the psychological crime."[8] Therapists view themselves as the self-made specialists on everything from infant bonding to social development to education to conduct. Some even recommend "cribside therapy" for babies as young as three months old.[9] Do you feel incomplete not having your recommended cribside therapy when you were three months old?

Psychology hasn't done much for the school system either. One columnist asks:

> What has gotten better in American schools after we flooded them with psychologists, counselors, "facilitators" and the like?... Academic performance certainly hasn't improved. We have yet to see test scores as high as they were 30 years ago. Maybe students are happier, healthier or something. But statistics on cheating, theft, vandalism, violent crime, venereal disease and teenage suicide all say no.[10]

Speaking of youth, researchers conducted a thirty-year study to study the effectiveness of psychotherapy on youth, billed as the Cambridge-Somerville Youth Study. *American Psychologist* shocked the psychology industry by publishing the study's results in 1978. The study found that those men who received psychotherapy treatment for an average of five years during adolescence turned out worse, based on the factors of alcoholism, criminal behavior and mental disorders, than those who did *not* receive psychotherapy.[11]

From personal development to marriage to children to youth, psychology has done its share of damage in people's lives. Well-known researcher Hans J. Eysenck, who has researched tens of thousands of psychological cases, estimates that a whopping *10 percent* of all psychotherapy produces harmful—not helpful—effects in the lives of clients.[12] Psychotherapy harms one out of every ten people! Instead of improving humanity, psychology has actually harmed it. So much for lofty promises.

A VICTIMIZED CULTURE

Psychology is not only ineffective and harmful on an individual level, but it also destroys our nation's morality and sense of justice. No longer is the law of the land "an eye for an eye." No longer are the righteous rewarded and the wicked punished. Through the influence of psychology in the courtroom, criminals who were once given jail time, prison or the death sentence for murder, rape, theft, drug possession and other serious crimes are now set free under the guise of psychological disorders and diseases. Here is just a sampling of the many crimes of injustice happening throughout courtrooms all over the world—you won't believe your eyes:

- **Battered wife syndrome:** A psychologist from London, Ontario testified that Karla Homolka participated in the abduction, sexual assault and murder of two teenage girls because her husband, Paul Bernardo, had battered her.

- **Premenstrual syndrome:** In December 1994 a jury in Liverpool, England found a woman not guilty in the killing of her husband after she was diagnosed as suffering from premenstrual syndrome.

- **Alcoholism:** This was Washington Mayor Marion Barry's defense against drug charges.

- **Computer addiction:** In Los Angeles, Kevin Mitnick, a computer hacker, pled guilty to theft after breaking into a corporate computer system and stealing software. The judge saw him as the victim of the insidious disorder of "computer addiction" and sentenced him to treatment for this "new and growing" impulse disorder.

- **Cultural psychosis:** A defense lawyer in Milwaukee argued that a teenage girl charged with shooting and killing another girl during an argument over a leather coat suffered from "cultural psychosis," which caused her to think that problems are resolved by gunfire.[13]

The justice system has bitten down on the bait of psychology in the courtroom to such an extent that in a recent California election, the state passed a proposition requiring "probation and drug treatment, *not incarceration*, for possession, use, [and] transportation of controlled substances and similar parole violations, except sale or manufacture. Authorizes dismissal of charges after completion of treatment."[14] No longer does possession of narcotics give you jail time, just a nice friendly drug treatment program provided by psychological experts. After completion of the program, you are free again…free to use more drugs.

As silly as this proposition sounds, California voters enthusiastically supported it. But did these voters research the effectiveness of drug treatment programs of the past before blindly accepting the notion that psychology could heal drug users? If they did, they would have realized that psychotherapy has been notoriously ineffective in treating substance abuse.[15] The "justice" system, in excusing so-called victims, has lost all sense of justice. Fortunately, some courts have caught on to the real truth behind psychology's facade of well-trained "experts" and scientific-sounding language, banning psychological evaluations and pleas of mental illness from their cases.

MURDER IN THE NAME OF MENTAL HELP

While criminals use psychology to excuse their crimes, some therapists reverse the trend: They use psychology to *commit* their crimes. Under the guise of psychology, some therapists try to get away with murder—literally. Candace's story illustrates the point…

After the adoption, ten-year-old Candace Newmaker had a new mom and a new home. To strengthen their relationship, her mom brought her to two therapists specializing in rebirthing therapy—a therapy symbolizing "rebirth" from the mother's womb to help bond the mother and child. The therapy, however, proved disastrous. After fifty minutes of gasping for air and trying to escape from blankets and pillows wrapped tightly around her, Candace cried out, "I'm going to die!"

27

The therapists coldly replied, "Go ahead and die."

In innocent confusion, Candace asked, "For real—die and go to heaven?"

"Yeah, die and go to heaven," the therapists said. Her struggling and squirming continued.

The mother asked Candace, "Do you want to be rebirthed?"

In her final breath, all Candace could say was, "No." The blankets ceased moving.

A Colorado court found these therapists guilty of murder and sentenced them to sixteen years in prison—a refreshing change from the typical victim mentality of our justice system. Under "Candace's Law," the State of Colorado now bans rebirthing therapy. Although a rare case, Candace's story shows psychology's frightening potential to destroy lives.

THE SEARCH CONTINUES

Psychology has influenced our culture at every level. One American history professor writes, "All the institutions of American life—schools, hospitals, prisons, courts—have been shaped by the national investment in feelings. Devotion to personal happiness and self-realizations has shaped American rhetoric."[16] Despite the saturation of psychology in American culture, results have been wanting. In the late 1970s, *Time* magazine quoted Ross Baldessarini, a psychiatrist and biochemist at the Mailman Research Center, as saying, "We are not going to find the causes and cures of mental illness in the foreseeable future."[17] More than twenty years later, his prediction still stands. Therapies once thought effective are now useless or even harmful.

The search for the causes and cures to our problems continues. Psychology books teach them, and conferences and seminars promise them. But will psychotherapy deliver them? Will we ever find a therapy that works after over a century of failure after failure? As help seekers move from one therapist to the next in search of the "why" and "how" of their lives, they only get the "what" in return. Where should we look in the quest to find the causes and cures to our problems?

CHAPTER 4

ANSWERING THE *WHY* OF LIFE

For over a century, psychology has attempted to answer the *why* of life: Why are we here? Why do we get unhappy? Why do we think and behave the way we do? Why do we experience problems and pain? These questions still continue to plague the field of psychology, with no theory standing the test of time. With all of the theories developed to explain human nature, wouldn't one of them get it right?

OUR FOUNDATIONAL PROBLEM

Unfortunately, the theories used by therapists to explain human nature lack one extremely important foundational truth: the fact that the human race is in rebellion against God the Creator. The Bible calls this rebellion sin, or a willful disobedience to God's commands. While psychology says that mankind is basically good, a brief look at the daily newspaper proves otherwise—that mankind is basically evil. If you are a Christian, you probably know this already. But with more and more pastors and Christian media lessening or even ignoring the concept of man's sin, a review of this foundational truth certainly doesn't hurt. If you are not a Christian, stick with me. I write this chapter especially with you in mind.

GOD KNOWS YOU WELL

So what does God have to do with the day-to-day intricacies of dealing with life's problems? Absolutely everything. The Creator knows His creation extremely well. He designed the universe with painstaking accuracy. The earth's gravitational pull is just enough to keep us on the ground but not too much to squash us. The distance from the earth to the sun is not too small to burn us up but not too large to freeze us. He designed the animal kingdom with loving creativity and endless variety. The awesome beauty of the mountains, the sea and the sky was no accident. He designed us with the most advanced DNA structure, eyesight and brain processes. In fact, medical experts consider the brain the most complex organ in the entire universe. The brain's billions of neurons and trillions of synapses make it more complex than the entire physical universe of planets, stars and galaxies.[1]

But perhaps most importantly, God knows our successes, our failures, our hopes and dreams, our likes and dislikes, our sources of stress, our marital problems, our fears, our emptiness, our loneliness and our guilt. He knows when we wake up, what we do throughout the day, how we treat our families and friends and when we go to bed at night. He knows the number of hairs on our heads. He even gave us the owner's manual for life, the Bible, so we can understand who we are, who God is and how to live life on this earth. If the Creator is this intimate with every aspect of our lives, shouldn't we allow Him to help us with our problems?

A VACATION GONE BAD

Our Creator really does want to help us. No problem is too small or too much for Him. Because of His great love for us, He stands ready with open arms to give us what we need to overcome all our problems. In fact, He created us for the sole purpose of knowing Him and pleasing Him. When we seek to know Him and please Him, He returns the favor with blessings and inner peace. He created the first man and woman, Adam and Eve, to have a relationship with them. He placed them in a tropical garden paradise for their enjoyment. Adam and Eve walked and talked with their Creator in perfect harmony—no problems, no worries. You could say Adam and Eve had the ultimate vacation getaway!

But just like a great vacation, it didn't last long enough. Adam and Eve willfully disobeyed God's commandment and ate of the tree of the knowledge of good and evil; then they hid themselves from God among the trees of the garden. Since God's holy, just nature could not tolerate their disobedience, He banished them from the lush paradise they enjoyed so much. More importantly, He banished them from a relationship with Himself. Their choice to disobey God reaped harmful physical and spiritual consequences. From now on they were to live a life of misery, frustration and hopelessness—a life separate from God.

ALL HAVE SINNED

Great story, you might think, *but what does this have to do with my life?* Unfortunately, since we have descended from Adam and Eve, we have inherited their sin nature, that is, their automatic, inward desire to rebel against God's commandments. The Bible says, "There is no difference, for all have sinned and fall short of the glory of God" (Rom. 3:22–23). At one time or another, every person on this earth has proven they were born sinners by doing or thinking something against God's commandments. We've all gone our own, independent, selfish way in life without considering God's requirements of us. If we claim we're the exception, we've just sinned by calling God a liar.

Sin explains our current condition—why we are dissatisfied with life and are seeking answers. The sin problem is the *foundational* problem from which all other personal problems in life originate—not just one of many complex problems afflicting the human race. The sin problem is the root cause of evil thoughts, murder, adultery, sexual immorality, theft, false testimony and slander. Sin originates in the heart of each person and then expresses itself in outward actions. Contrary to what psychology teaches, our hearts are not basically

31

good, but inherently evil: "The hearts of men, moreover, are full of evil and there is madness in their hearts while they live, and afterward they join the dead" (Eccles. 9:3). "The heart is deceitful above all things and beyond cure. Who can understand it? I the LORD search the heart and examine the mind" (Jer. 17:9–10). "Surely I was sinful at birth, sinful from the time my mother conceived me" (Ps. 51:5).

Our problem is not that we are victims of our low self-esteem, our unmet needs, our past hurts, other people's actions, our environment, our genetics, our brain or our unconscious tendencies. Our problem is not someone or something else outside of us. The problem is the sin in our hearts—humbling, but true all the same. Although we may have experienced hurt and pain in the past, and that may have affected our lives for the worse, the fact remains that God still holds us accountable for *our* sins and *our* shortcomings. We will have no excuses on judgment day, for *all* have sinned.

Sin is the big problem in our lives. Our sin nature separates us from knowing our Creator and His plan to make our lives better. Without a relationship with our Creator, we will continue to live lives of misery, frustration and hopelessness, just like our ancestors Adam and Eve. We will also be forever separated from our Creator after we die. Our sin nature keeps us out of the garden paradise of heaven where God dwells and instead sends us to hell, or separation from God in eternal suffering and shame. No matter how hard we try to live good, moral and upright lives, our sin-tainted efforts will never measure up to God's perfect standard. But if we can cure our sin nature, we can make peace with God, with others and with ourselves—for here and eternity.

MAN'S TREATMENT: HUMAN EFFORT

Now that we have identified the sin problem, how do we treat it? A therapist or other "expert" might propose these treatments:

- Believe in yourself and your power to change, and you will overcome your sins.
- Get more self-esteem to cure your illnesses and dysfunctions.
- Buy the latest self-help book to help you rise above your sins.

- Join a support group to bare your sins to others with similar struggles.
- Look into the past to understand the source of your sins.
- Blame your sins on other people, your environment or your genetic or biological makeup.
- Vent your frustrations to relieve the guilt of your sins.
- Try the latest groundbreaking psychological treatment method to help you feel better about your sins.
- Attend a twelve-step program and believe in a higher power to help you overcome your sins.
- Try yoga or meditation to gain peace over your sins.
- Achieve a state of godhood by discovering and harnessing your innate goodness.

Do any of these treatments sound familiar? Based on the last century of hopeful treatments gone sour, I would venture to say these treatments aren't too effective either. In fact, most of these treatments do more harm than good. Although some of these treatments sound like they could have potential, they will all fall short of curing our sin problem. We cannot cure our sin problem using man-made psychological theories or religious exercises. Man cannot fix his own sin problem; it must be dealt with by God Himself.

GOD'S TREATMENT: JESUS CHRIST

God knows that the human race is sinful and in need of restoration. He also knows that no amount of a person's self-effort or psychological insight can restore the broken relationship between Him and that person. So God took it upon Himself to fix a problem we couldn't because of His great love for us. Although God is a holy, just God who cannot tolerate sin, He is also a God of love who longs to have a relationship with us and make our lives worth living. His just nature demands punishment for our sins, but His loving nature desires a loving relationship with us. So what does God do in this paradoxical situation? *He takes our punishment for us.*

Two thousand years ago, God sent His only begotten Son, Jesus, from heaven to earth to be born of a virgin. Jesus was the only man in history who lived a perfect life without sin. He was crucified on a Roman cross to pay the price for the world's sins. Three days later He rose from the dead to prove He was God, and He appeared to many people, including over five hundred at one time. He ascended to heaven and is alive today at God the Father's right hand.

Why did God go through all the trouble to do this? Because He loves me, and He loves you. He has taken drastic measures to keep us out of hell. Make no mistake about it: God does not want you to go to hell. That's why He left the comforts of heaven to suffer in your place. The Bible says, "God demonstrates his own love for us in this: While we were still sinners, Christ died for us" (Rom. 5:8). He placed the punishment for our sins on His Son, Jesus Christ. Jesus became sin and tasted spiritual death for every person. On that cross, Jesus experienced the agony of hell—total separation from the Father—so we wouldn't have to. If we place our faith in Jesus as dying on the cross in *our* place to pay the punishment that *our* sins deserve, God will forgive us of our sins, heal us of our sin problem and restore our relationship with Him, just like Adam and Eve in the garden paradise. The Bible calls it God's gift to humanity: "For the wages of sin is death, but the gift of God is eternal life in Christ Jesus our Lord" (Rom. 6:23). The gift is free, but Jesus paid for the gift with His very life.

JESUS—THE ONLY WAY TO GOD

You may be wondering, "Why can't I have a relationship with God in my own personal way or in another religion besides Christianity? What makes Jesus so special—don't other religions give the same hope of a better life?" Although most of the world's religions teach similar ways to live and promise a better, "more spiritual" life, no religion except Christianity fully cures the problem of sin. No other religion promises complete and total forgiveness for the sinner by faith and only faith. Jesus claimed He was the only way to God when He said, "I am the way and the truth and the life. No one comes to the Father except through me" (John 14:6). The Bible also says about Jesus, "Salvation is found in no one else, for there is no other name under heaven given to men by which we must be saved" (Acts 4:12). Jesus is the only religious leader in history who overcame sin and death and rose from the grave to eternal life. While all other religious leaders still lie dead in their graves, a visit to Jerusalem reveals an empty grave where Jesus once laid. Jesus proved He was God in the flesh by rising from the dead. Only God can forgive sin, and Jesus is that God. Therefore, Jesus is the *only* one who can overcome our sin problem, restore our relationship with God and give us eternal life.

OUR RESPONSE

God took our sin problem upon Himself to fix. But we must administer the Jesus "treatment" personally before we can be cured of this foundational problem in our lives. A doctor's flu prescription won't help us if we just read the outside of the bottle. We must open up the bottle and take the recommended dosage to cure us of the flu. God's recommended dosage for curing sin consists of opening up His gift of salvation by:

- Agreeing with God about your sinful condition and admitting you have sinned against Him (Rom. 3:23)
- Believing that Jesus Christ died for your sins and rose from the dead (John 3:16, Rom. 10:9, 1 Cor. 15:3–4)
- Personally receiving Jesus into your life to forgive you of your sins (John 1:12)

Would you like to cure your sin problem *right now* with God's recommended dosage I just described? The Bible says, "Yet to all who received him [Jesus], to those who believed in his name, he gave the right to become children of God" (John 1:12). You can receive Jesus Christ into your life right now through a simple prayer before reading on. Pray something like this aloud to God, and He will hear you:

> *God, I admit that I have sinned against You and have lived my life apart from You. Thank You for sending Your Son, Jesus, to die on the cross in my place. Thank You, Jesus, for paying the penalty that my sins deserve and giving me eternal life. Jesus, please come*

into my heart and forgive me of my sins. Take control of my life, and help me to follow You from this point forward, until I see You face to face in heaven. Thank You for loving me and forgiving me. Amen.

NEW LIFE IN CHRIST

When you receive Jesus Christ into your life to forgive you of your sins, you restore your relationship with God. You now have direct access to God through Jesus Christ. Jesus replaces your emptiness, loneliness, guilt and fear of death with joy, comfort, peace, fulfillment and a secure place in heaven. Jesus removes your filthy unrighteousness and covers you with His perfect righteousness. God now sees you seated in heaven with Christ, who is perfect. In Christ, God accepts you unconditionally.

The Bible also calls you a new creation. Old things have passed away and all things have become new! Before receiving Jesus, your old, destructive sin nature ruled over you and you were a slave to it. After receiving Jesus, you rule over your sin nature, and you are a master over it through the power of God now living inside of you. From this point forward, "it is God who works in you to will and to act according to his good purpose" (Phil. 2:13). You will soon agree from personal experience that Jesus Christ is the only way to effectively overcome life's problems.

THE BOOK

We can trust the claims of Jesus Christ found in the Bible. The world's all-time bestseller, the Bible is truly an amazing book: a collection of sixty-six books written by over forty authors from different backgrounds and eras, over a period of at least fifteen hundred years. Yet its consistency of thought and message remains intact throughout—that God, made known to man through Jesus Christ, desires to have a relationship with us and bless our lives. The only conceivable explanation for this thematic consistency between the books of the Bible is that God Himself, who exists outside of time and space, inspired men to write these books by His Holy Spirit. God has given us the Bible to reveal His character and His plan for the human race. He has given us the Bible to show us our sinful condition, God's remedy in Jesus Christ and God's will for how to live the Christian life. Once we begin following God's plan for our lives and not our own, we will begin to see our lives turn from frustration and chaos to inner peace and order.

Many great men in history have loved and respected the Bible. Abraham Lincoln said, "I believe the Bible is the best gift God ever gave to man." George Washington said, "It is impossible to rightly govern the world without God and the Bible." Robert E. Lee said, "In all my perplexes and distresses the Bible has never failed to give me light and strength." Napoleon said, "The Bible is no mere book; it is a living creature with a power that conquers all who oppose it." Patrick Henry said, "The Bible is worth all other books that have ever been printed."[2]

PROPHECY IN THE BIBLE

Through prophecy, archeology and science, the Bible has been proven accurate, trustworthy and true. The Bible is full of predictions about Jesus in the Old Testament Jewish Scriptures written *hundreds of years* before He ever walked the earth:

- His virgin birth (Isa. 7:14)
- His birthplace (Mic. 5:2)
- His entry into Jerusalem on Palm Sunday (Dan. 9:24–26; Zech. 9:9–10)
- His crucifixion (Ps. 22; Isa. 53)
- His resurrection (Ps. 16:10; 30:3, 9; 40: 1–2; Isa. 53:10; Hos. 6:2)
- His ascension to sit at the right hand of God the Father (Ps. 16:11; 24:3–10; 68:18; 110:1; Prov. 30:4)

The odds of just three of these predictions being fulfilled in one person in history is astronomical, yet Jesus fulfilled over three hundred prophecies of the Old Testament Scriptures![3] These 100 percent accurate predictions about Jesus made by men of God hundreds of years before Christ's birth prove that Jesus really was who He said He was: God in the flesh, the Savior of the world, the giver of new life. No other book dares to base its authenticity on predicting the future, yet the Bible not only dares to predict the future; it does so with 100 percent accuracy! Fulfilled prophecies like these give us confidence in the divine inspiration of the Bible, for only God knows the future with 100 percent accuracy since He exists outside of time and space.

ARCHAEOLOGY IN THE BIBLE

We can also trust the accuracy of the Bible because of the many archaeological discoveries affirming its authenticity. With over five thousand copies uncovered that were written just two hundred twenty-five years after the original manuscripts, the New Testament has greater documented accuracy than the combined writings of Plato, Herodotus' *History* and Homer's *Iliad*, all highly respected and trusted historical works.[4] Dr. Nelson Glueck, one of the greatest twentieth-century authorities on biblical archaeology, concluded:

> No archaeological discovery has ever controverted a biblical reference. Scores of archaeological findings have been made which confirm in clear outline or in exact detail historical statements in the Bible. And, by the same token, proper evaluation of biblical descriptions has often led to amazing discoveries.[5]

Each time we find a ruin in the Holy Land, we can trace it back to the Bible. Conversely, each time we look to the Bible for clues, we discover what the Bible says should be there.

SCIENCE IN THE BIBLE

Many scientific disciplines of today find their roots in the basic phenomena and processes described in the Bible. For example, the Book of Job (which some scholars believe is the oldest book of the Bible) makes references to condensation, precipitation, run-off, snow, the hydrologic balance, the rotation of the earth, gravitation, rock erosion, the glacial period, the size of the universe and radio waves.[6] The Bible also speaks of many medical practices now considered mandatory. In Genesis 17:12, God told Abraham to circumcise every male eight days old. Today doctors consider circumcision of male babies a standard practice after birth, for it has been found to result in lower rates of penile problems, urinary tract infections, sexually transmitted diseases and cancers.[7]

If the Bible can accurately describe history, science and the future, we should have no problem trusting its sufficiency in helping us deal with our daily struggles.

GOD HAS THE ANSWERS

Why are we here? Why do we think and behave the way we do? Why do we experience problems and pain? God gives us the answers to the *why* of life in the Bible. Why are we here? We live to get to know our Father in heaven and to make Him known, now that our relationship is restored. We can get to know God through reading the Bible, praying to God and worshiping God. We can make Him known by loving others and telling them about Jesus. Why do we think and behave the way we do? The sin in our hearts causes our corrupt thoughts and evil behaviors, but in Jesus we can live in fellowship with God and overcome our sinful nature. Why do we experience problems and pain? We live in a world full of sinful people just like us, so there's bound to be problems! But God uses suffering in our lives to mature us as Christians.

Knowing God and making Him known as our Creator, Savior and Lord sums up the meaning of life. The Bible says about knowing God:

> I consider everything a loss compared to the surpassing greatness of knowing Christ Jesus my Lord, for whose sake I have lost all things. I consider them rubbish, that I may gain Christ and be found in him, not having a righteousness of my own that comes from the law, but that which is through faith in Christ—the right-eousness that comes from God and is by faith.
>
> —Philippians 3:8–9

While knowing God is the supreme goal of Christianity, knowing self is the supreme goal of psychology. We will look at this and other differences between Christianity and psychology in the next section.

PART II

PSYCHOLOGY AND CHRISTIANITY: WHAT'S THE DIFFERENCE?

With Jesus in our hearts and Bibles in our hands, should we continue to look to therapists, psychiatrists, support groups and twelve-step programs for guidance? Do we need both Christianity and psychology to understand how to live effectively? Does one complement the other, or do they contradict each other? In this section we will analyze the principles used in psychology and compare these with the Bible. The principles we believe about ourselves, others and God determine how we live our lives and what kind of consequences our lives will produce. What we believe really matters. So let's take a closer look at how the beliefs of psychology and Christianity compare.

CHAPTER 5

TWO
OPPOSING
FAITHS

In a sense, psychology and Christianity are two belief systems on life. Psychology tells us to put faith in ourselves and others for fulfillment in life, while Christianity tells us to put faith in Jesus Christ for fulfillment in life.

ANOTHER RELIGION

Psychology literally means, "study of the psyche" or "study of the soul." Psychology and Christianity each provide a view of the soul and how the soul should live. Each attempts to explain who we are, why we are here, how to meet our needs, how to solve our problems and how to achieve fulfillment. But while psychology is a worldview or philosophy of life with man at the center and with man as his hope, Christianity as characterized in the Bible is a worldview or philosophy of life with *God* at the center and with *God* as man's hope. Paul Vitz, an associate professor of psychology at New York University, makes these strong comments about the religious nature of his own profession in his book *Psychology as Religion*:

> Psychology has become a religion: a secular cult of the self. By this I mean an intensely held worldview, a philosophy of life or

ideology. More specifically, contemporary psychology is a form of secular humanism based on the rejection of God and the worship of the self... Psychology as religion exists, and it exists in strength throughout the United States.[1]

One American history professor observes that the rise of psychology may have coincided with the decline of religion in America. She says, "The decline of religion may also account for the devotion to the psyche. As Americans began to lose faith in salvation from above, they put more faith into self-glorification. This new psychological gospel insisted on scrutiny of the psyche and devotion to personal happiness."[2] Psychology's motto is, "I am my own salvation." Even the past president of the well-known American Psychological Association, George Albee, admits the religious nature of the field:

The old conventional sources of explaining the mysteries of human existence, such as religion and science, no longer hold much water for a lot of people. So people have turned largely to psychology as one field which attempts to answer questions about the meaning of life.[3]

Psychology claims to have answers to the meaning of life. Therapists and psychiatrists now handle issues once reserved for pastors and theologians.

The fathers of the field actually conceived psychology as an alternate religion to Christianity—one where you no longer needed God to change yourself. It became the religion of self. The fathers of psychology—including Freud, Jung and others—criticized the beliefs of Christianity because Christianity emphasized a God-centered view of man, which directly opposed their man-centered view of man. Their theories about man's thoughts, attitudes and behaviors strongly contrasted with biblical Christianity, promising self-improvement and personal fulfillment apart from God.

As an alternate religion, psychology has its own religious leaders. The priest of Christianity is Jesus Christ, while the priest of psychology is the therapist. While the Bible tells us to worship God and obey His written Word, psychology tells us to worship the therapist and obey their treatment plans. Whether intentionally or ignorantly, many clients view their therapists as secular priests, or even as idols of worship. With these pseudo-religious leaders come religious teachings.

"BELIEVE IN YOURSELF"

The pervasive teaching of psychology is to believe in oneself. Do any of these colloquialisms used by therapists sound familiar?

- "You've got to look out for number one and do what's best for you."
- "It starts with you—you can't help others unless you first help yourself."
- "Follow your gut and you'll never go wrong."
- "Just do what feels right for you."

Man throughout the ages has always believed in himself and strived for self-improvement. You would think that after the thousands of years that man has existed we would have attained perfection by now! No, instead we still see the same problems in our homes, workplaces, communities and country: hatred, discord, jealousy, anger, selfishness, wars, factions, envy, frustrations, irritations and resentment. Nothing has changed after all these years of believing in ourselves and striving for self-improvement. Why hasn't believing in ourselves worked? Because psychology fails to take into account the presence of sin in human nature.

While the Bible centers around the doctrine of sinful man and God's plan to redeem man from sin through Jesus Christ, psychology centers around the inherent goodness of man. Those in the psychology field, such as this psychiatrist, openly admit this: "Psychiatry has a quarrel with only those forms of religion which emphasize the doctrine of original sin. Any belief that tends to focus on the idea that man is inherently evil conflicts with the basically humanistic approach to problems that psychiatrists must follow."[4]

Psychology attributes our problems in life not to original sin, but to environmental, hereditary, biological and unconscious influences. The therapist will tell us how we can overcome these influences by our own efforts instead of through the power of God the Holy Spirit. "If we believe in ourselves," the therapist would say, "we can overcome anything." We soon find, however, that this advice backfires, damaging us spiritually.

When we believe in ourselves, we become self-sufficient and independent of God's help or direction. This type of living sounds attractive, since we naturally find it much easier for us to live life our own way than to swallow our pride, humble ourselves before God and live His way. But the results get much worse when we take God out of the picture. The oldest lie ever told to mankind promised self-sufficiency. Way back in the Garden of Eden, the serpent told Adam and Eve that they could be like God (i.e., they would be self-sufficient, have knowledge and wisdom and would no longer need God) if they ate of the fruit of the tree. Of course, they fell for Satan's lie, sin came into the world, and the human race has been miserably self-sufficient ever since.

This lie has even infiltrated the church. Christian polls have revealed that most Christians believe the Bible says, "God helps those who help themselves."

Contrary to popular opinion, the Bible *never* tells us to believe in ourselves. Over and over, through principle and illustration, the Bible portrays the self as utterly sinful, hopeless and useless. Every one of us is desperately wicked inside. The only good thing we have in us is God, and nothing more. As Christians, our sinful nature (our self) continuously wages war against the Holy Spirit inside us (Gal. 5:17). This passage of Scripture goes on to list all the detestable things we can do because of our sinful nature. Why would we look to our self if our self continually rages against God inside us? Jesus said, "Apart from me you can do nothing" (John 15:5), but Paul said about Jesus, "I can do everything through him who gives me strength" (Phil. 4:13). We look to Jesus—not ourselves—to help us live life.

THE SELF-ESTEEM DECEPTION

Believing in ourselves has birthed the all-too-popular concept of self-esteem. Therapists tell us that high self-esteem forms the key to our happiness. Karen and Keith's therapist from chapter one proposes

46

that Karen's unhappiness with her home life stems from her low self-esteem:

Karen: I know I spend a lot of time with my mom, but *[to Keith]* at least she accepts me as I am—unlike your parents.

Therapist: Karen, does it make you happy to feel accepted?

Karen: Of course!

Therapist: I wonder if there are other people in your life who don't accept you the way your mother does. Can you think of anyone close to you who, for example, puts you down or doesn't praise you frequently?

Karen: Sure, my husband and my kids. They always seem to whine and complain. I feel very unappreciated in my home.

Therapist: OK, let's go with that...

Karen: Well, I'm always trying to please them, but they never seem to want to please me. Some days I feel like a complete failure as a wife and a mom—especially when Keith's parents visit. I just don't measure up with any of them.

Therapist: I understand. It sounds like Keith and your kids are simply not fulfilling your need for greater self-esteem and value. So, you turn to your mother to restore your self-worth. She makes you feel valuable. Would you say this is true?

Karen: Yes, I would.

"If only Karen had more self-esteem...if she only thought more highly of herself...she would have been happier and wouldn't abandon her husband and children every weekend," reasons her therapist. But Jesus tells us the truth: "Blessed are the poor in spirit...Blessed are those who mourn...Blessed are the meek..." (Matt. 5:3–5). Jesus identifies the happy people as low, humble and meek—not arrogant, proud and loud. The issue here is not whether we have high or low self-esteem, but that our self-esteem turns into Christ-esteem. Although Jesus makes this point very clear, we still hear therapists, talk-show hosts and even some misinformed Christians insisting that we just don't have enough self-esteem! Oprah Winfrey made this startling claim during one of her shows: "What we are trying to change in this one hour is what I think is at the root of all the problems in the world—lack of self-esteem."[5]

But is a lack of self-esteem really our problem?

REVEALING RESEARCH ON SELF-ESTEEM

To answer this burning question, the California state legislature created the California Task Force to Promote Self-Esteem and Personal and Social Responsibility in the late 1980s. This task force believed that high self-esteem would reduce social ills such as crime, alcohol and drug abuse, welfare dependency, teenage pregnancy, child and spousal abuse, and children's learning problems in school. After much research from University of California professors, the task force released a book containing the study's results. One syndicated writer for the *San Francisco Examiner* summed up the report: "Save yourself the 40 bucks the book costs and head straight for the conclusion: There is precious little evidence that self-esteem is the cause of our social ills."[6] The report admitted, "One of the disappointing aspects of every chapter...is how low the association between self-esteem and its consequences are in research..."[7]

Leaders of the popular DARE (Drug Abuse Resistance Education) program, which used methods that included building self-esteem to keep kids off of drugs, came to the same conclusion. They admitted their programs failed.[8] But we still hear the empty claims of psychology that self-esteem helps society to this day, and self-esteem programs like Michigan's POP (Power of Positive Thinking) program for elementary school students, youth programs like STOP (Stand Tall on Positiveness), and Massachusetts' "I Am a Good Person" curriculum continue to operate with false hopes of success.[9]

Other research shows no direct relationship between self-esteem and positive or negative behavior. According to the *American School Board Journal*, "No reliable evidence supports the utility of self-esteem scores to predict important behaviors."[10] Neither does self-esteem relate to problem-solving capability. Researchers at Purdue University concluded, "Self-esteem is generally considered an across-the-board important attitude, but this study showed self-esteem to correlate negatively with performance…The higher the self-esteem, the poorer the performance."[11]

Common sense confirms these findings. If people always tell me I'm a wonderful person and I do everything great, I have no incentive to work hard or improve. America's schools have reaped the repercussions of this way of thinking. We have the highest self-esteem in the world, but rank among the Third World countries in terms of high school graduate test scores. The Koreans rank first in math, and they have low self-esteem!

A Biblical Look at Self-Esteem

Despite the research that self-esteem does not improve behavior or performance, some Christians use the word like a central doctrine of the Christian faith. We hear some Christians telling us to have high self-esteem, a sense of self-worth, healthy self-concept, deep self-understanding, strong self-acceptance and plenty of self-love. We should actualize ourselves in order to achieve self-realization and self-fulfillment. We hear these terms from respected Christian pastors and leaders and think, *Sounds good to me. No harm in thinking highly of oneself—that's only healthy,* without considering what the Bible has to say about them. Scripture has no place for these blatant psychological concepts.

Instead of high self-esteem, we should esteem Christ and His loving sacrifice for us on the cross. Does that mean we think low of ourselves? Of course not, for our self doesn't even enter into the picture. The light of Christ's presence overshadows any thought of self, since we no longer live, but Christ lives in us (Gal. 2:20).

Instead of a sense of self-worth, we should count Jesus worthy to receive power, honor, glory and praise (Rev. 5:12). Does that mean we are worthless? No. Although we are unworthy, we are not worthless. Christ loved us enough to die for us.

Instead of healthy self-concept, we should view ourselves as sinners saved by grace (Rom. 3:23; Eph. 2:8–9). Does that mean we delve into despair over our sinfulness? No, because Christ's righteousness hides our unrighteousness, and God has justified us in His sight (Rom. 8:30).

49

Instead of deep self-understanding, we should have a deep understanding of God's character and will for our lives (Phil. 3:10–11). Does that mean, then, that we cannot understand ourselves? No, we *can* understand ourselves, but only in proportion to our understanding of God. The clearer Christ becomes, the clearer we become in relation to Him (Eph. 1:17–19). The clearer the holiness of God becomes, the clearer our wretchedness, wickedness and sinfulness become. If we think we are something when we are nothing, we deceive ourselves (Gal. 6:3).

Instead of strong self-acceptance, we should not become satisfied with our current condition, but strive to be holy as God is holy (1 Pet. 1:15–16). Does that mean we can't rest in God's unconditional love? No, it just means we should desire to grow closer to God in response to His unconditional acceptance (Rom. 12:1).

Instead of self-love, we should love God and others as we already love ourselves (Matt. 22:37–40). Does that mean we hate ourselves? No, for Paul said to not *only* look to our own interests, but also to the interests of others (Phil. 2:4). In this verse he implies we should not hate ourselves.

Instead of actualizing ourselves, we should deny ourselves in preference to others for the glory of God (Matt. 16:24). Does that mean we become miserable human beings? Not at all, but to the contrary, we will find fulfillment (Matt. 10:39).

Instead of achieving self-realization, we should realize that apart from Christ, we cannot produce good fruit (John 15:5). The self produces rotten fruit; Christ produces good fruit. Does that mean we play no part in realizing good "mental health"? Not at all. Realizing our full potential as Christians requires a team effort between God and us as we put our faith into action (Phil. 2:12–13).

Instead of striving for self-fulfillment, we should seek to fulfill God's will and purpose in our lives (Rom. 12:2). Does that mean God will call us into a South American jungle as missionaries? Not necessarily, for God's will is good, pleasing and perfect, and He will give us the desires of our hearts as we seek Him.

CHRIST-ESTEEM

We don't need more self-esteem, self-love, self-[fill in the blank]; we need Christ-esteem! I wonder what today's Christian therapist would have told Moses when he complained about not being a good speaker and leader of the people of Israel. God certainly didn't tell him to have better self-esteem! Instead, it pleased God to receive glory through the surrendered vessel of Moses. The less self in our lives, the better, in God's book. God wants us to focus on Him and become humble, not focus on ourselves and become prideful. We should care about how God esteems us, not how we esteem ourselves. God says, "This is the one I esteem: he who is humble and contrite in spirit, and trembles at my word" (Isa. 66:2).

Jesus' parable of the Pharisee and the tax collector gives us insight into God's opinion of self-esteem. During prayer the Pharisee boasted to God about his own righteousness, while the tax collector wouldn't even look up to the sky, but beat his breast and said, "God, have mercy on me, a sinner." Which person did God hear? The tax collector! God is not impressed with our self-esteem. Rather, He despises it. But God does not despise our humility: "The sacrifices of God are a broken spirit; a broken and contrite heart, O God, you will not despise" (Ps. 51:17). What the Christian therapist would consider low self-esteem, God considers a pleasing sacrifice.

Paul had high self-esteem for a while. Paul thought of himself as "a Hebrew of Hebrews; in regard to the law, a Pharisee...as for legalistic righteousness, faultless" (Phil. 3:5–6). He actually thought he was perfect! The Christian therapist would call Paul the model example of high self-esteem. But after meeting Christ, Paul became a new creation and saw himself as the chief of sinners (1 Tim. 1:15). Paul counted all of his self-esteem as dung compared to knowing Christ (Phil. 3:8). What the Christian therapist would consider admirable, Paul considered dung.

LET MY WILL BE DONE

When we rip off the psychological covers of self-esteem and expose its nakedness, we recognize self-esteem as just another form of self-worship. Low self-esteem is self-pity—a sin—and high self-esteem is pride—another sin. Martin Luther wrote, "Against this secret villain we must pray God daily to suppress our self-esteem."[12] Luther knew the dangers of self-esteem's idolatry, where instead of idolizing statues of gods and goddesses, we idolize ourselves. One theologian writes, "When an idol is worshiped, man is worshiping himself, his desires, his purposes and his will...As a consequence of this type of idolatry man was outrageously guilty of giving himself the status of God and of exalting his own will as of supreme worth."[13] Psychology puts man at the helm, making him the god of his personal universe. Some theories of psychology now adopt the New Age beliefs of the divinity of man and the power of man to tap into this divinity in order to change himself. New Age is self-worship taken to its extreme. Psychology and New Age both tell us to look within for guidance—to "let my will be done."

God didn't wire us this way, however. God created us to do His will—not our own. God made us with a big hole in our soul for the very purpose of filling it with His presence and His love. That hole remains empty and void if we live by faith in ourselves. But if we trust in Christ and humbly depend on Him for our strength, God fills us with His power to overcome. We won't find true contentment until this happens. When we look to God for guidance, our self-sufficiency dies along with its baggage of emptiness, loneliness, guilt and fear, and God-sufficiency takes over with its peace, order and direction. Instead of trusting in ourselves, we believe in, trust in and cling to Jesus with all our hearts, all our minds, all our souls and all our strength. The Holy Spirit—not our self-effort—will help us change and give us fulfillment.

A DANGEROUS THREAT

The religion of psychology has become a dangerous threat to Christianity. A psychiatrist admits, "The human relations we now call 'psychotherapy' are, in fact, matters of religion—and that we mislabel them as 'therapeutic' at great risk to our spiritual well-being...It is not merely a religion that pretends to be a science; it is actually a fake religion that seeks to destroy true religion."[14] Its doctrines of self-esteem and believing in self have polluted the minds of Christians and blurred their discernment of what is of God and what is not. Are you one of these Christians?

Contrary to psychology, we are not to "look out for number one" or to seek pleasure, but we are to trust in God and glorify Him in everything we do. God doesn't exist to make us happy; *we exist to please Him*. In other words, it's not all about me; it's all about God. What does God say about believing in yourself? "He who trusts in himself is a *fool*, but he who walks in wisdom is kept safe" (Prov. 28:26, emphasis added). We don't look to ourselves to fix problems around us; we look to God to fix the problems inside of us.

CHAPTER 6

WHO
IS AT
FAULT?

The tendency to pass blame instead of admitting our fault is as old as mankind itself. After Adam ate the forbidden fruit, God asked Adam, "Have you eaten from the tree that I commanded you not to eat from?" Adam responded, "The woman you put here with me— she gave me some fruit from the tree, and I ate it." He blamed his disobedience on his wife. So God turned to Eve and asked, "What is this you have done?" Eve responded, "The serpent deceived me, and I ate" (Gen. 3:11–13). She passed the blame for her disobedience to the devil.

Today psychology continues the age-old tradition of passing the blame. By focusing on the actions of others and the traumatic events of the past, psychology calls us the victims of our environment. He who was once a sinner is now a victim.

LOOKING BACK

Psychology places a heavy emphasis on analyzing the past, expressing emotions from the past and blaming personal problems on the people and environments of the past. Therapists believe that successful treatment of the present depends on analyzing and understanding the past. Let's take a closer look at Karen and Keith's therapy session from chapter one, focusing on those parts of the session devoted to the past.

Therapist: *[After a long, pensive pause]* I can see that both of you are feeling neglected. You feel like the other doesn't care about your needs and doesn't think you're important. You want your needs to be taken seriously, and you want to be viewed as valuable. The resentment and hurt you are feeling is nothing new for either of you. Keith, did you ever feel neglected as a child?

Keith: *[Awkwardly]* Uh, I don't remember my childhood too well.

Therapist: Did your parents buy you nice things as a child?

Keith: *[Resentfully]* Nope, just the necessities.

Therapist: OK, can you remember times when your parents took time out to spend with you, to play a game or go to the park? Did they ever let you know how special and important you were to them?

Keith: No, not really. They were pretty busy.

Therapist: Keith, you seem to have had a self-sufficient childhood. Did your parents have anything to do with this?

Keith: Well, my dad left my mom when I was nine years old, and my mom had to raise the four of us alone.

Therapist: How did she handle that?

Keith: She had to go to work full-time to make ends meet, but I think she handled it well. She didn't have much time to spend with us—she was always working, cooking or cleaning. So the four of us entertained ourselves, and it worked out all right, I guess.

Therapist: It sounds like your mother needed you to be in the background, and you respected that need.

Keith: *[Solemnly]* Yeah, that's probably true.

Therapist: Keith, it sounds like you've reached a point in your life when you just won't be in the background anymore. You want more attention, more quality time. I think that when you see Karen spending all her time with her mother, you get very frustrated—especially when you work so hard to provide for her. You've decided that it's time to stop putting your own needs aside in order to take care of others.

Keith: I'd agree with that.

The therapist and Keith spent most of the therapy session analyzing the past, expressing emotions from the past and blaming current problems on the past. Keith feels pain from Karen's lack of attention because of his neglected childhood. He departs from his ninety-dollar session momentarily satisfied, for now he has a convenient scapegoat on which to place blame for his problems. Satisfied? Yes. Resolved? No. His problems with Karen remain, with no resolution in sight. Keith and Karen will most likely return to therapy the following week and continue to make excuses for their behavior toward each other.

Passing the Blame

When Karen and Keith weren't joining the therapist in blaming people from the past, they were busy blaming each other. Unfortunately, many therapy sessions do not emphasize enough personal responsibility of one's actions. If the client does admit feeling guilt about something, the therapist reassures, "No need for you to feel guilty—that's unhealthy." Instead, the therapist should ask, "What have you done that would make you feel guilty inside?"

We need to view guilt as a positive feeling. God gave us the capacity to feel guilt to tell us when we have sinned, just as He gave us the capacity to feel heat to tell us how to avoid getting burned. Feeling guilt is the first step toward taking responsibility for our sin and asking for God's forgiveness and healing. If we never feel guilty, we will never take responsibility! When a therapist relieves a client's guilt, that client never takes responsibility.

To relieve guilt, therapists usually have clients blame their problems on their spouse, their friends, their job, their childhood or some other environmental factor. Although our childhood determines much of our personality as adults, focusing on our childhood and then using this as an excuse to continue with unhealthy behavior denies any personal responsibility and willingness to change. Therapists have us visualize, imagine, recover and relive our past and our "memories" using techniques that even border on the occult. Whatever the therapist drums up from the past, whether true or purely imagination, becomes the scapegoat for the present.

Because of the victim mentality that psychology has ingrained in our culture, hardened criminals like the Menendez brothers use claims of childhood abuse to justify murdering their own parents. I can murder you because of my sugar overdose from too many Twinkies (true testimony of former San Francisco city supervisor Dan White).

Psychology's victim mentality has replaced right and wrong with "situational ethics," where everything is relative to what works for me. If I feel tired, I have the right to leave work early and still get paid. If I have a bad marriage, I have the right to beat up my wife and children to take out my anger. If it pleases me to cheat on my spouse, I have the right to fulfill my desires. When my chief goal is personal happiness, God's laws of right and wrong and good and evil no longer have relevance in my life. A late-nineteenth-century psychology pundit explained it this way: "Let this be our test: the indulgence of any feeling that causes unhappiness to ourselves is always wrong."[1] The flip side of this statement then also applies: "The indulgence of any feeling that causes happiness to ourselves is always right." As psychology continues to replace moral absolutes with victimization and situational ethics, our blame-shifting culture careens faster and faster down the road to self-destruction.

ADMITTING THE TRUTH

Although adverse environments may negatively impact our lives and affect us in harmful ways, we still must answer to God for our own actions. A son who experiences abuse and neglect by his father must still answer for the way he treats his own children when he grows up. God treats the sins of each person as their own—no one else's. The Bible makes this point clear:

> The soul who sins is the one who will die. The son will not share

the guilt of the father, nor will the father share the guilt of the son. The righteousness of the righteous man will be credited to him, and the wickedness of the wicked will be charged against him.

—Ezekiel 18:20

If we blame others for our sinful behavior instead of ourselves, we will never recognize our need for God's forgiveness. Blaming others has eternal consequences.

On judgment day we won't have any psychological disorder, abusive parent or terrible job to hide behind. Instead we will stand exposed before a holy God and His Son, Jesus Christ. The Bible tells us that we shouldn't blame God, the devil or others on our sins, but only ourselves: "Each one is tempted when, by his own evil desire, he is dragged away and enticed. Then, after desire has conceived, it gives birth to sin; and sin, when it is full-grown, gives birth to death" (James 1:14–15). Instead of creating excuses for our behavior and blaming others, we just need to admit our guilt, and then repent and ask Jesus to cleanse us from our sins.

FINDING FORGIVENESS

Cassie Bernall, one of the Christian martyrs in the Columbine High School shootings of April 20, 1999, understood what it meant to take responsibility for her actions and ask God for forgiveness and help. Before receiving Jesus into her life, Cassie was involved in self-mutilation, hateful music, witchcraft, drug and alcohol abuse, and suicidal thoughts. She wrote in an English essay, "I hated my parents and God with the deepest, darkest hatred. There are no words that can accurately describe the blackness I felt… "[2] She and her friends even planned to murder her parents, complete with graphic pictures of how it would happen. One friend told her, "Kill your parents! Murder is the answer to all your problems. Make those scumbags pay for your suffering."[3]

But she also had another friend named Jamie, a Christian, who cared enough for her to tell her the truth about her suffering. Cassie recounts in another essay:

Jamie told me very gently, and in such a noninvasive and inoffensive

59

manner, about Christ, and how what had happened to me was not God's fault. He might have allowed it to happen, she said, but ultimately I had brought it upon myself. We are given a free will, Jamie told me, and I had chosen to make decisions I would later regret. I found truth in her words and began to listen... Then, on March 8, while I was on a retreat with Jamie and her church, I turned my life around. It was only then that I was really able to see where I had gone astray. I had made bad choices, and *there was nobody to blame but myself*—something I had denied constantly throughout my suffering.[4]

Once Cassie stopped blaming her parents and took responsibility for her sinful behavior, she recognized her need for Christ to cleanse her of her sins and give her a fresh start. When she returned from the church retreat, she exclaimed to her mom, "Mom, I've changed. I've totally changed." Her mom noted:

From then on, Cassie became a totally different person... [There was a] change in her spirit—her gentleness, her humility, and her happiness. She seemed to have found a freedom she had never had before, and it changed the entire atmosphere in our house... Her whole character was somehow transformed... She had found something that was going to fulfill her in a way that nothing else had up till then, and if I think about it, the thing that showed it most was her smile. She began to smile.[5]

Cassie Bernall was not the result of her surroundings, the product of her upbringing or the innocent victim of her unconscious psyche. Cassie admitted her responsibility for her sin, and God was willing and able to take Cassie, in just the condition she was in, and completely and radically change her life for the better. Her mother bears witness to this fact: "If I've learned anything from Cassie's short life, it is that *no adolescent, however rebellious, is doomed by fate*. With warmth, self-sacrifice, and honesty—with the love that ultimately comes from God—every child can be guided and saved."[6]

If God can change a rebel like Cassie, He can change anyone.

New Creations

Psychology tells us to look into the past and blame others in order to understand the present, but the Bible calls us new creations in Christ—the old is gone and the new has come (2 Cor. 5:17). The Christian understands that his or her past is crucified with Christ—forgiven and forgotten. If our old lives are buried with Christ by His burial and our new lives are resurrected with Christ by His resurrection (Rom. 6:4), why should we dig up the dirt that should remain buried? Lot's wife illustrates the tragic consequences of looking back to our lives before we met Christ. Although warned by the angels of God not to look back when they destroyed Sodom and Gomorrah for their wickedness, "Lot's wife looked back, and she became a pillar of salt" (Gen. 19:26). Like Lot's wife, we will suffer if we look back at the wickedness of our past in order to find hope for the present.

If our past is crucified, we shouldn't take it down off the cross and analyze it. The Bible says, "*Forgetting* what is behind and straining toward what is ahead, I press on toward the goal to win the prize for which God has called me heavenward in Christ Jesus" (Phil. 3:13–14, emphasis added). We are running a race to the finish line of heaven. If we look back, we will stumble and fall behind. We will drudge up emotions from our former life before Christ that will take our eyes off of the finish line. We should only look back to remember God's blessings and deliverance to carry us through tough times. *This* kind of looking back motivates us to complete the race.

Trouble in Paradise

God wants to make sure we understand that our problem is us and not our environment. So much so, that He will give us one thousand years of perfect peace on earth to prove it. According to the Book of Revelation, this period of one thousand years will occur immediately after the Second Coming of Christ to the earth. Satan will be bound in a prison, Jesus will rule and reign as Lord of the earth, and we will be like Adam and Eve in the Garden of Eden all over again. We will have no more tears, no more injustice, no more problems—just pure paradise. "*Then*," you might say, "*then* our problems will go away and we will be happy." You would think so, but in actuality, the Bible tells us a different story. God releases Satan from his prison, and he deceives the nations across the world to follow him and fight against Jerusalem, the world capital where Jesus rules. Despite the peace and prosperity of a world ruled by Jesus Himself, people all over the world will remain discontented and will fight against Him.

Our problem is not with our environment; our problem is with our sinful hearts. No amount of self-improvement, global cooperation or visualizing world peace will change this fact. God gave us a perfect environment at the beginning of mankind, and He will do it again at the end of mankind. But the results remain the same. We have all fallen short of God's standard. We have all sinned against God. The sooner we humble ourselves and admit this, the better... for our families, our schools and our country.

CHAPTER 7

WHICH FIGUREHEAD DO YOU FOLLOW?

Psychology and Christianity also differ in the person providing help to the client—the figurehead, for lack of a better term. Psychology's figurehead is the therapist, whereas Christianity's figurehead is Jesus Christ. Both claim they can help us understand and solve our problems, so which person should we trust? To answer this question, I will play the role of a client and consider each person's qualifications in five areas: experience, intimacy, knowledge, counsel and strength.

WHO IS MORE QUALIFIED?

First, let's look at experience. A therapist probably has an average of twenty years of experience working in the field with clients like myself—an extremely generous estimate. Jesus, on the other hand, has amassed over four thousand years of experience in dealing with all of mankind ever since recorded history began. With an impressive résumé like that, Jesus rises to the top as the expert on human behavior.

Next we should take into account how well each person knows me as a person—my personality, likes and dislikes, hopes and dreams, talents and gifts, and so forth. Their counsel should line up with who I am. A therapist spends fifty minutes a week with me until my therapy stops. The therapist only knows me for the duration of my therapy treatment. Jesus, on the other hand, created me and has known me intimately since before the day I was born (Jer. 1:5). He knows every thought I have and every word before I speak it. He knows the desires of my heart and my hopes for the future. He even knows the number of hairs on my head! Jesus wins in the intimacy category.

We should also consider what each person knows about the situations I face. They should know all the details surrounding my problems. A therapist knows only what I have told him or her since I began my therapy sessions, and nothing more. Jesus, on the other hand, has the big picture. Since He is all knowing, He knows my entire situation. Even the things I didn't see, hear or know, He has seen, heard and known. Since He has the master plan, Jesus seems better qualified to counsel me in my situations.

We shouldn't forget about the quality of the guidance and suggestions that each person provides. After all, if the counsel doesn't work, why even seek it in the first place? A therapist tries hard to provide good counsel based on the latest therapeutic technique, past counseling successes, personal experience and even personal opinion. The therapist's personal issues and problems may get in the way as well. If I get him or her on the right day, I may get lucky. Jesus, on the other hand, has the perfect love and wisdom to tell me just what I need to hear at that moment. His motives are pure and true, and He will never fail me. He created me and knows how I tick. Cast another vote for Jesus.

Finally, we must consider the strength I need from each person to help me carry out his or her counsel. I can't do this alone, you know. A therapist has a cell phone and office hours. I can call every time I run into problems and hope they answer (and hope they are in a good mood). Jesus, however, lives inside of me as a believer to strengthen me when I need it. I always have access to His resurrection power and comfort, just for the asking. That's a deal I just can't refuse. I'll choose Jesus on this one, too.

Looking at the five crucial qualifications of experience, intimacy, knowledge, counsel and strength, Jesus Christ unanimously wins over a therapist as the counselor of choice. We should have no reservations about placing our complete trust and confidence in Him.

ONLY GOD KNOWS THE HEART

Human counselors are people just like us. They don't have what God has to help people effectively on an intimate and personal level. We are the creation, not the Creator. Only the Creator knows how to counsel His creation. Only God knows the makeup of a person's immaterial domain of heart, soul and spirit. A therapist cannot analyze and treat this part of a person. A pastor agrees:

> [The fathers of psychology] were guessing about invisible, internal matters that only God can see and explain. Furthermore, they were doing such from a philosophical perspective on life that purposely left God out of the equation. Only God can look on the heart of man, evaluate it, and supply the remedy for the needs of the heart.[1]

The Bible tells us that God alone is the expert on the human heart: "The heart is deceitful above all things and beyond cure. Who can understand it? I the LORD search the heart and examine the mind" (Jer. 17:9–10). "O LORD Almighty, you who examine the righteous and probe the heart and mind..." (Jer. 20:12). Therefore a human counselor will not give us what Jesus Christ, the heavenly Counselor, will give us. Jesus has the unique qualifications to assess our problems and provide solutions because He sees inside our hearts.

WORLDLY WISDOM

Although God is the only One who truly knows what we need and when we need it, people still run to the figureheads of the world for answers to their problems. Figureheads of the world abound in type and flavor, offering the latest man-made programs, services and techniques. Therapists provide the latest treatments for self-transformation; self-help authors write books on self-healing techniques; seminar presenters charge hundreds of dollars telling people how to live successful, fulfilling lives; twelve-step program facilitators promote a set of rules and a "higher power" to help people overcome addictions; advertisers promise self-fulfillment through materialism; yoga and meditation gurus offer peace and relaxation to their anxious clients; talk-show hosts throw public pity parties, give their philosophies about their guest's dilemmas and provide built-in support groups of applause; and psychics give hope to those who fear the future.

Unfortunately, these figureheads of the world promote belief systems and views on life founded on man-made theories and worldly wisdom. Worldly wisdom constantly changes to fit the trends of the times. Have you ever wondered why so many self-help books sell in today's bookstores? Which ones are correct? Which ones can we trust? Why do self-help books from ten years ago no longer sell? Does the advice in self-help books have a shelf life of ten years and then mysteriously expire?

We can ask the same questions about psychological theories, talk-show spirituality or any other form of worldly wisdom. Why has psychology's master list of disorders changed so much since its inception? Why do psychological theories come and go so quickly? The answer to all of these questions is simple. Theories based on people's opinions and cultural perspectives will always change. Man-made theories all pass away with time.

GODLY WISDOM

God's Word, on the other hand, will never pass away with time. One pastor proclaims:

> The Bible, like its Author, is the same yesterday, today, and forever. It never changes its message; it never changes its methods; it never changes its positions on right and wrong, truth and error, good and evil. It never fails to fulfill what it promises; it never fails to accomplish what it predicts; it stands forever.[2]

The Creator is the only one qualified to tell the creation how to live, and He has done this for us in His Word. Unlike material from the "experts," God's Word will always remain the same. The Bible says, "Your word, O LORD, is eternal; it stands firm in the heavens" (Ps. 119:89). We can apply God's Word to our lives just as much today as when it was first written, for its Author never changes. God's Word transcends the cultures, traditions, preferences, philosophies and technological advances of the ages because the Bible exposes man's heart, and man's heart has always been the same.

God despises man-made psychological theories and worldly wisdom because they rob people of the truth that will set them free. He actually calls worldly wisdom foolishness. The Bible says, "Do not deceive yourselves. If any one of you thinks he is wise by the standards of this age, he should become a 'fool' so that he may become wise. For the wisdom of this world is foolishness in God's sight" (1 Cor. 3:18–19). The Bible also warns, "See to it that no one takes you captive through hollow and deceptive philosophy, which depends on human tradition and the basic principles of this world rather than on Christ" (Col. 2:8). Instead of worldly wisdom, God wants us to have godly wisdom: "We have not received the spirit of the world but the Spirit who is from God, that we may understand what God has freely given us. This is what we speak, not in words taught us by human wisdom but in words taught by the Spirit, expressing spiritual truths in spiritual words" (1 Cor. 2:12–13). We have this godly wisdom in Jesus Christ: "Christ, in whom are hidden all the treasures of wisdom and knowledge" (Col. 2:2–3). God wants our faith to "not rest on men's wisdom, but on God's power" (1 Cor. 2:5).

BLIND SHEPHERDS AND THE GOOD SHEPHERD

When I first decided to study psychology, I sincerely wanted to help people improve their lives. I thought that with the proper schooling, training and self-analysis, I could adequately help others. But everything I learned consisted of man-made, worldly wisdom. I accepted certain sinful, harmful behaviors as "normal" because the psychology field classified them as such. Apart from Jesus and with no biblical knowledge, I could no more lead someone else to a better life than they could lead me. I was a blind shepherd leading my sheep down the road to destruction.

As the good shepherd, however, Jesus makes us lie down in green pastures, leads us beside still waters and restores our souls. Jesus said, "I am the good shepherd; I know my sheep and my sheep know me" (John 10:14). Instead of going to a sinful therapist, we can take our problems straight to Jesus, our perfect High Priest. Jesus knows exactly what we are going through and how we feel because He lived as a man on this earth. Jesus ate, drank and slept like everyone else. He had a job and a family. He experienced grief, exhaustion, persecution, temptation and suffering—and He overcame it all. The Bible says, "For we do not have a high priest who is unable to sympathize with our weaknesses, but we have one who has been tempted in every way, just as we are—yet was without sin" (Heb. 4:15).

THE WONDERFUL COUNSELOR

Since Jesus sympathizes with us, we can take our problems to Him through confident prayer: "Let us then approach the throne of grace with confidence, so that we may receive mercy and find grace to help us in our time of need" (Heb. 4:16). Not only did Jesus die on the cross to save us from hell, but as High Priest He continuously waits to hear from us and help us from His throne in heaven: "Because Jesus lives forever, he has a permanent priesthood. Therefore he is able to save completely those who come to God through him, because he always lives to intercede for them" (Heb. 7:24–25).

As the constant intercessor for our souls, Jesus is truly our Wonderful Counselor. His office never closes. We don't have to make an appointment; we can meet with Him wherever we are. Best of all, His services are absolutely free! He has already paid a costly price for our office visits on the cross. Seven hundred years before Jesus walked the earth, the prophet Isaiah predicted the birth of this Wonderful Counselor: "For to us a child is born, to us a son is given, and the government will be on his shoulders. And he will be called *Wonderful Counselor,* Mighty God, Everlasting Father, Prince of Peace" (Isa. 9:6, emphasis added).

JESUS PLUS NOTHING

We are complete in Jesus Christ. Not Jesus plus psychology, or Jesus plus self-help—just Jesus. We "have been given fullness in Christ" (Col. 2:10). When we approach Christ through the Word of God and prayer, God promises mercy and grace to help us in our time of need. God's Word helps us understand who we are and the problems we face. It cuts to the heart and judges our thoughts and intentions so we can walk in a right relationship with Him and with others (Heb. 4:12). The Bible says, "Every word of God is flawless; he is a shield to those who take refuge in him. Do not add to his words, or he will rebuke you and prove you a liar" (Prov. 30:5–6). When we add worldly wisdom to God's Word, we send a message to God that His words are not enough to help us—we need worldly figureheads to fill in the missing pieces. We lie to ourselves to our own detriment, as the fallacies of worldly wisdom blur our understanding of God's perfect will for our lives.

Have you been trusting in the priests of psychology, or the Counselor of Christianity? Have you been living by the wisdom of the world, or the wisdom of the Word? One will disappoint; the other will deliver. When it comes to seeking counsel, it is better to take refuge in the Lord than to trust in man (Ps. 118:8).

CHAPTER 8

WHERE
IS YOUR
FOCUS?

Have you ever noticed that people who tend to focus on themselves never seem happy or content? They strive for more power, a better car, a different mate or a thinner body, expecting these things to bring happiness. But when they finally get what they want, they still want more. Nothing seems to satisfy their desires. Those who always focus on others, however, seem to have real peace and joy in their lives.

TRYING TO BE HAPPY

Despite this ironic phenomenon, psychology contends that our unhappiness results from *our* unmet needs. Psychology puts the focus on ourselves—how *we* feel, the plans *we* have and the needs and desires *we* want fulfilled. Treatment revolves around how to restore a client's happiness and pleasure in life. Therapists fail to realize that most of our problems result directly from self-focus. The deeper we introspect and the harder we try to be happy, the more miserable and depressed we become! It has been said, "The pursuit of happiness is the chief cause of unhappiness." Self-focus manifests itself in many ugly ways:

- The need to be in control
- Disregard for the welfare of others
- Making oneself a standard of conduct
- Obsessions with possessions
- A spirit of unforgiveness
- A lack of humility
- The need for excessive praise
- The problem of pleasure seeking[1]

SELFISHNESS IN THE LAST DAYS

The Bible lists these very traits as describing people in the last days in which we live. Paul warns Timothy:

> But mark this: There will be terrible times in the last days. People will be lovers of themselves, lovers of money, boastful, proud, abusive, disobedient to their parents, ungrateful, unholy, without love, unforgiving, slanderous, without self-control, brutal, not lovers of the good, treacherous, rash, conceited, lovers of pleasure rather than lovers of God—having a form of godliness but denying its power.
>
> —2 Timothy 3:1–5

Psychology has helped fulfill the biblical prophecy that in the last days, people would be "lovers of themselves," "lovers of money" and "lovers of pleasure." Messages that cater to pleasure, happiness and living the good life permeate our culture. Advertising convinces us, "It's all about you." Our culture believes that the meaning of life is to please *ourselves* and make *ourselves* happy. Psychology embodies this same value system of self-focus and selfishness.

SELFISHNESS IN THE FAMILY

Selfishness spreads its deadly poison first within the family unit. The nuclear family has undergone a nuclear war, as families act more like busy roommates running their own separate agendas than tightly bonded units focused on pleasing Christ and each other. Then, when families suffer from the fallout, they seek therapists who make the problem worse by telling them to focus on their own needs first. The president of the California Association of Marriage and Family Therapists sees nothing wrong with selfishness:

> I have come to the place in my life where I have a standard answer to others who declare me selfish. "Thank you," I respond. I have been working toward that goal for years. I have been co-dependent all my life and have not known how to look out for myself and my needs; I have given in to others and lost the appropriate concept of placing value upon myself and my needs. So your judgment of me being 'selfish' is a compliment. It shows I have grown.[2]

Therapists like the one in Karen and Keith's marriage therapy session from chapter one now elevate selfishness to an admirable virtue. As you read their session below, note in bold the overall themes of wanting, needing and feeling, as well as the many occurrences of the words *I* and *me*:

Therapist: Tell me about the last fight you had.

Karen: Well, **I spent all afternoon last Sunday preparing a full-course meal** for Keith's parents. Keith sat on the couch watching football while **I slaved over the stove** and his parents talked my ear off. Keith's mom watched my every move. She was always quick to point out faults in my cooking techniques. When she wasn't criticizing my cooking, she would wait until she thought I wasn't looking and then wipe her finger across the top of every conceivable cabinet and countertop she could find. Then, **if that wasn't enough to push me over the edge, Keith's dad reprimanded me** for taking away the kids' dessert when they wouldn't eat their dinner.

Keith: *[To Karen]* C'mon, Karen, they were just being kids!

Karen: *[To Keith]* Kids need discipline, and **I don't appreciate your parents telling me how to raise my kids!**

Therapist: **How does that make you feel, Karen?**

Karen: **I am sick and tired of Keith's parents never accepting me and treating me with respect.** I'll never be good enough for them.

Keith: *[To Karen]* How can you be good enough when you never see them? It took two years for you to finally have them over for dinner. But you can see your parents every weekend.

Therapist: Tell me more about that, Keith.

Keith: She's never around! **I work all week to put food on the table,** and when the weekend comes **I expect some quality time together.** But off she goes with the two kids to grandma's house, to "shop 'til they drop" as they always say. *[Long pause]*... Then the credit card bills come rolling in, and **who has to pay them? Me!** In fact, we're maxed out on nothing short of nine credit cards right now. **I see her bills more than I see her.** And it's not like the bills are for things we need. No, she always has to have the latest everything—clothes, shoes, jewelry—and it piles up in the closet. Then she buys our kids everything they ask for. **But when it comes around to me, it's socks and underwear, socks and underwear.**

Therapist: *[After a long, pensive pause]* **I can see that both of you are feeling neglected. You feel like the other doesn't care about your needs** and doesn't think you're important. **You want your needs to be taken seriously, and you want to be viewed as valuable. The resentment and hurt you are feeling** is nothing new for either of you. **Keith, did you ever feel neglected as a child?**

Keith: *[Awkwardly]* Uh, I don't remember my childhood too well.

Therapist: Did your parents buy you nice things as a child?

Keith: *[Resentfully]* Nope, just the necessities.

Therapist: OK, can you remember times when your parents took time out to spend with you, to play a game or go to the park? Did they ever let you know how special and important you were to them?

Keith: No, not really. They were pretty busy.

Therapist: Keith, you seem to have had a self-sufficient childhood. Did your parents have anything to do with this?

Keith: Well, my dad left my mom when I was nine years old, and my mom had to raise the four of us alone.

Therapist: How did she handle that?

Keith: She had to go to work full time to make ends meet, but I think she handled it well. She didn't have much time to spend with us—she was always working, cooking or cleaning. So the four of us entertained ourselves, and it worked out all right, I guess.

Therapist: **It sounds like your mother needed you to be in the background, and you respected that need.**

Keith: *[Solemnly]* Yeah, that's probably true.

Therapist: Keith, it sounds like you've reached a point in your life when you just won't be in the background anymore. **You want more attention, more quality time.** I think that when you see Karen spending all her time with her mother, you get very frustrated—especially when you work so hard to provide for her. **You've decided that it's time to stop putting your own needs aside** in order to take care of others.

Keith: I'd agree with that.

Karen: I know I spend a lot of time with my mom, but *[to Keith]* at least **she accepts me as I am**—unlike your parents.

Therapist: **Karen, does it make you happy to feel accepted?**

Karen: Of course!

Therapist: I wonder if there are other people in your life who don't accept you the way your mother does. Can you think of anyone close to you who, for example, puts you down or doesn't praise you frequently?

Karen: Sure, my husband and my kids. They always seem to whine and complain. **I feel very unappreciated in my home.**

Therapist: OK, let's go with that…

Karen: Well, I'm always trying to please them, but **they never seem to want to please me. Some days I feel like a complete failure as a wife and a mom**—especially when Keith's parents visit. I just don't measure up with any of them.

Therapist: I understand. **It sounds like Keith and your kids are simply not fulfilling your need for greater self-esteem and value.** So, you turn to your mother to restore your self-worth. **She makes you feel valuable.** Would you say this is true?

Karen: Yes, I would.

Karen and Keith's therapist encouraged self-fulfillment to improve their marriage relationship. But as long as both partners focus on themselves, conversations like these will never end. Their marriage will continue in frustration and defeat.

Instead of considering ourselves as most important, God's Word tells us to "do nothing out of selfish ambition or vain conceit, but in humility consider others better than yourselves. Each of you should look not only to your own interests, but also to the interests of others" (Phil. 2:3–4). If in our marriages we simply yield up our self-centered rights to the other person, arguments will diffuse and our godly example will influence our spouses. For marriages and other relationships to improve, at least one person must decide to stop pointing the finger and humbly say, "I was wrong. Please forgive me." Whenever that happens, the road to healing begins.

SELF-LOVE AND SACRIFICIAL LOVE

Psychological love is the love of self. Self-love leads only to disorder and chaos. One author describes our bent toward self-love by quoting a sixteenth-century Swiss Reformer by the name of Ulrich Zwingli: "Man unceasingly loves himself, seeks to please himself, trusts in himself, credits everything to himself, thinks that he sees what is straight and what is crooked, and believes that what he approves everyone ought to approve, even his Creator."[3] When we get selfish in our relationships, we resemble a flock of seagulls more than we resemble Christ. Seagulls yell at each other, fight with each other and demand their rights. After they've exhausted their possibilities for gain, each goes their own independent direction, looking for something else to devour. Have you ever seen seagulls on a beach blanket or in a trash bin? It's pure chaos.

The Bible, however, talks about a different kind of love—a sacrificial love that focuses on others and not on us. Jesus referred to this sacrificial love when He said, "If anyone would come after me, he must deny himself and take up his cross and follow me" (Matt. 16:24). Denying yourself and taking up your cross means you deliberately take your focus off of yourself and onto others, as Jesus did when He deliberately denied His own life and went to the cross for our sins. Columbine martyr Cassie Bernall knew this kind of sacrificial love. One of her friends recalls:

> When I think of Cassie I always think of what Saint Francis said about how you shouldn't seek to be loved as much as you should just love. That thought was embedded in her. I think Cassie felt that only God was going to be able to fulfill her, and that was probably the thing that kept her from going crazy about her image or from getting caught up looking for a boyfriend, or whatever. She refused to give in, and *she was determined to overcome her problems by looking past them.*[4]

Cassie didn't spend hours of therapy focusing on her self-image and why she didn't have a boyfriend. Instead she trusted God and looked beyond her own problems to help others.

GOD'S LOVE

The kind of sacrificial love that Cassie lived out has more power than you could ever imagine. The power of sacrificial love breaks down walls, builds trust and heals relationships. Sacrificial love never fails, for it is God's kind of love:

> Love is patient, love is kind. It does not envy, it does not boast, it is not proud. It is not rude, it is not self-seeking, it is not easily angered, it keeps no record of wrongs. Love does not delight in evil but rejoices with the truth.
>
> —1 Corinthians 13:4–6

> [Love] bears all things, believes all things, hopes all things, endures all things. Love never fails.
>
> —1 Corinthians 13:7–8, NKJV

These verses define what it means to say, "God loves you." Let's look at the previous verses in greater detail to appreciate God's love for us and the power of expressing God's love to others.

Love is patient.

God showed patience toward us while we rebelled against Him and lived life our own way. With God's example, we can show patience toward hard-to-love people who seem to rebel against us. Our patience will melt their hearts as God's patience melted ours. Impatience, on the other hand, results from irritation—a symptom of self. These irritations make up the topics of discussion for most therapy sessions.

Love is kind.

Before we surrendered our lives to Christ, God gave us food, clothing, shelter, a job and other necessities out of His kindness, although we did not deserve it. God's loving-kindness eventually led us to repentance. In the same way we can show kindness to those who don't deserve it in the hopes that they will repent. This requires self-lessness. Our kindness quickly turns to coldness when we consider our self-interests—how *we* are treated—above the other person's well-being. Most therapy sessions focus on our self-interests instead of showing kindness toward others.

Love does not envy.

When we realize that our sins deserve death and that Jesus took this punishment upon Himself and forgave us, we rest content with our new lives in Christ. We have no room in our hearts for envying what others have, what others do or what others look like. If we do envy, we have shifted our focus from Jesus to our own selfish, covetous desires. Therapists empathize with envious clients, but the Bible calls it sin.

Love does not boast.

When we receive Jesus into our lives, we cannot boast about anything but the love God has showed us at the cross. The Bible says, "For it is by grace you have been saved, through faith—and this not from yourselves, it is the gift of God—not by works, so that no one can boast" (Eph. 2:8–9). Boasting focuses on self, whereas love focuses on Jesus and others. In marriage therapy sessions I would frequently hear such boasting as, "I clean up after you every day, and you don't say a word about it!" Even Keith had his share of boasting: "I work all week to put food on the table."

Love is not proud.

The opposite of humility, pride says, "I'm better than you." Psychology encourages pride by placing more importance on the selfish needs of the client than on humble submission to one another. But when we consider the awesome power and greatness of the Creator of the universe who humbled Himself and became a man...who considered others better than himself...and who willingly died on a Roman cross for us...we have no other choice as mere human beings but to humble ourselves as Jesus did and lay aside our pride and our selfish needs.

Love is not rude.

Since Jesus died for all people and not just for us, we should treat others with the same courtesy and kindness that Jesus showed us. If we act rudely toward others, we imply that our feelings and concerns are more important than theirs—another sign of selfishness.

Love is not self-seeking.

Jesus knew that He had to suffer and rise again three days later to restore the relationship between God and mankind. The night before His crucifixion, He struggled with what lay before Him. He knew He would be whipped, punched, hit over the head with a rod, spat upon, His beard plucked from His face, crowned with thorns, mocked, scorned and finally nailed to a rough wooden cross by His hands and feet. Worse than the physical suffering he would endure, however, was the knowledge of his imminent separation from the Father. Thirty-three years of perfect oneness with the Father would soon end when He would become sin for us. He could have saved His own life and told God the Father, "I've done no wrong. I don't deserve this. This isn't fair...forget it. I'm bailing out and going back to heaven where I'll be happy and comfortable." But instead He said, "My Father, if it is possible, may this cup [the cross] be taken from me. *Yet not as I will, but as you will*" (Matt. 26:39, emphasis added). Jesus intentionally laid aside His concern for self, for the joy of setting the world free. He showed us the perfect example of selflessness. While psychology says, "Look out for number one," Christianity says, "Nobody should seek his own good, but the good of others" (1 Cor. 10:24).

Love is not easily angered.

Even in the midst of excruciating pain and anguish, Jesus had compassion on those who crucified Him. While hanging on the cross, Jesus said, "Forgive them, Father, for they do not know what they are doing." The rest of us would have yelled out, "You fools! All of you! You let a murderer go free and you crucify me instead? You're going to pay for this!" Our anger would have consumed us. While angry feelings are normal, we can handle these feelings in either loving or hateful ways. God's love in our hearts can turn our selfish, hateful reactions to others' wrongs into compassion on those who truly "do not know what they are doing." While psychology teaches alternative methods to deal with hate such as punching a pillow and going to the gym (which don't work, by the way), the Bible teaches us to cover others' wrongs in love: "Hatred stirs up dissension, but love covers over all wrongs" (Prov. 10:12).

Love keeps no record of wrongs.

When we put our faith in Jesus' death as payment for our sins, God gives us a clean slate. Jesus' blood completely washes away our past. The Bible says:

> Seek the LORD while he may be found; call on him while he is near. Let the wicked forsake his way and the evil man his thoughts. Let him turn to the LORD, and he will have *mercy* on him, and to our God, for he will *freely pardon.*
>
> —Isaiah 55:6–7, emphasis added

> If we confess our sins, he is faithful and just and will forgive us our sins and purify us from all unrighteousness.
>
> —1 John 1:9

> As far as the east is from the west, so far has he removed our transgressions from us.
>
> —Psalm 103:12

If the God of the universe has forgiven and forgotten our sins, shouldn't we also forgive and forget the sins of others made in God's likeness? Psychology teaches us to look back into the past and analyze the wrongs of others and how they have affected us. Karen and Keith spent most of their therapy session analyzing the wrongs of the other and the wrongs of their parents.

These historical reflections actually backfire and produce even more resentment and bitterness in our hearts. Christianity, on the other hand, teaches that we should forgive others as God has forgiven us. When we forgive others, God replaces our resentment and bitterness with peace and love. God doesn't say, "All right, that's the tenth time you've done that. I've had enough with you!" Instead He continues to love us sacrificially and unconditionally.

Love does not delight in evil but rejoices with the truth.

Jesus takes no delight in seeing His children sin. But how often we delight in someone else's faults and misfortunes because it makes us look better in comparison. In therapy we bring up our spouse's faults to lessen our own. This delighting in evil has selfish roots. God rejoices in all of His new creations whom He has purchased, justified and set apart for heaven. We can do the same by rejoicing in the positive aspects of others' lives and encouraging them as they run the race to heaven. While delighting in evil tears people down, rejoicing in the truth builds them up.

Love bears all things.

God bears all things for us by protecting and sheltering us from the storms of life. When a storm suddenly dumps on you in the wilderness, what do you do? Jump inside the tent! God is our spiritual tent that we can run to when a storm hits. Whenever we're in danger, we just dial 911 for help—Psalm 91:1: "He who dwells in the shelter of the Most High will rest in the shadow of the Almighty." David continues, "I will say of the LORD, 'He is my refuge and my fortress, my God, in whom I trust'" (v. 2). Husbands should be a refuge and fortress for their wives as God is for us by protecting their wives from exposure, ridicule or harm. Psychology, however, can emphasize the husband's happiness at the expense of the wife's protection. When a husband bears all things, he no longer focuses on his own happiness but on that of his wife. God made woman from the side of man so that man would wrap his arm around her and provide protection and comfort.

Love believes all things.

God declares Christians not guilty, righteous and perfect in Christ. He sees the final product—what we will be when we reach heaven. The apostle Paul chose to consider his fellow brothers and sisters in the same manner. Paul regarded no one according to their sinful nature, but rather according to their identity in Christ (2 Cor. 5:16–17). He loved others by believing in their potential for spiritual growth and service.

Instead of "believing all things," psychology assumes the worst in people. Therapists can give diagnoses that cripple clients for life. When I was working as a mental health worker, I had one client who saw a marriage family therapist to help her mood swings. Susan blamed her mood swings on her therapist-imposed bipolar disorder (a mood disorder). Instead of believing in Susan and helping her work through her mood swings, Susan's therapist stuck a label on her that haunts her to this day. But love doesn't see people for who they are today, but for who they will become tomorrow in Christ.

Love hopes all things.

As Christians, we have the greatest hope ever known to man: the hope of heaven through Jesus Christ. Even in the trials of life we have hope because we know that "in all things God works for the good of those who love him, who have been called according to his purpose" (Rom. 8:28). We can encourage others with the promises of God and renew their hope. If someone has exhausted all of the possibilities or has reached the seeming "point of no return," we can still hope for the best for that person, knowing that God can do the impossible. Self-love, on the other hand, would simply give up hoping for that person. Self-love would not care enough to continue hoping when all of the facts say "no way." Since psychology has no hope apart from humanity, a therapist cannot instill hope in a client facing a seemingly impossible situation.

Love endures all things.

True love endures all things. It doesn't give up when the going gets tough. Jesus on the cross paints the most powerful picture of enduring love. He could have given up, taken the easy road and not gone to the cross. But because of His infinite love for us, He endured the cross and bore its shame. His enduring love continues to this day. Has God ever divorced us? Has He ever said, "I can't deal with your faults and shortcomings any more. You've crossed the line. I no longer consider you My child. I'm giving you up for adoption"? Of course He wouldn't. God loves us unconditionally, because God *is* love. So too we should never give up on our marriages, because God will never give up on us. Instead we need to persevere.

But, as you can guess, psychology takes a different approach. A therapist on television told a couple in marriage trouble, "How do you put up with this? One thing you have to consider is that you may be finished as a married couple. Some wounds don't heal." Without the knowledge of Christ's enduring love for us, our wounds drive us to divorce. When my friend and her husband sought out marriage therapy, the therapist told them, "Based on our time together, I feel you two just aren't compatible. You would probably be happier apart. Have you considered divorce?" This sounds more like cowardice than counsel. Therapists don't promote a love that endures, but a love that quits—which isn't love at all.

Love never fails.

I have seen many ineffective therapy sessions, but I have never seen ineffective love. The love that Jesus showed us on the cross has resulted in millions of changed lives over two thousand years. Costly love produces priceless results. The Bible tells us, "Above all, love each other deeply, because love covers over a multitude of sins" (1 Pet. 4:8). Love diffuses disagreements, fuels forgiveness and reaps restoration. When marital problems strike (and they will), remember, LOVE NEVER FAILS.

JOY IN THE LORD

As contrary to human reasoning as it may sound, if we focus on God and others before ourselves, we will experience a more fulfilling life. God's formula for joy is JOY: Jesus first, others second, yourself last. Any other combination won't give us JOY! First, we "fix our eyes on Jesus, the author and perfecter of our faith" (Heb. 12:2), and we "seek first his kingdom and his righteousness" (Matt. 6:33). We remember that "nobody should seek his own good, but the good of others" (1 Cor. 10:24). Finally, we take care of our own needs.

But some would like the acronym to read JYO (Jesus first, yourself second and others third) because they misinterpret Jesus' two greatest commandments: "'Love the Lord your God with all your heart and with all your soul and with all your mind.' This is the first and greatest commandment. And the second is like it: 'Love your neighbor as yourself.' All the Law and the Prophets hang on these two commandments" (Matt. 22:37–40). They adopt the psychological view that we can't love our neighbor unless we first love ourselves. In other words, if our needs are met, and if it seems convenient for us to help someone, and if it costs us nothing to do so, then and only then should we love our neighbor. However, Jesus encourages us to love others even when inconvenient and painful: "But I tell you who hear me: Love your enemies, do good to those who hate you, bless those who curse you, pray for those who mistreat you" (Luke 6:27–28). This kind of sacrificial love puts our self-interests last, not first.

"Love your neighbor as yourself" means loving others in the way we already love ourselves. Jesus doesn't have to remind us to take care of ourselves because we already do (Eph. 5:29; Phil. 2:4). He commands us to turn our attention away from ourselves and love others, just as we already love ourselves. Although this command can prove difficult to keep at times, we can do it with God's power and our submission and obedience.

SERVANT OF ALL

Jesus summed up self-focus this way: "Whoever finds his life will lose it, and whoever loses his life for my sake will find it" (Matt. 10:39). These are radical words. If you spend all of your effort focusing on your life, you will remain empty and frustrated. But when you lose your life in service to others for Jesus' sake, your life will fall in line with God's wonderful plan.

It can be shocking to step out of ourselves for a moment and take inventory of how much of the last twenty-four hours we spent focusing on ourselves and how much time we spent focusing on the needs of others. Jesus reminds us that the greatest in the kingdom of heaven will be the servant of all: "Whoever wants to become great among you must be your *servant,* and whoever wants to be first must be *slave of all.* For even the Son of Man did not come to be served, but to serve, and to give his life as a ransom for many" (Mark 10:43–45, emphasis added). Jesus lived a life of focusing on others in humble servitude. Jesus said, "No servant is greater than his master" (John 13:16). If our Master came to serve, then as His servants we must do the same. Let's make it a priority to spend less time focusing on our own selfish desires and more time "[washing] one another's feet" (John 13:14).

PART III

PSYCHOLOGY IN THE CHURCH

God made marriage for people; He didn't make people for marriage. He didn't create this institution so He could just plug people into it. He provided this so people could enjoy each other to the fullest. If you have two people who are not thriving healthfully in a situation, I say remove the marriage. Let them heal.[1]

A well-known Christian in marital strife received this advice from a Christian therapist. Now divorced, this person fell for the psychological thinking that if a couple does not "enjoy each other to the fullest" and is not "thriving healthfully," the couple should get divorced in order to "heal." This case illustrates the dramatic influence of psychology on the church.

In this section we will look at how much psychological thinking has seeped into the church with its disorders, medications, Christian therapists, support groups and twelve-step programs. God has a better way for us to handle our problems, and He gives us the choice of which road to take: the road of self-serving Christian psychology or the road of God-serving biblical living.

CHAPTER 9

MY DISORDER
MADE ME
DO IT

A friend of mine showed me a bulletin from a church he visited listing the following weekly activities for its members:

- Freedom from depression support group
- Grief recovery group
- Anger support group
- Compulsive overeaters support group
- Group for parents of children with ADHD (attention deficit hyperactivity disorder)
- Compassionate (nonviolent) Communication Workshop, a six-week course taught by a psychotherapist who asks attendees, "Would you like to experience the power of using words to create affection, trust and respect—to watch anger, frustration and hurt fade away?"

Somewhere stuck in between all of these support groups I managed to find listings for a Bible study and a prayer meeting. Tragically, this church focuses on grief, depression and anger more than on Christ. While they wallow in self-pity, support groups and worldly wisdom, the Lord waits patiently for them to acknowledge His sufficiency and seek His face.

SPIRITUAL SHORT-CIRCUIT

The church today has allowed the worldly ideas of psychological disorders and diseases to stroll into our lives virtually unnoticed. Self-pity has replaced prayer and petition. Support groups have replaced trust in God's power. Many Christians believe they have no power over their mental-emotional-behavioral problems, when all the while God waits for us to unleash His indwelling power through confession and simple, childlike faith in Him.

Thanks to psychology, instead of confessing our sins, we call our sinful behaviors by the more politically correct and scientific-sounding terms of disorders, diseases, illnesses and addictions. We confess our addictions to one another and receive salvation through recovery that never really ends. Without true confession and forgiveness through the Lord Jesus Christ, we cut off fellowship with God and short-circuit His power to help us overcome our problems. We cheat ourselves out of God's blessings by throwing up our hands and surrendering to the claims of psychology. But should we take disorders and diseases seriously? Are they real, and do they have any scientific validity? Who decides what behaviors qualify as disorders or diseases in the first place?

DISORDERS AND DSM

Our American culture obsesses on psychological disorders and diseases. If I experience anxiety, I must have an anxiety disorder. If I drink too much, I must have the disease of alcoholism. If I get depressed, I must have a mood disorder. If I eat too much, I must have an eating disorder. If I can't sleep, I must have a sleep disorder. If I become stressed out over my new job in a new city, I must have an adjustment disorder. The psychology industry uses the disorder/disease concept to convince people of their need for psychological help—slap an impressive-sounding label on a life problem, call people who have that problem "victims" of "disorders" and "diseases" and claim to have the cure.

You can find every psychological disorder imaginable in psychology's bible, the *Diagnostic and Statistical Manual of Mental*

Disorders, or *DSM*. This reference book, published by the American Psychiatric Association (APA), compiles the most common syndromes and disorders observed over the years in psychological practice. The fourth revision since its initial publication in 1952 lists no less than 340 different psychiatric conditions.[1]

Some disorders in this manual of labels include:

- Eating disorder
- Anxiety disorder
- Mood disorder
- Sleep disorder
- Adjustment disorder
- Narcissistic personality disorder
- Avoidant personality disorder
- Obsessive-compulsive personality disorder
- Antisocial personality disorder
- Paranoid personality disorder
- Dependent personality disorder
- Attention deficit hyperactivity disorder[2]

DISORDER MANIA

Psychology seems to have a disorder for every possible human condition. "If you're not feeling 100 percent perfect, you must have some sort of disorder in your life," says the therapist or psychiatrist. Psychology turns the common experiences of life, like depression, anxiety and fear, into permanent conditions that require extensive psychological treatment. Even religious people have a "religious addiction" if they are using it to escape real life or avoid painful feelings. If you take all of the possible disorders in the *DSM* and research the number of people in America who have been diagnosed with each disorder, you will come up with a population more than two times larger than the entire population of America.[3] In other words, the average person in America has at least two disorders! Perhaps you have happiness anxiety—when happy, you are keenly aware of the potential for unhappiness that could soon occur, causing intense anxiety. Or perhaps you call yourself one of the 5,600,000 Americans who have the UFO abduction syndrome...[4]

If you or someone you know has been diagnosed with a psychological disorder or disease, these statistics should ease your concern about what the "experts" think. Even if you don't think you have a disorder, the therapist or psychiatrist will make sure you have one by the time the session ends. First, the therapist and psychiatrist will ask you a series of questions that deal with thoughts, emotions and behaviors. Then he or she will try to fit your responses into a label to make a diagnosis. If you don't agree with the therapist's or psychiatrist's psychological label, you are labeled as being in denial until you accept that label. Either way, you need help.

The labels of the *DSM* actually serve the therapist and psychiatrist more than the client. Psychology has succeeded in duping the American public into believing that if they don't feel right in some way, they must have a disorder and must get it treated by a professional. They have created their own market to sell their services, resulting in a win-win situation for all parties involved: The therapists and psychiatrists make money diagnosing clients; the pharmaceutical companies make money developing prescription drugs; and the clients get a convenient excuse for their behavior from an "expert" in the field.

CULTURAL SCIENCE

How does the APA determine the disorders and diseases of the *DSM* in the first place? A historical event may shed some light on this question. In 1973, the APA removed homosexuality from the *DSM* manual of disorders in response to threats from a group of homosexuals outside the building on the day of the vote. The APA caved in to the pressure, removed the disorder and included a work-around statement that excluded those conditions that "have strong cultural or subcultural supports or sanctions."[5]

This event, along with other similar politics, has led many to believe that the *DSM* does not compile verified results of in-depth scientific research and testing, but instead merely reflects what our culture considers normal and abnormal. Therapists and psychiatrists observe client symptoms, describe them, attach a label to them and add the label to the *DSM*. Personal viewpoints and opinions determine exactly how to describe symptoms and whether or not to consider a symptom "normal" (whatever that means). Disorders appear and disappear based on the subjective opinions of a body of psychological decision-makers.

DISEASE OR DECEPTION?

Cultural influences aside, does scientific research substantiate the claims of the *DSM*'s disorders and diseases? Take for example the disease of alcoholism. The psychology industry claims that twenty-five million people in the United States are alcoholics.[6] But Dr. Herbert Fingarette, a professor at the University of California and well-known scholar, disagrees with this statistic: "*No* leading research authorities accept the classic disease concept. One researcher puts it quite boldly: 'There is no adequate empirical substantiation for the basic tenets of the classic disease concept of alcoholism.'"[7] Harold Mulford, director of alcohol studies at the University of Iowa, exposes this truth:

> I think it's important to recognize that the alcohol disease concept is a propaganda and political achievement and not a scientific achievement. Science has not demonstrated that alcoholism is a disease by defining it, nor has science or technology demonstrated it to be a disease by coming up with an effective treatment or preventative.[8]

But the general public still believes the unscientific notion of a disease called alcoholism, mainly due to entire organizations and multimillion-dollar industries built around this false concept who would go out of business if the truth were told. The same holds true for depression, manic-depression, schizophrenia and other so-called diseases that have no scientific basis. *Time* magazine reported on a panel at a psychotherapy conference in 1985, citing that three out of four "experts" said there is no such disease as schizophrenia.[9]

Psychiatrist Gary Almy describes a true medical disease in this way:

For a true disease, the cause, course of illness, and outcome can be predicted. For any specific disease, there will be a specific recommended treatment that can be expected to lead to the disappearance of abnormal signs, the lessening of symptoms and, ideally, a cure...The syndromes and disorders [of psychiatry] have no known cause, no predictable course of illness, no specific and reliable treatment, and no reliable response to treatment...The diagnoses left to psychiatry, such as depression, schizophrenia, passive-aggressive personality, and narcissism, fail to fit the definition of true diseases.[10]

MY DISORDER IS CONTAGIOUS

With no predictable cause, course, treatment and outcome, most of psychology's diagnoses *do not* qualify as disorders or diseases. In other words, most psychological disorders and diseases simply do not exist. Anxiety, then, becomes an accountable behavior and not an excusable disorder or disease. So why does the psychology industry still base their therapy treatments and medical prescriptions on disorders that do not exist? Part of the problem stems from psychology's insistence in treating the mental just like the physical. The words *mental illness* prove the point. Think about those terms. Can you catch a mental illness the way you can catch a cold? No, because symptoms of a cold are physical and symptoms like anxiety are mental. You cannot call a mental behavior an illness or disease and then treat it like a physical condition. For example, alcoholism is not a physical disease, but a mental choice. On the other hand, cancer and Alzheimer's disease are physical diseases, not mental choices.

We need to make the differentiation between the mind and the brain. The mind is not an organ that can contract a disease, disorder or illness. Many mental-emotional-behavioral symptoms once classified as purely soul-related (mental) now get classified as brain-related (physical), although no scientific evidence supports the presumption that mind equals brain. Psychology uses medical-sounding disorders and diseases that describe what really amounts to mental-emotional-behavioral problems. "But what about chemical imbalances?" you might ask. In the next chapter we will examine the claim that chemical imbalances cause psychological disorders and diseases.

A BROKEN LINK

Do we have a spiritual component to our mental conditions? Since we cannot consider depression a disease and anxiety a disorder, could these conditions result from a broken link between God and us, where we no longer have a faithful, obedient relationship with God? The life of King David helps us answer this question.

David was a man after God's own heart—a king, a warrior and a lover of God. When David's relationship with God thrived, he would praise and worship God day and night. He couldn't wait to go to the temple of God. He had a peace in his heart and hope for the future. Basically, he had an abundant, overcoming life. But when David sinned against God with his pride, adultery with Bathsheba and murder of her husband Uriah, suddenly life wasn't a blessing anymore. David's sin cut off his relationship with God, and as a result his bones "wasted away" (Ps. 32:3). He actually had physical manifestations of his broken relationship with God.

We can experience the same manifestations when we cut off the living water of Christ in our hearts with unconfessed sin. Depression and anxiety replace joy and peace. Only Christ can fix the problems causing these symptoms, not a therapist.

TAKE A SPIRITUAL INVENTORY

More often than not, I have found that our mental conditions stem from deeper problems relating to our relationship with God. We should take a spiritual inventory and evaluate our relationship with God. We should ask ourselves, "Am I rightly related to God and others in my life at this very moment?" Yes, we are forgiven and righteous in God's sight because of Jesus, but sin has a sneaky way of building up in our hearts and clogging the flow of the Holy Spirit's living water in and through our lives. When the water stops flowing, we begin to notice our spiritual lives drying up. Suddenly life turns from wonderful to burdensome. We begin to see things through the filter of self instead of through the filter of God. God seems more distant, people seem more annoying, and we seem more focused on ourselves and what makes us happy. Once we stop surrendering to and trusting in Christ moment by moment, our lives begin to bear bad fruit, because "everything that does not come from faith is sin" (Rom. 14:23), and sin produces bad fruit. To produce good fruit again, we, like David, should confess and repent of our sins to restore our fellowship with God.

BIBLICAL SOLUTIONS

As Christians, we have control over our behavior. No so-called disorder or disease has power over us, regardless of what psychological "experts" claim. Instead of blaming our behavior on disorders and diseases, we should admit our fault. Once we take responsibility for our actions, we can trust in the Lord to help us, and He will give us the power to overcome our sinful behavior.

Without Jesus we are slaves to sin. We can become so steeped in a particular sinful activity—pornography or gambling, for example—that it controls us and we become addicted to it. But if the Son sets us free, we will be free indeed! For the Son to set us free, we need to heed His heavenly treatment by practicing trust and obedience. Let's take a look at how a lack of trust in God and obedience to His commands can contribute to the mental, emotional and behavioral problems many of us experience. We can diagnose and treat many of the behaviors described in the *DSM* in a biblical way.

Eating disorders: In Christ, we are no longer slaves to the sinful nature—the sinful nature no longer has control over us (Rom. 6:6–7). We can trust God to help us gain control over this problem. I met one young woman who went to the best therapists available to gain control over her bulimia, a type of eating disorder. After literally years of therapy, she made no progress whatsoever. Then she met the Counselor who would help her overcome her sinful nature in this area—Jesus Christ.

Anxiety disorders: Everyone experiences anxiety at one time or another. But if we really trusted God's sovereignty over every situation, we wouldn't become anxious. Instead we would rest in God's hand, casting every care upon Him (1 Pet. 5:7). The more we practice trusting God, the less frequently we will become anxious.

Mood disorders: We all experience depression as a normal part of life. Frequently, however, depression results from focusing on ourselves. We need to remember that we no longer live, but Christ lives within us. We live our lives by faith in the Son of God who loved us and gave Himself for us (Gal. 2:20). We have crucified our self-life and focused our mind's eye on Him.

Sleep disorders: Not being able to sleep relates to anxiety. We should pray, give thanks to God and read His Word, and God will give us a supernatural peace and rest in our hearts (Phil. 4:6).

Adjustment disorders: Worry and stress often come upon us during times of adjustment and transition. Jesus tells us not to worry about our lives, but to trust in the One who never changes (Matt. 6:25, 34; John 14:1; Heb. 13:8).

Narcissistic personality disorder: Those who want all the attention, praise and adoration act prideful. The sin of pride banished Lucifer from heaven (Isa. 14:12–15). We must confess pride when the Holy Spirit brings awareness of this sin into our minds. God has a way of humbling those who exalt themselves when pride remains unchecked (Dan. 4:33; Luke 14:11).

Avoidant personality disorder: These people feel inadequate, insecure and highly sensitive to what others say and think about them. As a result they avoid others. God wants us to realize that He is for us, so who can be against us (Rom. 8:31)? We trust in the full acceptance and security we have in Christ (Eph. 1:6). We care more about what God thinks of us than what people think (Rom. 2:29).

Obsessive-compulsive personality disorder: Obsessive-compulsive people are controlling perfectionists. They do not trust God's sovereign hand in all situations and therefore have a difficult time letting go (Ps. 103:19). If we call Jesus the Lord of our lives, we will surrender control to Him in all things and recognize that if we could attain to perfection, then Jesus died for nothing (Gal. 2:21).

Antisocial personality disorder: These people take selfishness to a new level. They will deceive and manipulate others in order to get what they want. Paul tells us to avoid such people in the church (Rom. 16:17–18). As we have already seen, selfishness is sin. If we focus on satisfying only ourselves, we do not live by faith in God (Gal. 5:16–21). God's heavenly treatment? Deny yourself, take up your cross and follow Christ (Matt. 16:24).

Paranoid personality disorder: Paranoia has to do with fear of other people. But God has not given us a spirit of fear, but a spirit of power, love and a sound mind (2 Tim. 1:7). We can trust God because He helps us deal with other people (Heb. 13:6).

Dependent personality disorder: We don't have to become overly dependent on others to help us function in life. With Christ living inside us, we can depend on Him in all things (2 Pet. 1:3). We can do all things through Christ, who strengthens us (Phil. 4:13). Depending solely on others reveals our independence from God. God wants us to trust Him and Him alone.

Attention deficit hyperactivity disorder (ADHD): Children that always find it difficult to sit still and pay attention prove their undisciplined nature. Parents simply have to discipline their children, as sitting still and paying attention require a disciplined mind (Prov. 22:15).

The Bible provides simple yet profound solutions for all of these "disorders." By trusting our Lord's promises, we can overcome the behaviors that once overcame us. An uncontrollable sin before Christ can become a controllable choice in Christ. But we must make that choice—an act of the will—to place our trust in Christ and obey Him moment by moment in every situation we face.

The supposed diseases and disorders of psychology keep us from realizing the true problem—our relationship with God. Instead of recognizing sin, repenting of it and trusting in the cross of Christ for forgiveness and cleansing, we never hit stage one. Why? Because psychology no longer calls sin "sin," but sickness, illness, addiction, syndrome, hurt, trauma, dysfunction, disorder, disease—you name it. Diseases and disorders actually drive us away from God. Instead of attaching a convenient label to ourselves and using this label as an excuse for sinful behavior, let's just call it for what it really is: sin for which Christ died. Christ wants us to come to Him with our sin. We cannot begin to fathom the depths of Christ's love and forgiveness. He never runs out of forgiveness for us, for His fountain of grace never ceases to flow.

CHAPTER 10

SHOULD I
TAKE PSYCHIATRIC
MEDICATION?

Hannah tried everything. Even though she was in and out of therapy for over ten years, her depression continued to get worse and worse. Although a Christian since a young age, Hannah's depression seemed insurmountable. Her psychiatrist eventually put her on Prozac, a popular antidepressant medication. But the Prozac only deepened her depression. On two separate occasions Hannah tried to kill herself while on the medication. Eventually Hannah decided to turn her entire life over to God and follow Him with all of her heart. Christ's resurrection life began to take over. Her faith, hope and love continue to increase as God has brought her through many serious family-related trials since this recommitment. As a result of her recommitment to Christ, Hannah has stopped being depressed and now uses her time praying to God and serving, loving and encouraging others.

BLAME IT ON THE BRAIN

Fortunately, Hannah committed her life to Christ before attempting suicide for a third and perhaps final time. But some Christians continue to risk their spiritual and physical health by trusting the claims of psychiatric medications more than the claims of Christ. Although research has *not* scientifically proven psychological disorders and diseases, many in the psychology industry claim that disorders and diseases stem from genetic or biological traits that cause chemical imbalances in the brain. Disorders once classified as purely soul- and mind-related (mental) are now considered brain-related (physical). As a result, people now turn to psychiatric medication to cure so-called chemical imbalances that cause mental disorders.

In this chapter, we will discover the truth behind chemical imbalances, popular medications and the pharmaceutical industry at large. You may ask, "I've tried everything else with little success—should I resort to psychiatric medication?" This chapter will help you answer this question.

As a former psychotherapist, I have no real-world experience in psychiatry of which to speak. (Psychiatry is the medical practice within the psychology field responsible for prescribing medications to clients seeking psychological help.) However, a portion of my schooling required a thorough understanding of how to diagnose clients for treatment purposes, including knowing when to refer clients to psychiatrists for medication. In this chapter I share my views on when we should take medication and when we should not, and I cite research from others in the medical profession as well. I hope that as Christians, we will only take medication when it makes medical sense to do so.

JUST POP A PILL

As a culture we view "popping a pill" as the solution to almost every inconvenience we face. We pop a pill to relieve stress, put us to sleep, control menstrual cycles and even kill an unwanted baby. We have come to trust in medication to conquer anything that gets in the way of our comfort and pleasure in life, including mental, emotional and behavioral problems.

It's not surprising then that anti-anxiety and anti-depression medications surpass every other kind of psychiatric medication in number of sales. In fact, worldwide sales of Prozac, a popular antidepressant medication, totaled $2.3 billion in 1996.[1] The number of Prozac users reached an astounding twenty-five million in less than ten years.[2] People now flock to medications for even the most minor feelings of discomfort. They take Prozac for fatigue; Paxil or Zoloft for apathy and aimlessness; Xanax, Klonopin or Ativan for anxiety and nervousness; and Ritalin, Dexedrine or Adderall for lack of focus or children's misbehavior. Even some Christians now place their faith in pills instead of God to solve their mental-emotional-behavioral problems.

CHEMICAL IMBALANCES AND GENETIC INHERITANCE: FACT OR FICTION?

Most people resort to psychiatric medications because they believe in the popular notion of biochemical imbalances (or simply "chemical imbalances") in the brain. Many therapists and psychiatrists now view most (if not all) disorders and diseases of the *DSM* as biological or genetic in nature, claiming chemical imbalances or genetic inheritance as the culprit. Brace yourself, because research reveals a very different story.

Contrary to popular belief, *chemical imbalances do not cause mental disorders like depression, anxiety and attention deficit disorder.* The media bombard us with messages that adrenaline, hormonal and serotonin imbalances and deficiencies cause our mental-emotional-behavioral problems. However, research has either not confirmed this claim or retracted earlier proof as inconclusive. Psychiatrist and Harvard instructor Joseph Glenmullen tells us, "In every instance where such an imbalance was thought to have been found, it was later proven false...A serotonin deficiency for depression has not been found."[3]

Psychiatrist Peter R. Breggin, known as the ethical voice of psychiatry, and his associate David Cohen note, "In the field of mental health, not a single physical explanation has been confirmed for any of the hundreds of psychiatric 'disorders' listed in the *DSM-IV*."[4] Not only has research never proven disorders and diseases on a mental level, as we have already seen, but it has also never proven them on a physical (biochemical) level. In fact, "All the talk about biochemical imbalances is pure guesswork...No biochemical imbalances have ever been documented with certainty in association with any psychiatric diagnosis."[5]

If your therapist or psychiatrist doesn't attribute your disorder or disease to chemical imbalances, he or she may point to genetic inheritance, claiming that your depression could run in your family. Dr. Glenmullen describes how, in recent decades, researchers claimed to have discovered the gene for manic depression on multiple occasions, only to retract the announcements after closer scrutiny. He concludes, "No claim of a gene for a psychiatric condition has stood the test of time, in spite of popular misinformation."[6] In spite of what you may have heard from your doctor, the research shows that we do not inherit our mental-emotional-behavioral problems from the family tree.

THE MYSTERY OF THE HUMAN BRAIN

Why haven't all of our advances in modern medicine revealed how chemicals in the brain affect our behavior and mental state? Because we are dealing with the most complex creation in the universe: the human brain. Although researchers have discovered some knowledge of how chemical messengers (called "neurotransmitters") work, they still don't understand how they work together to produce brain functions. Drs. Breggin and Cohen admit:

> The public is told that a great deal of science is involved in the prescription of psychiatric drugs, but this is not so—given that we know so little about how the brain works. The knowledge that we do have about the effects of psychiatric drugs on the brain is largely limited to test-tube studies of biochemical reactions utilizing ground-up pieces of animal brain. We simply do not understand the overall impact of drugs on the brain. Nor do we have a clear idea about the relationship between brain function and mental phenomena such as "moods" or "emotions" like depression or anxiety.[7]

Psychiatrist Dr. Gary Almy agrees: "Science understands little about the function of the brain and even less about how the various psychiatric medications affect the brain."[8] Even the researchers themselves admit they don't know much about the human brain. After reviewing the biochemical disease models of depression, the director of the depression research program at the Massachusetts General Hospital confessed in 1997, "The dark side of all of this is that we have many elegant models, but the real fact is that [when it comes to] the exact mechanisms by which these things work, *we don't have a clue.*"[9]

ANIMAL TEST RESULTS

Any claims of chemical imbalances in the human brain stem from animal research conducted on healthy, normal animal brains—not on people with supposed chemical imbalances in their brains. According to Drs. Breggin and Cohen, "We lack the technical capacity to measure biochemical concentrations in the synapses between nerve cells [of human brains]." Dr. Glenmullen adds, "Nor can one measure serotonin at specific synapses."[10] Not only have researchers failed to measure levels and locations of serotonin and other chemicals in the human brain, but they also have no way of predicting the results of medication in treating people with these elusive "chemical imbalances."[11]

On the contrary, animal research *has* shown that *all* psychiatric drugs disrupt and impair normal brain functions and actually *cause* chemical imbalances.[12] Many psychiatric symptoms actually result from the psychiatric drugs themselves. The FDA (Food and Drug Administration) knew this before approving Prozac, but thanks to deceitful product marketing, the FDA approved this drug, and the drug companies popularized it as a cure to "biochemical depression."[13] Since most psychiatric drugs *cause* chemical imbalances in animal brains, many people experience prolonged or even permanent brain damage as a result. The medication causes the very problems it should cure!

PRESCRIPTION BY OBSERVATION

If chemical imbalances did actually exist, wouldn't the psychiatrist need to measure the type, location and amount of chemical imbalance in the brain in order to prescribe the correct medication? One would expect medical testing to take place to diagnose and treat a medical condition properly. For example, if I had sharp pains in my lower back, the doctor would take an X-ray to examine vertebrae alignment and then propose a proven treatment plan. But in the world of mental problems, the psychiatrist takes a different approach...

Picture yourself walking into a psychiatrist's office, hoping to get cured from your anxiety. First the psychiatrist spends a few minutes with you asking you questions and observing your behavior. The psychiatrist then makes an educated guess of your "disorder" based on his or her observations and knowledge of the *DSM*. The psychiatrist explains to you that your disorder results from a chemical imbalance in your brain and recommends you take a medication to fix your chemical imbalance. You leave with prescription in hand and with the hope that your medication will really do what the experts say it will do.

But when do you take the tests that measure the chemical imbalance? The answer is never. Psychiatrists perform absolutely no medical testing for chemical imbalances to understand the type of chemicals you lack, how much of them you lack and where you lack them. You won't get a brain scan, a blood test, a spinal tap or any other medical test to detect a chemical imbalance. In its place you get an external observation of your symptoms and behavior by an "expert," followed by a drug prescription. The traditional medical profession would outlaw this kind of medical practice, but the psychology profession gets away with it.

After filling your prescription, you blindly begin taking medication for your condition, without any measurements proving a chemical imbalance actually exists and without any knowledge of expected results. You have placed your life in the hands of your psychiatrist who has given you mind-altering drugs for a disorder that doesn't even exist in the first place.

What can you expect from drugs prescribed by a psychiatrist?

PSYCHIATRIC MEDICATION:
OVER-PROMISED AND UNDER-DELIVERED

Does medication produce effective results? A recent television commercial puts it into perspective. The commercial promotes a research study for those who may have "treatment-resistant depression." They say, "If you've taken this and that type of antidepressant medications for x months or more and are *still* depressed, you may have 'treatment-resistant depression.'" Boy, this one sounds like a doozy—a disorder on top of a disorder. You don't just have depression; you have *treatment-resistant depression*. It's going to take a real miracle drug to cure that one. The company advertising this product must have discovered a huge market of people who have taken depression medication with little or no success.

Researchers at the University of California, San Diego have even come up with a surgical implant hoping to cure people suffering from severe depression. A pacemaker-looking device, the implant targets people who have had no success with therapy and medication. A doctor inserts the implant into a person's chest to send electronic pulses from the chest, through the neck and to the brain stem to increase brain activity. Studies like these shed light on the ineffectiveness of therapy and medication in treating depression, the most common "disorder" in America.

Since disorders and diseases do not exist, the medication used to treat a client's conditions will not produce the desired results. Medication has proven no more effective than plain sugar pills, especially when measured over periods lasting more than a few weeks or months.[14] On the contrary, research done over the long term has actually shown that these drugs make people's mental conditions increasingly worse.[15] With results like these, we should no longer think of medication as a last-resort treatment when all else fails.

I have seen medication's ineffectiveness firsthand while working at psychiatric wards in hospitals. At first I thought the patients had real disorders that only medication could improve. But soon I noticed the same patients getting refills month after month with very little or no improvement. Their behavior remained unchanged. Some even got worse from their medication. The psychiatric ward became a revolving door for patients hooked on prescription drugs.

Predicting the results of psychiatric medications can be a real challenge. One person may respond to the same dosage completely differently than another person, even though both receive the same psychiatric diagnosis. If the medication doesn't produce the desired results, the psychiatrist may blame the client's persistent "mental illness" instead of blaming the drug itself. Without an objective, scientific basis for prescribing medication, psychiatrists must provide hit-or-miss treatments.

TRADE-OFF OR RIP-OFF?

When you take psychiatric drugs, you open yourself up to innumerable side effects that make medication less of a trade-off and more of a rip-off. Have you ever noticed that the television advertisements for medication promise to help one condition but then go on to list ten other problems you may experience? "Get maximum relief from your pain with new Krypton from XYZ Labs... may cause headaches, nausea, dizziness, dry mouth, sweating and insomnia." They fix one problem but create ten others!

Psychiatrists tell us the most commonly reported side effects from psychiatric drugs include "confusion, memory difficulties, dulled emotions, artificial feelings of euphoria, depression, anxiety, agitation, personality changes, and psychosis."[16] These conditions sound remarkably similar to the conditions for which people take medication in the first place. Psychiatric drugs can also make a person less sensitive, less in touch with reality, more distant, and vacant and unloving. They can even produce permanent personality changes and psychosis.[17]

FOURTH LEADING CAUSE OF DEATH

Not only does medication cause side effects, but many types of medication can also lead to more serious complications or even death. *The Journal of the American Medical Association* (*JAMA*) reported that prescription drugs may be the *fourth* leading cause of death in hospitalized patients, killing one hundred thousand people each year. The association revealed, "We are more likely to die from a medication than from most diseases."[18] The *JAMA* report showed that prescription-drug-related deaths followed only heart disease, cancer and stroke in number.[19]

Even with these startling statistics, many in the psychology field figure the benefits outweigh the risks. They claim that psychiatric drugs can prevent suicides and violence by changing a person's outlook on life. But research has shown just the opposite results: "There is no convincing evidence that any psychiatric medication can reduce the suicide rate or curtail violence. But there is substantial evidence that many classes of psychiatric drugs...can cause or exacerbate depression, suicide, paranoia, and violence."[20] Andrea Yates drowned each of her five children in rapid succession in the bathtub of her Houston, Texas home while on antidepressants. Instead of curing her postpartum depression, the six months of antidepressants drove her to methodically murder her own children, who ranged in age from six months to seven years old.

WITHDRAWAL AND BRAIN DAMAGE

As if these dangerous side effects and the possibility of death weren't enough, we haven't even considered what happens when you want to stop taking medication. Some psychiatrists compare the withdrawal symptoms of psychiatric drugs with those of alcohol, marijuana and even heroin.[21] If you are fortunate enough not to experience any serious side effects with a particular medication, you will most likely experience withdrawals when you try to stop. Due to the addictive nature of many psychiatric drugs, the withdrawal symptoms are frequently much worse than the symptoms you experienced before taking the drugs.

If you do succeed in withdrawing from a drug, you may experience brain damage of varying degrees, depending on the type of drug, dosage amount and length of time you took the drug. As I mentioned earlier, most psychiatric drugs cause chemical imbalances in animal brains. After the brain wears itself out compensating for these imbalances, it gives up and remains in an altered state for an indefinite period of time. People could experience brain alterations and damage that affects them years after quitting medications.[22]

DRUGS DU JOUR

People take the advice of psychiatrists who confidently recommend medication but who have little clue as to the permanent physical damage that medication could do to the brain. The most popular medications today include antidepressant medication, anti-anxiety medication, stimulants and herbs. Each has its own unique risks.

Antidepressant medications

Even though research has never proven the cause of depression medically, the psychology industry tells the general public otherwise. One brochure in a drug store overconfidently states, "Depression is a medical disorder, like diabetes or heart disease, and is treatable."[23] People trust these claims and get a prescription for an antidepressant medication to treat their "medical disorder" that really doesn't exist. Drug companies market antidepressants by claiming them "selective" for serotonin, meaning that the drug selectively targets areas of the brain deficient in serotonin. However, according to a Harvard instructor and psychiatrist, "There is, in fact, no known depression center in the brain. Rather, the drugs have global effects owing to serotonin's vast influence."[24] As a result, antidepressants affect the entire brain—even those areas that it shouldn't affect. Experts believe that increasing serotonin levels in the brain inadvertently decreases dopamine levels, leading to the dangerous side effects that have been reported.[25]

Prozac sales lead all antidepressant medications to date. Some experts in the field believe that long-term use of Prozac can produce changes in brain structure and chemistry leading to irreversible tics, dependency, emotional desensitization and even intense irritability sometimes leading to suicide.[26] The FDA warns that the drug causes psychotic mania behaviors like extreme overactivity, insomnia, racing thoughts, frantic outbursts, violence, paranoia and suicide.[27] Research has also shown Prozac to cause obesity and *worsening* depression,[28] a perfect example of how a psychiatric drug can actually cause the very symptoms the drug claims to cure. The makers of Prozac now market this medication under an additional name, Sarafem, to treat so-called premenstrual dysphoric disorders in women.[29] They have also created a liquid mint version of Prozac for children, as well as a Prozac pill for depressed dogs and cats.

Other popular antidepressants accompany Prozac in the antidepressant category, such as Zoloft, Paxil, Luvox, Celexa, Wellbutrin, Effexor, Serzone and Remeron. All of these antidepressants have serotonin-boosting effects on the brain similar to Prozac, resulting in equally debilitating and dangerous side effects.[30]

Anti-anxiety medications

Like depression, anxiety is categorized as a medical illness instead of a mental state of mind. Anti-anxiety medications have also been watched with scrutiny for their highly addictive qualities. Many compare the addictive qualities of anti-anxiety medications to heroin. As I write this, a Christian friend of mine is taking Xanax, a popular anti-anxiety medication. He wants to stop taking the medication and start trusting in the Lord again. Unfortunately, when he tries to stop, he experiences tics and other uncontrollable physical manifestations. His attempts to stop taking Xanax have failed because, in his words, "I'm addicted now. When I stop I experience *ten times* the amount of anxiety that I had when I first started taking it." His experience confirms the research done on Xanax: "Marginal positive results are erased by the eighth week, at which time many or most patients experience more anxiety than before they began taking the drugs."[31] The disappointing and often dangerous results of anti-anxiety medications have motivated many people to file lawsuits against drug companies. In fact, I recently saw a television advertisement telling users of certain anti-anxiety medications how to receive a monetary refund in connection with a lawsuit settlement.

Stimulants

Stimulants like Ritalin and Adderall have gained popularity as the drug of choice for controlling children who are hyperactive, impulsive and inattentive. Those in the psychology field diagnose these children as having ADHD (Attention Deficit Hyperactivity Disorder), a disorder that, according to the psychology industry, "is due to a chemical imbalance in the brain. Genetics may play a role in determining who gets ADHD... "[32] Although the psychology industry claims that ADHD results from medical conditions, research has never confirmed this claim.

The ADHD disorder disturbs Ryan and me more than any other. My husband has seen what stimulants do to children diagnosed with this disorder. The teenagers he knows who take stimulants act like robots—they show dulled emotions and seem disconnected and in a continuous drug-induced trance (because they are). They perform on command, without any life or individuality about them. They spend their teenage years in a drug haze not brought on by independent rebellion, but by parental request.

Comments from this doctor being interviewed by *Reason* magazine will make us think twice before stuffing Ritalin down our children's throats for their misbehavior:

> The [ADHD] epidemic doesn't exist. No one explains where this disease came from, why it didn't exist 50 years ago. No one is able to diagnose it with objective tests. It's diagnosed by a teacher complaining or a parent complaining. People are referring to the fact that they don't like misbehaving children, mainly boys, in the schools. The diagnosis helps tranquilize the parent, tranquilize the school system... We may not know all of the medical consequences [of prescribing Ritalin to kids] for another 20 or 30 years... I don't know if the average person on Main Street realizes that if a 30-year-old man has a pocketful of Ritalin, he can go to jail for years. This is called "speed." And this is what they give as a treatment to schoolchildren when there's absolutely no laboratory or medical evidence that they are sick.[33]

Ritalin and other stimulants can cause insomnia, seizures, agitation, irritability, nervousness, confusion, disorientation, personality changes, apathy, social isolation, sadness, depression, paranoia and mania. Ritalin can also disrupt growth hormone production. Cylert, another stimulant, has even caused death due to liver failure in some cases. Emotional effects of stimulants include flattened emotions and robotic behavior. Ironically, Ritalin and other stimulant drugs can cause the very problems parents want to fix. They can produce hyperactivity, loss of impulse control and diminished concentration and focus.[34] How sad that we would rather turn our kids into obedient robots to make our lives easier than take the effort to discipline them and the time to love them and get involved with their lives. We'd rather "debark"[35] our kids than put them through obedience school.

Some parents give Ritalin to their kids to help improve their grades. Perhaps the media and some psychiatrists claim Ritalin can expand the mind, but the psychiatric research proves otherwise. Research has shown that stimulants like Ritalin do not improve a child's academic performance, mental functions or learning ability, but rather impair them.[36] Let's reject psychiatric drugs like Ritalin and return to what has worked for thousands of years: time, love and discipline.

Herbs

We have little documented research on the use of herbs such as St. John's Wort as an alternative treatment of mental, emotional and behavioral problems. While initial findings on the effectiveness of St. John's Wort have been positive, its long-term effects are not yet known. Years down the road, we may discover that herbs are harmful and that all the marketing hype about herbal treatments was just that—hype. In fact, some herbal medicines have already been pulled from the store shelves due to dangerous reported side effects.

SUPPRESSING THE TRUTH

After all of this research revealing the harmful side effects and serious dangers of psychiatric medications to treat "disorders," why haven't you heard about it? Thanks to drug companies that ignore or twist research to sell more drugs, the American public believes that lengthy, objective and proven research goes into developing safe and effective psychiatric medication.

Marketing from drug companies and psychology industry groups has convinced us that chemical imbalances in our brains cause our mental-emotional-behavioral problems. Since they claim to know the cause, they also claim to have the answer—a big cure in a small package. Drs. Breggin and Cohen boldly expose this shameful truth: "Many educated Americans take for granted that 'science' and 'research' have shown that emotional upsets or 'behavioral problems' have biological and genetic causes and require psychiatric drugs... Few if any people realize that they are being subjected to one of the most successful public relations campaigns in history."[37] Later they say, "The campaigns to promote 'mental illness' have been so successful that, within a matter of a few years, millions of Americans have come to believe that they have 'biochemical imbalances,' 'panic disorder,' or 'clinical depression,' and that their children have 'ADHD.'"[38]

Dr. Glenmullen thinks similarly: "In the past decade, hypothetical biochemical imbalances have been presented to the public as established fact. The result is an undue inflation of the drug market..."[39] Drug companies and psychology industry groups ignore the research findings concerning chemical imbalances, drug side effects and permanent brain damage in favor of making money off of people's problems.

The APA's reaction to results of an international survey presented at their prestigious 1998 meeting prove just how far the psychology field will go to suppress the truth for selfish gain. The results revealed that *over 50 percent* of clients discontinue psychiatric drug treatment due to side effects, including drug-induced "sleep problems, anxiety and agitation, and sexual dysfunction." Despite these alarming results, the APA recommended a "worldwide campaign to *encourage* more people to seek psychiatric treatment."[40] Could the APA be in "denial" to keep their industry alive?

Although the FDA must approve all new psychiatric drugs before release to the market, the drug companies themselves perform the research on effectiveness and safety, and that research only lasts six to eight weeks. The drug companies frequently produce vague, biased research that intentionally fails to reveal the adverse and sometimes fatal side effects of the new drug to the FDA. In addition, the long-term side effects of the drug remain unknown upon FDA approval. Therefore you cannot trust a psychiatric drug just because the FDA approved it. Instead of asking, "Did the FDA approve this drug yet?" or even "Do I trust my psychiatrist?", you should ask, "Should I trust the drug company whose livelihood depends on sales of this drug?" By falsely influencing psychiatric organizations, the FDA, the media and the general public, drug companies have deceived and destroyed the

114

lives of millions of people with brain-damaging medications.

We cannot do much to stop the momentum and influence of the drug companies. However, each of us has the power to reject taking psychiatric medication and giving these types of medication to our children.

To Medicate, or Not to Medicate

While psychiatry's disorders and diseases have not been medically proven, diseases like Alzheimer's, Parkinson's, epilepsy and dementia *have* been proven to have a true medical origin. We should certainly take medication to treat these cases of true diseases.

How can we know whether we have a true disease or a psychiatric "disease"? We should get medical testing for any perceived illnesses. Testing may include blood tests, brain imaging and other objective measurements. If testing is positive, we should take the doctor's recommended medication and follow the appropriate treatment plan. If testing is negative, we do not have a medical condition but a mental one. As we've seen previously, our mental problems are really spiritual problems that we can diagnose and treat biblically.

The God of Medication

Unfortunately, we seldom realize that many of our problems result from our lack of trust in and obedience to God. Instead many Christians now look to the god of medication to fix a spiritual problem that only God can fix. In fact, research shows that a whopping 90 percent of those seeking medical assistance have an emotional component at the root of their problem.[41] Instead of humbling ourselves before God, admitting our sin, receiving His forgiveness and cleansing, and resuming our trust in Him, we take the easier road of masking our problems with drugs.

One pastor witnessed how a lack of obedience to God produced the mental problems of a few people from his congregation: "Some of my counselees have been treated with antidepressants. One had been incorrectly diagnosed as a schizophrenic, and another had been in psychiatric therapy for more than fourteen years, without cure. In both cases, the cause of their problems was deep anger and bitterness. Drugs were not the solution."[42]

Taking drugs to cover up deeper spiritual issues puts us in serious danger physically and spiritually. Medication blinds us to our real need for God. Medication becomes our god in place of the one and true God. The god of medication keeps many from experiencing a living, abiding relationship with Jesus Christ. Many in the field of psychiatry now agree that, thanks to the propaganda efforts of drug companies, "nowadays the ultimate Higher Power is medication."[43] I'm sure God grieves when He sees Christians trusting in this higher power.

One summer day I spoke with a woman about her bouts with depression. I asked her about her relationship with God, and she admitted neglecting it. She knew she needed to get back on the right track spiritually. But every time I would encourage her to return to the open arms of God, she would refocus on her depression and her need for medication. Her god was her medication—she trusted more in her medication than she did in God Himself.

Psychiatrists also admit that people use medication to avoid addressing the real issues in their lives: "If used to solve emotional problems, [psychiatric medications] end up shoving those problems under the rug of drug intoxication while creating additional drug-induced problems."[44] If you want to numb yourself and escape from your problems, take psychiatric medications. In this context, psychiatric medications "work," not by restoring a perceived chemical imbalance, but by impairing brain functions to dull your suffering and escape from your problems. You could call them a high-society, socially accepted version of marijuana. Like marijuana and alcohol, psychiatric drugs give us an escape from reality and, like Andrea Yates, open us up to demonic influence beyond our control. Psychiatric drugs are the gods we turn to when we have problems we can't bear. The living God waits with open arms to receive us, but like Adam and Eve, we run and hide instead.

TRUST AND OBEDIENCE

God desires that we confess our sins to Him instead of hiding from

Him. When we resume trusting God and obeying Him moment by moment, we will find that our mental-emotional-behavioral conditions will miraculously disappear, and the fruit of love, joy and peace will grow once again. This shouldn't surprise us, because God is the source of our life! He wants to fill us with His life—that's why He sent His Son to restore our broken relationship. Jesus has not only provided a way to heaven; He is our source of overcoming life in the present. We simply need to trust and obey Him.

One pastor received a letter from a radio listener about the power of obedience over "mental illness:"

> I am a 27-year-old female. When I was 14, I began to experience depression frequently. I was not a Christian, nor was I raised by Christian parents...My depression continued as I grew older, and as a result became worse as time passed. I became a chronic suicide case...
>
> When I was 20 I went to a psychiatrist, who diagnosed me as a manic depressive. He put me on lithium and told me I would be this way for the rest of my life. The drug therapy kept me from going into a severe suicidal depression. However, the deep feelings of depression and despair were still a reality.
>
> I finally came so low that there was nowhere to turn but to the Lord. I heard the Christian life was supposed to be the only way to live, but God was not real to me. I decided I was going to seek God with my whole heart, as Jeremiah 29:13 says. Then if I found this to be nothing but an empty endeavor, I would give up living.
>
> I fed upon tapes of your Bible teaching. The Lord began His work in me. Through His Word, as you taught, the Holy Spirit showed me just exactly what my problem was, and what I needed to do about it.
>
> My problem was sin—a heart that would not forgive, and it was making me bitter...I turned to the Lord and asked Him to help me forgive. I continued in the Word diligently, and the transformation process took place. The Lord delivered me...
>
> The memorizing of Scripture is renewing my mind. This is the only key for anyone suffering emotional problems, because it is the Living Word of God, it is the supernatural power to transform

anyone's life and mind...No doctor, no drugs can do what the Bible had done for me in changing my life.

P.S. By the way, I have been off all medication for three years now! Obedience is the key![45]

WE ARE GOD'S TEMPLE

We are the temple of the Holy Spirit, who lives in us. The Bible says, "You are not your own; you were bought at a price. Therefore honor God with your body" (1 Cor. 6:19–20). Everyone who calls himself or herself a Christian has the words "Property of God" branded on their soul. If we are God's property, does it please God for us to take brain-damaging substances into our bodies? The Holy Spirit doesn't need the help of psychiatric drugs to give us an over-coming life. He has done just fine for the past two thousand years without them. When we pollute our bodies with psychiatric drugs, the good fruit of the Holy Spirit grows rotten. Instead of love, joy, peace, patience, kindness, goodness, faithfulness, gentleness and self-control, we experience insensitivity, depression, anxiety, hyperactivity, isolation, psychosis, suicide, violence and seizures.

We can classify problems as either medical (physically measurable) or spiritual (physically immeasurable). Psychology misses the mark with its medical approach to spiritual issues. Instead of popping a pill, we should bring our mental-emotional-behavioral problems to the Wonderful Counselor, Jesus Christ, and discover the cause of our problems and feelings.

Are you not trusting God in a certain area of your life? Are you disobeying Him in some way? Think about your relationship with God before running to prescription drugs. After examining what God has to say about your problems as revealed in His Word and by His Holy Spirit, if you honestly confess where you have strayed and get back on course, God will cure you. That's His promise.

CHAPTER 11

WHAT ABOUT "CHRISTIAN" PSYCHOLOGY?

Professional Christian counseling, which I will hereafter call Christian psychology, has become extremely popular in the Christian community. A quick browse through any Christian newspaper will reveal countless advertisements of Christian therapists selling their counseling services. Psychology-based books on self-improvement and marriage and family relationships take up entire sections of Christian bookstores. Many larger churches have full-time licensed Christian therapists on staff. One pastor observes:

> Evangelicalism is infatuated with psychotherapy. Emotional and psychological disorders supposedly requiring prolonged analysis have become almost fashionable...Virtually everywhere you look in the evangelical subculture, you can find evidence that Christians are becoming more and more dependent on therapists, support groups and other similar groups.[1]

Even senior pastors dismiss their own knowledge in the doctrine and application of God's Word by referring their congregation to Christian therapists. But is "Christian" psychology Christian? Does God want us to see Christian therapists with our problems? Let's meet Mr. Churchgoer to answer this question.

MEET MR. CHURCHGOER

Mr. Churchgoer, a Christian man, has been experiencing debilitating depression for the last three months. He has been out of work for almost a year, his marriage has become distant and cold, and he feels more and more hopeless about life. He hasn't learned how to apply the Bible to his life effectively since becoming a Christian. In fact, he hasn't spent much time reading the Bible at all. He wants to change, but he doesn't know where to begin. His wife recommends asking the church about it.

So Mr. Churchgoer consults his pastor, Mr. Scripture, about his bouts with depression. After meeting with Mr. Churchgoer, Mr. Scripture decides that his extensive knowledge in the doctrine and application of God's Word cannot adequately meet this man's complex needs. Mr. Scripture refers Mr. Churchgoer to the professional Christian psychologist on staff with the church.

Mr. Churchgoer walks into Dr. Insight's office and immediately notices the impressive psychology credentials on the wall. Mr. Churchgoer says to himself, "This man will certainly have the answers I've been looking for. He has the psychological training, *and* he's a Christian!" After sitting down, Dr. Insight begins to ask questions about Mr. Churchgoer's depression. After hearing out his symptoms, Dr. Insight asks, "What were your parents like?"

Mr. Churchgoer wondered what his parents had to do with his depression, but he figured Dr. Insight knew what he was doing. So Mr. Churchgoer answers, "They were good parents. They brought me up in the church—it was a tradition, you know. They would always tell us to be on our best behavior whenever we were in public. I attended only the best schools and was consistently at the top of my class—my parents always made sure of that. I really have no complaints about them."

"Hmm..." After a few minutes of reaching back into his "secret knowledge" gained through extensive psychological training and experience, Dr. Insight concludes, "It sounds like your depression may stem from the large amount of pressure placed on you since you were a child to increase the prestige of your family." Shifting gears,

Dr. Insight continues. "Let's move on. Tell me about your marriage. How's that going?"

"My wife is wonderful, although lately we haven't been getting along. She's always complaining to me about how I never want to do anything anymore. She gets frustrated and yells at me when I struggle making simple decisions," replies Mr. Churchgoer.

Dr. Insight notes, "You may be suffering from a mood disorder. In any case, it sounds like your wife is contributing to your poor self-esteem. The Bible says that the wife is supposed to submit to the husband as unto Christ. By yelling at you, she is certainly not submitting."

Mr. Churchgoer smirks and says, "That's right! She never submits to me. I don't know very many Bible verses, but I made sure to memorize that one. I tell it to her all the time, but she never listens!"

After a few minutes of contemplation, Dr. Insight firmly states, "I believe your depression stems from your parents' high expectations and your wife's verbal abuse. I have three recommendations for you as we begin our six-month treatment plan. First, you need to see me once a week for individual therapy so we can help restore your normal mood and repair any damage done to your relationships and career that has resulted from this disorder. You can start on the road to recovery by remembering your self-worth every morning when you wake up. God loves you and thinks you're the most important person in the world, and you should, too! After all, you can't love others until you first love yourself."

Dr. Insight continues, "Second, in addition to our weekly individual therapy, you and your wife must visit weekly for marriage therapy. In addition to helping improve your marriage, these sessions will help your wife understand the nature and treatment of this potentially chronic disorder." Pulling out a stack of workbooks from his desk, he says, "Start reading through these marriage workbooks I've written." Taking a deep breath and leaning back into his leather chair with his hands clasped behind his head, Dr. Insight confidently concludes, "We'll also get you started on an antidepressant medication. There are minor side effects, but most people do just fine."

A relieved and beaming Mr. Churchgoer stands up and shakes Dr. Insight's hand. On the way out of the church office Dr. Insight reassures Mr. Churchgoer, "Don't you worry. With the right amount of treatment and medication, mixed with lots of faith in yourself and God, you'll conquer this disease of depression in no time." Mr. Churchgoer leaves the church with renewed hope that, with Dr. Insight's expert treatment plan, his bouts with depression will soon end. Before going to bed that night, Mr. Churchgoer thanks God for Dr. Insight's help.

Six months later, after a depleted bank account from thousands of dollars of therapy sessions and psychotropic medication, more intense feelings of hopelessness and apathy and a knockout fight with his parents about their child-rearing failures, Mr. Churchgoer's depression has only worsened. While taking the medication he experienced stomach discomfort, diarrhea, weight gain, hair loss, severe acne and memory loss. The side effects became so severe that Dr. Insight recently discontinued the medication. Now, however, Mr. Churchgoer is undergoing major drug withdrawal, complete with symptoms of restlessness, insomnia, racing thoughts, increased talkativeness and excessive pleasure seeking.

Concerned about Mr. Churchgoer's well-being, Mr. Scripture visits him at his home, where Mr. Churchgoer stays most of the day. Mr. Scripture offers his prayers and his love and encourages Mr. Churchgoer that his fellow worker in the Lord, Dr. Insight, would like to offer extended treatment for his depressive disease. In the meantime, Mr. Churchgoer will miss this weekend's message from Mr. Scripture on the sufficiency of God's Word in all of life's circumstances.

A BETTER WAY

This sequence of events and the tragedy that resulted has become all too real in the church today. How different this exchange would have sounded and its results would have been if Mr. Scripture used God's Word, by the power of the Holy Spirit, as the *sole* treatment for Mr. Churchgoer's depression. Instead of referring Mr. Churchgoer to a Christian psychologist, Mr. Scripture could have used his knowledge of Scripture to help Mr. Churchgoer understand the reasons behind his depression and the ways to conquer it. Instead of considering the past as crucified with Christ, Dr. Insight brought up memories of Mr. Churchgoer's childhood and then blamed his depression on his parents. Instead of telling Mr. Churchgoer that he should love his wife as Christ loved the church and gave Himself for her, Dr. Insight blamed his depression on his wife's "verbal abuse" that contributed to his "poor self-esteem."

Dr. Insight's treatment centered more on psychology than on the Bible. Instead of remembering his self-worth, Mr. Churchgoer should have denied himself and, trusting Jesus, looked after his wife's needs. Instead of reading man-made materials on the treatment of depression, Mr. Churchgoer should have consulted the Bible. Instead of taking medication, Mr. Churchgoer should have restored his relationship with God.

TWISTED SCRIPTURE

This Christian psychologist's vocabulary overflows with psychological terms like "mood," "disorder," "recovery," "disease," "self-esteem," "self-worth" and the like. But Dr. Insight also throws out a few biblical concepts to make his psychology sound Christian—concepts like the wife submitting to the husband, the love of God and the love of others. Dr. Insight skillfully takes these verses out of context and twists them to fit the situation at hand. The wife submits to the husband, but the husband should also sacrificially love the wife. Our life centers around God, not ourselves; we should sacrificially love others before ourselves.

From this account you can easily see how the Bible can get distorted when placed in the context of psychology. This dangerous mixture of contradictory theories produces futile—if not tragic—treatments that ultimately rely on worldly wisdom and "professional" insight over the power and purity of God's Word. Christian psychology is just another belief system that twists God's Word for its own benefit, taking verses from God's Word out of context to support man-made psychological theories. The cults twist God's Word, and we take notice. Why then, does Christian psychology get away with it?

PSYCHOLOGY WITH CHRISTIANITY ON TOP

What exactly is wrong with the concept of Christian psychology? In theory, going to a Christian therapist with my problems seems logical. As a Christian experiencing mental, emotional or behavioral problems in my life, I would naturally want to go to someone trained in providing counseling and who uses the Bible as the standard from which they work... right?

However, in practice, official Christian flavors of psychology do not exist. Most Christian therapists consider themselves therapists who just so happen to be Christian. They still use the man-made theories of psychology, but they add the Bible when possible and call it Christian. Just as Mormonism adds the Bible to their other doctrinal books and claims their beliefs are Christian, so too Christian psychology adds the Bible to their doctrinal theories and claims their beliefs are Christian. One pastor sees right through this deception: "Though almost all [evangelical psychological clinics] claim to offer biblical counsel, most merely dispense secular psychology disguised in spiritual terminology."[2]

Remember the counseling advertisement from chapter three?

WE OFFER SPECIALIZED PSYCHOTHERAPY
TO HELP YOU OVERCOME:

- Anxiety
- Depression
- Addictions
- Eating Disorders
- Childhood Abuse
- Marriage/Family Problems
- Ministry Issues

Did you find it immediately obvious that this advertisement represented a Christian counseling service? Probably not, for the majority of the advertisement comes from psychology, while the last line gives a hint of Christianity. Christian therapists build their counseling foundation on psychological theories, not the Word of God. Paul warned the Corinthians about building on a foundation other than Jesus Christ: "But each one should be careful how he builds. For no one can lay any foundation other than the one already laid, which is Jesus Christ" (1 Cor. 3:10–11). Christian psychology lays a faulty foundation with a few Bible verses on top—a building bound to collapse.

CHRISTIAN WITCHCRAFT

There is no such thing as Christian psychology. These two words are polar opposites. If the therapist is Christian, he or she should not use psychology. If the therapist uses psychology, he or she should not use the Bible. Have you ever heard of Christian witchcraft or Christian evolution? Like Christian psychology, these phrases are oxymorons.

As we've already discovered, psychology is a man-centered view of life, whereas Christianity is a God-centered view of life. Take for example the biblical doctrines of sin, salvation and sanctification. The Bible says that:

- Sin = our innate wickedness that separates us from knowing God.
- Salvation = placing faith and trust in Christ to cleanse us of sin and restore our relationship with God.
- Sanctification = setting ourselves apart from the world and obeying God as the Holy Spirit makes us more like Christ.

But some Christian therapists say that:

- Sin = sickness, illness, dysfunction or anything that lowers our self-esteem.
- Salvation = curing our illness by boosting our self-image and self-esteem and getting in touch with our inner goodness.
- Sanctification = producing good mental health by our own psychoanalysis and self-effort.

CHRISTIAN PSYCHOLOGY: A BAD MIXTURE

Even psychology professors in the educational ranks question the compatibility of psychology with Christianity. Paul Vitz, an associate professor of psychology at New York University, says, "Psychology as religion is deeply anti-Christian."[3] William Kirk Kilpatrick, associate professor of educational psychology at Boston College, says:

> Psychology and religion are competing faiths. If you seriously hold to one set of values, you will logically have to reject the other...True Christianity does not mix well with psychology. When you try to mix them, you often end up with a watered-down Christianity instead of a Christianized psychology. But the process is subtle and is rarely noticed.[4]

Since psychology and Christianity differ so widely, those who attempt to add the Bible to their psychological views must, by necessity, water down or ignore Scripture to make the two work together. Integration of the two is impossible, as one author aptly puts: "One cannot make Christian that which is essentially anti-Christian, no matter how Christian its practitioners may be."[5]

ANTI-CHRISTIAN ROOTS

We can easily identify psychology's anti-Christian roots by studying the views of its founders. Sigmund Freud called religion a form of neurosis and affectionately referred to himself as "the godless Jew who founded psychotherapy."[6] In fact, Freud and other psychology icons, including Jung, Adler, Maslow, Fromm, Rogers and Janov, did not believe in Jesus Christ and intentionally based their theories on their own opinions about mankind and how to change him. Freud believed that religion, inherently evil in his opinion, actually caused mental illness. Jung called religion an imaginary coping mechanism for mental illness. Both Freud and Jung participated in idolatry and the occult. Although we couldn't imagine seeking godly advice from men like this, many Christians do this very thing when they see Christian therapists who use psychological theories in treatments.

AA AND THE GOD OF PERSONAL EXPERIENCE

Freud and Jung weren't the only fathers of psychology who dabbled in mysticism and the occult. The founders of Alcoholics Anonymous (AA), one of today's most popular psychological recovery programs, frequently contacted and communicated with the dead. Bill Wilson and Bob Smith held séances and used Ouija boards on a regular basis.[7] Wilson even took LSD to better understand psychic phenomena.[8] Many people falsely believe that these men were Christians just because they attended meetings of the Oxford Group, a so-called Christian movement that focused on personal experience instead of the Bible.[9] Wilson's "conversion," however, was anything but Christian.

After crying out to God about his drinking problem, Wilson had a mystical experience that would later form the foundation of his twelve-step recovery program. An "indescribably white light" filled the room and he was "seized with ecstasy beyond description."[10] He sensed a great peace and finally "knew that [he] was loved and could love in return."[11] In Wilson's supernatural experience, he never recognized his sinfulness and separation from God. He never exercised faith in the blood of Jesus Christ for forgiveness of his sins. Nevertheless, Wilson believed this presence represented God.

Wilson reflected this vague, universal God in his twelve steps, frequently referring to "God as we understood Him." While the Bible of Christianity teaches that faith in the death and resurrection of Jesus Christ provides the *only* way to God, Bill Wilson's biography states that he "felt it would be unwise for AA as a fellowship to have an allegiance to any one religious sect. He felt AA's usefulness was worldwide, and contained spiritual principles that members of any and every religion could accept, including the Eastern religions."[12] According to AA, your personal experience and beliefs—not the Bible—define the identity of God. Many Christians who attend AA-like recovery meetings fail to realize that Wilson's twelve steps never originated from the Bible, even though Bible verses now appear in some "Christianized" versions of the twelve steps.

Furthermore, the humanistic exercises that make up the twelve steps completely omit any faith in God's transforming grace by the Holy Spirit. Improvement depends solely on your sheer will power to succeed. You can imagine the hopelessness that prevails in this sort of program when people place themselves under such burden and expectation, with no assurance of success. Overcoming any of life's problems without the Holy Spirit cannot be considered a Christian practice. Nevertheless, the explosion in popularity of AA's twelve steps in both Christian and non-Christian circles has spawned more than 260 twelve-step programs in America.[13]

PSYCHOLOGY AND THE OCCULT

More and more psychological programs like AA contain mystical components that rely on subjective experience over biblical truth. These forms of psychology open people up to harmful influences: "Psychological methods, concepts and conclusions are channels through which satanic, occult and Eastern mystical influences enter Western society...There is evidence that occult practices have been accepted by a large and perhaps growing number of psychological professionals."[14] For example, one clinical psychologist observed that "I Ching, Tantra, Tarot, alchemy, astrology and other occult practices could be useful for producing mental health and giving meaning to life."[15] I find it hard to believe that some Christian therapists have integrated these forms of Eastern religious practice into their treatments. The once-pagan practices of yoga, meditation and hypnotism have grown extremely popular, even in the toolbox of some Christian therapists. You can imagine the confusion and danger that results from this smorgasbord method of treatment, when clients blindly open themselves up to demonic powers. They take a little bit of Jesus, a little bit of yoga and a little bit of meditation, creating a whole lot of spiritual confusion.

PSYCHOLOGICAL INVASION

Although those with any knowledge of the psychology field understand psychology's anti-Christian roots, Christian psychology's sinful yeast still spreads unchecked throughout the church, harming the spiritual lives of too many misinformed Christians. Some pastors have witnessed Christian psychology's harmful influence firsthand. Dr. J. Vernon McGee, a well-known Bible-preaching pastor now with the Lord, made this alarming prediction about psychology's invasion of the church: "I see that this matter of psychologizing Christianity will absolutely destroy Bible teaching and Bible churches."[16] The destruction has begun. Pastor and evangelist Greg Laurie illustrates how the language of psychology has woven its way into our everyday vocabulary:

> Secular psychology has invaded the church with many concepts that are wrong—terms that are used even in sermons: wholeness, healthy, enable, dysfunctional, and making amends. What do these terms mean? They're not biblical terms. For example, one might say, "We're having problems...I don't think this is a *healthy* relationship...We haven't really found a state of *wholeness* in the commitment we made to one another...I feel that we're somewhat *dysfunctional*...Perhaps we need to make *amends*." Many Christians know more about self-esteem than they know about self-denial. They know more about inner healing than they do about outward obedience. They know more about getting in touch with their inner child than they do about reckoning the old man dead.[17]

Another pastor also sees the recent shift in the church from biblical to psychological thinking: "Contemporary opinion is more utilitarian [than God's grace], valuing physical comfort more than spiritual well-being, self-esteem above Christlikeness, and good feelings over holy living."[18] The way a Christian campus ministry leader at Harvard University described the problems of his students reeks of this kind of psycho-babble: "... student counselees exhibit feelings of guilt, addictive sexual relationships, low self-esteem, disrespect for parents, cynicism, depression, anger carried inside for years, eating disorders, drug abuse, alcoholism, compulsive shopping, and 'emptiness under our feet.'"[19] I'd like to know exactly what it feels like to have "emptiness under my feet." Sounds pretty surreal.

JUST LIKE THE WORLD

Christian therapists sound just like their secular counterparts, and their mode of operation resembles those of secular therapists as well. If I have a problem for which I need guidance, I open the yellow pages, locate a Christian counseling center or church and schedule an appointment with a therapist or church psychologist. As I enter the therapist's office, I can't help but notice the walls lined with textbooks and periodicals on psychology and covered with framed degrees and certificates. I lean over a large desk to shake the hand of the therapist whom I am paying to listen to me for fifty minutes. I return a week later to start the whole process over again. It seems the only things differentiating a Christian therapist from a secular one are the fish logo in their advertisements and the occasional positive Bible verses used to help their clients feel better.

PSYCHOLOGICAL MARRIAGES

Marriage seminars blur the differentiation even further. Today you seldom find a marriage seminar based solely on the Word of God. Instead, a typical marriage seminar receiving rave reviews from Christians will be hosted, not by a pastor or Bible teacher, but a licensed psychotherapist! One popular Christian counseling center specializing in marriage prides themselves on their psychological bent. Their motto reads, "Integrating the truth of Christianity with the best of psychology in caring for the souls of people." If they really told the truth, their motto would read, "Integrating the truth of Christianity with the myths of psychology in confusing the souls of people."

CHRISTIAN SUPPORT GROUPS

In a continuing effort to become just like the world, some churches have adopted secular psychology's "support group" concept, trying to attract the 40 percent of Americans, or seventy-five million adults, who belong to one of more than three million support groups.[20] Groups from recovering drunkards to drug addicts to overeaters have popped up all over Christendom in an effort to attract people with similar struggles. Although this practice seems logical on the surface, the Bible never mentions believers splitting up into recovery groups based on past sins and going through twelve steps to heal. Although the apparent success of recovery programs like AA remains unproven,[21] churches still adopt this worldly method of helping its members overcome their sins.

My husband and I attended one Bible study with handouts titled "The Ten Decisions of Wholeness" and "The Twelve Steps—a Spiritual Discipline for All Christians," a "Christianized" version of AA's 12 steps. The handouts failed to mention the cross of Jesus Christ anywhere. The God "as we understood Him" told us to stop attending that Bible study.

The Bible considers the body of Christ a whole unit, made up of believers from many different backgrounds and lifestyles. In 1 Corinthians 6:9–11, Paul described the various sins the Corinthians had committed in the past, including excessive drinking, sexual immorality, adultery, stealing, greed and so forth. But then he concluded with, "And that is what some of you *were*. But you were washed, you were sanctified, you were justified in the name of the Lord Jesus Christ and by the Spirit of our God" (emphasis added).

Paul implied that instead of identifying ourselves with past sins, we should identify ourselves as in Christ, focusing on the victory we have through the "one step" of faith in the blood of Christ shed on the cross. Support groups hurt us spiritually because they center on problems instead of Christ; in doing so, they perpetuate identification with sins that Christ has completely cleansed and forgotten. Support groups also foster a form of gossip and slander when sins are advertised to uninvolved parties.

PSYCHOLOGICAL MISSIONS

Christian psychology has even spread its tentacles of worldly influence into the mission field. Numerous missions organizations now force those God has called into the mission field to undergo psychological screenings, interviews and personality tests. These missions organizations deny support to those who refuse to participate in these unscientific and unbiblical activities.[22] In the name of psychology, these organizations have assumed authority over the Holy Spirit as the final decision-makers on who can and who cannot take the simple gospel of Jesus Christ to the ends of the earth.

CHRISTIAN PSYCHOLOGY IN THE REAL WORLD

Let me take a moment to tell you about some real-world experiences I had with Christian psychology when I hit the streets as a new Christian just out of graduate school. With Bible in hand, I sought out a counseling position at a local Christian counseling center where I could use the Bible to help people with their problems.

During one interview, a Christian therapist asked me bluntly, "How do you think you can help people?"

I answered, "Well, by using the Word of God."

She confidently replied, "No, that's not what I mean. See, I'm divorced so I can help people who are divorced. Are you divorced?"

Feeling a bit awkward at this point, I said, "Uh, no, I am not divorced."

"OK, well I have kids. Do you have kids?"

"No, I'm not even married yet."

"Well, you need to identify areas in your past that you've experienced so that you can help others who are going through the same things."

Needless to say, I didn't accept this job. Looking back on this interview, I realized this Christian therapist believed you could only help others through your personal life experiences instead of through God's Word. In other words, whatever happens to you becomes the standard by which to live. You are now the final authority on life, and other people need to glean from your superior wisdom and experience. Instead of moral absolutes, everything is relative to your subjective past experience.

It saddens me to think of how many sincere Christians this woman has misled with her empty, futile advice. Christian psychology has become a field where "'there are as many psychotherapies as there are psychotherapists,' where there is no authoritative manual or guidebook, where each therapist brings to the client his own home-grown wisdom and advice."[23] Truth is relative to the therapist.

My wake-up call with Christian psychology did not end there. I discovered that an increasing number of Christian therapists who advertise their Christian orientation now prohibit use of the very Bible they claim to believe! At my request to use the Bible during counseling sessions, one therapist who interviewed me responded, "We don't do that here."

I replied, "But this is a Christian private practice. Don't people come here for biblical advice?"

He answered, "That's what churches are for. They can get that stuff at church. You'll need to stick to the psychological theories you learned in school."

Taken aback, I said, "Well, I *would* like to use the Bible if people request it."

The look on his face made me quickly realize where he stood with the Bible. At the same interview he eventually told me, "This isn't going to work."

So I politely got up and shook his hand. Before I could leave, he thrust into my hand his business card with a big Christian fish on it and exclaimed, "Good luck!"

After much interviewing, I finally found a Christian private practice that allowed me to use the Bible *only* with clients who requested it; otherwise I had to use psychology. As the weeks passed, I realized that those who worked in this Christian private practice didn't care about helping people—they only cared about making money. Staff meetings consisted of marketing brainstorm sessions, where we asked each other questions like, "How do we attract more clients?" and "How do we keep clients coming back?" We didn't focus on helping people, but on growing the business.

THE BUSINESS OF CHRISTIAN PSYCHOLOGY

These three experiences typify today's Christian psychology scene. It makes me wonder why these therapists call themselves Christian counselors in the first place if they do not use God's Word. Christian counseling without the Christian Book is simply not Christian. They should remove the fish if they depend on past experiences and psychological theories. I truly believe they retain the popular Christian symbol to attract the Christian community, increase market share and grow their businesses. For these therapists, it's not about helping people grow closer to Christ—it's about making money from people's hurts.

The Bible speaks of this type of person who uses the name of Christ for their own benefit: "Unlike so many, we do not peddle the word of God for profit. On the contrary, in Christ we speak before God with sincerity, like men sent from God" (2 Cor. 2:17). The Greek word for *peddle* can also mean "adulterate for gain." These therapists adulterate Christianity for their own selfish gain.

Of course, many Christian therapists primarily desire to make a difference in people's lives over making a lot of money. They sincerely believe that integrating the Bible with their professional training will do more to help their clients than hurt them. These people may be sincere, but as the saying goes, they can also be sincerely wrong. If they took a serious look at the roots and beliefs of psychology and compared these with biblical doctrine, they would soon realize the two cannot coexist in any way. Integration hurts the church more than it helps it, for when the church adopts worldly belief systems, they also adopt worldly lifestyles. Being a friend of the world makes one an enemy of God (James 4:4).

DID PAUL NEED PSYCHOLOGY?

With the popularity of Christian psychology continuing to grow, many in the church do not share my views of Christian psychology. These "integrationists" claim that integration of psychology and the Bible gives us even more insight into human behavior. To these people I pose the following argument. Consider the fact that psychology didn't even exist until the 1800s. How did Christians possibly live for eighteen hundred years without psychology? They lived just fine. Do we know more about living the Christian life to the fullest than Paul, John or Peter? Obviously not, but Christian therapists think they do. No longer do God's Word, God's Spirit and God's people provide sufficient help with the problems of life. Now we need the "secret knowledge" of the all-knowing Christian therapist to reveal truth about the human soul that God seemed to have left out for us modern folks.

You may say, "But we live in such hectic times. The environment is so different, with over-filled schedules, working parents, day care, traveling demands and keeping up with technology. Plus, people are more wicked today, with family abuse, rape, drugs and alcohol, divorce—the list goes on!" We do live in crazy times in the twenty-first century, but a good, close examination of the Bible will reveal that previous generations faced a harsh environment and low morality of their own. People in biblical times didn't have the modern conveniences we do. They had to grow their own food, make their own clothes and build their own houses. We just get a job and pay for someone or something else to do the work. People in biblical times also had their share of wickedness. A glance through the Book of Judges and other historical Old Testament books proves the point. They murdered, raped, abused family, divorced and got drunk. People are people, with the same hearts, the same hurts and the same needs for fulfillment, meaning and purpose. From Adam and Eve up to today, people have always struggled to discover the *why* of life.

You may also ask me, "We use other advances in our modern age that weren't available to those in biblical times, so why not use psychology?" True, but what kind of advances are they? If they are advances that have no effect on our spiritual well-being, then praise God for them. But if they are a false gospel that seeks to add to or undermine the Christian faith, then we should say with Paul, "But even if we or an angel from heaven should preach a gospel other than the one we preached to you, let him be eternally condemned!" (Gal. 1:8). Christian therapists preach a false gospel that contradicts Scripture and follows the opinions of men who hated religion and subtracted God out of all of their theories of human behavior.

JESUS IS THE TRUTH

Integrationists also justify using Christian psychology by claiming that "all truth is God's truth." To accept this claim, we would then have to adopt portions of the religions of Buddhism, Islam, Hinduism, Mormonism and Jehovah's Witnesses, since these religions contain a measure of truth, right? Not a chance! By definition, Christianity excludes all other religions and "truths" by the very words of Jesus Christ Himself: "I am the way and the truth and the life. No one comes to the Father except through me" (John 14:6). Jesus did not say He is *a* truth; He said He is *the* truth. Instead of "all truth is God's truth," a more accurate statement of truth is "*Jesus* is God's truth." Jesus also said, "Sanctify them by the truth; your word is truth." (John 17:17), telling us that we grow in godliness by the truth of God's Word only. Jesus did not say, "Your word, plus psychological theories, are truth."

JESUS IS SUFFICIENT

We seem to have this underlying belief that if a Christian individual has secular training in counseling people, he or she will have more readiness and effectiveness than an untrained Christian, despite the overwhelming secular evidence to the contrary. Why do we ignore the evidence and determine to see the "professionals?"

We believe Satan's lie that we need more than God's Word and God's indwelling Spirit to give us full lives, so we abandon fact for fiction by trusting the so-called experts of this world. We think that the Bible *plus* a counseling degree, or the Bible *plus* years of counseling experience somehow demands more respect. People who discover my past counseling experience wonder why I do not use it in a Christian setting. I simply explain to them that psychology, Christian or otherwise, denies the sufficiency of Christ to meet our every need in life. Jesus said, "I have come that they may have life, and have it to the full" (John 10:10). Jesus Christ is sufficient to give us all we need for a full life.

GRACE FOR LIVING

The Bible makes it clear that God's grace, or provision, is sufficient for living:

His divine power has given us *everything* we need for life and godliness through our knowledge of him who called us by his own glory and goodness.

—2 Peter 1:3, emphasis added

And God is able to make *all* grace abound to you, so that in *all* things at *all* times, having *all* that you need, you will abound in *every* good work.

—2 Corinthians 9:8, emphasis added

And my God will meet *all* your needs according to his glorious riches in Christ Jesus.

—Philippians 4:19, emphasis added

If God gives us *all* we need for life, why would we go elsewhere? Do we trust man's psychological theories—the wisdom of this world—more than God's flawless Word? Do we blindly trust Christian therapists without investigating their claims in Scripture? Do we trust in self-effort and not in the living God who dwells inside of us? Do we want the quick, easy fix instead of counting the cost of being a true disciple of Christ? The words of Timothy ring true today: "For the time will come when men will not put up with sound doctrine. Instead, to suit their own desires, they will gather around them a great number of teachers to say what their itching ears want to hear. They will turn their ears away from the truth and turn aside to myths" (2 Tim. 4:3–4). More and more of today's Christians want their ears tickled by the godless myths of psychology wrapped in familiar, non-threatening Christian packaging, while their Bibles gather dust on the shelves.

DID CHRIST DIE FOR NOTHING?

Like the Galatian church, we have learned to depend on our own fleshly resources to live the Christian life instead of depending on God's grace. The Galatians began their Christian lives in the Spirit, receiving God's saving grace through simple faith. Eventually, however, some from the church tried to "pervert the gospel of Christ" (Gal. 1:7) by requiring them to perform outward rituals in order to please God. The Galatians reverted back to their own efforts, living miserable Christian lives of self-sufficiency.

Perplexed, Paul asked the Galatians, "Are you so foolish? After beginning with the Spirit, are you now trying to attain your goal by human effort?...Now that you know God—or rather are known by God—how is it that you are turning back to those weak and miserable principles?" (Gal. 3:3, 4:9). We are being asked this same question today in light of Christian psychology's perverted gospel of self-sufficiency. Paul set the example: "[We] put no confidence in the flesh" (Phil. 3:3). "Not that we are sufficient of ourselves to think of anything as being from ourselves, but our sufficiency is from God" (2 Cor. 3:5, NKJV) By setting aside the grace of God in favor of self-sufficiency, the church has effectively said, "Christ died for nothing" (Gal. 2:21). If Christ died for nothing, we're in serious trouble.

"RETURN TO ME"

As He did for idolatrous Judah, God is calling us back to the purity and simplicity of His Word: "Stand at the crossroads and look; ask for the ancient paths, ask where the good way is, and walk in it, and you will find rest for your souls" (Jer. 6:16). Judah had been looking to other gods, not unlike the god of Christian psychology, to guide and help them, but their "broken cisterns" (Jer. 2:13) came up dry. God sent prophets again and again to warn them of His judgment on their idolatry, but Judah wouldn't listen. Truth disappeared and idolatry took its place: "This is the nation that has not obeyed the LORD its God or responded to correction. Truth has perished; it has vanished from their lips" (Jer. 7:28). The unadulterated truth of the Word of God is quickly perishing at the hands of Christian psychology and its followers.

What kind of correction is God using in these last days to turn our hearts back to him? Could God have used the Columbine High School disaster and other school shootings since then to show us what our departure from God's Word has done to future generations of America? I believe God is disciplining us to turn us back to His Word alone for all of our needs. God's eventual judgment of Judah at the hands of the Babylonians was "because they have forsaken the covenant of the LORD their God and have worshiped and served other gods" (Jer. 22:9).

With the heavy influence of the false religion of psychology on the church, America is heading down the same path to destruction as Judah. We need to remember our godly heritage as a nation, repent of our idolatry and return to the power and life of God's Word. As we humble ourselves, pray, seek His face and turn from our wicked ways, God will hear our prayers, forgive our sin and heal our land (2 Chron. 7:14).

A FAITHFUL FEW

Fortunately, some people have not turned away from God and bought into Christian psychology. A few Christians in the field of psychology have questioned the scientific validity and biblical basis for Christian psychology, and they have been ostracized from their spheres of influence as a result. Even those within the church experience judgment and criticism for taking a biblical stand on the authority of God's Word and His Spirit to address the issues of life. It also encourages me that more and more church members oppose the psychology movement within the church. Shortly after the Columbine tragedy, an interviewer asked Michael Shoels, father of martyr Isaiah Shoels, "Are you going to seek counseling to help you get through this time?" Michael firmly replied, "No. We are Christians. We have God to get us through this."

Michael Shoels understood and heeded God's warning about trusting in man. He trusted in God instead.

> This is what the Lord says: "Cursed is the one who trusts in man, who depends on flesh for his strength and whose heart turns away from the LORD...But blessed is the man who trusts in the LORD, whose confidence is in him."
>
> —Jeremiah 17:5, 7

One can never say God doesn't care about us. He cared enough to send His only begotten Son to earth to pay the price for our sins. He cares enough to give us everything we need to live life to the fullest. He cares enough to prepare a place for us in heaven that will last forever. Praise God for His mercy and grace for living!

CHAPTER 12

A
ROYAL
PRIESTHOOD

If seeing a Christian therapist isn't the answer, then what should we do when we need to share our problems with someone? We can confide in a trusted Christian friend. God loves to use other Christians to minister to us and carry out His will in our lives. Many times God sends someone into our lives at just the right time to help us and to say the things we long to hear. We can also do the same for others. If we have placed our trust in Jesus Christ and have surrendered to the Holy Spirit, God can use us to minister to other Christians.

PRIESTS OF GOD

As Christians, we have all the tools we need to minister to others. No buildings, no textbooks, no training manuals, no degrees, no offices, no fees—just God working through us to help other people. God actually considers us priests. Don't worry—no black robes and white collars are required. God calls us priests because of Jesus in our hearts, not because of the clothes we wear or the degrees we hold. The Bible says, "But you are a chosen people, *a royal priesthood*, a holy nation, a people belonging to God, that you may declare the praises of him who called you out of darkness into his wonderful light" (1 Pet. 2:9, emphasis added). We no longer need to bring in the "professionals," for we already have an army of counselors in the ranks. God has given us the organization of the body of Christ and how each interacts with the other:

> It was he who gave some to be apostles, some to be prophets, some to be evangelists, and some to be pastors and teachers, *to prepare God's people for works of service, so that the body of Christ may be built up* until we all reach unity in the faith and in the knowledge of the Son of God and become mature, attaining to the whole measure of the fullness of Christ.
>
> Then we will no longer be infants, tossed back and forth by the waves, and blown here and there by every wind of teaching and by the cunning and craftiness of men in their deceitful scheming. Instead, speaking the truth in love, we will in all things grow up into him who is the Head, that is, Christ. *From him the whole body, joined and held together by every supporting ligament, grows and builds itself up in love, as each part does its work.*
>
> —Ephesians 4:11–16, emphasis added

The apostles, prophets, evangelists, pastors and teachers prepare God's people—the royal priesthood—to do the work of the ministry, which consists of building up the body of Christ in love through mutual care.

PRIESTLY DUTIES

Priests have a very special twofold function: They represent God to man through their lives, and they represent man to God through their prayers. As priests, we have the God-given privilege to use our lives to reveal Jesus Christ to others and to pray about others to God. If we have made the Bible and the Holy Spirit our firm foundation in our personal lives, then God can use us to help others, and He can use others to help us. This concept of mutual care makes the church—the formation of believers in Christ—crucial to our livelihood. As the church, we depend on each other to help each other through the tough times in life and keep each other on the right path with God. Instead of backbiting, gossiping, slandering and competing, we should comfort, encourage, warn, uphold, teach, reprimand, correct, disciple, build up, pray for, forgive, submit to, serve and love other believers in Christ. These actions make up the essential duties of our "priesthood" to other believers:

> Praise be to the . . . God of all comfort, who comforts us in all our troubles, so that we can *comfort those in any trouble* with the comfort we ourselves have received from God.
>
> —2 Corinthians 1:3–4, emphasis added

> *Carry each other's burdens,* and in this way you will fulfill the law of Christ.
>
> —Galatians 6:2, emphasis added

> *Encourage one another* daily, as long as it is called Today, so that none of you may be hardened by sin's deceitfulness.
>
> —Hebrews 3:13, emphasis added

> Now we *exhort* [encourage] you, brethren, *warn* those who are unruly, *comfort* the fainthearted, *uphold* the weak, be *patient* with all.
>
> —1 Thessalonians 5:14, NKJV , emphasis added

> *Warn* him as a brother.
>
> —2 Thessalonians 3:15, emphasis added

> All Scripture is God-breathed and is useful for *teaching, rebuking* [reprimanding], *correcting* and *training in righteousness* [discipling], so that the man of God may be thoroughly equipped for every good work . . . Preach the Word; be prepared in season and out of season; *correct, rebuke* [reprimand] and *encourage*—with great patience and *careful instruction* [teaching].
>
> —2 Timothy 3:16–17, 4:2, emphasis added

> Each of us should please his neighbor for his good, to *build him up.*
>
> —Romans 15:2, emphasis added

> Brothers, *pray* for us.
>
> —1 Thessalonians 5:25, emphasis added

Be kind and compassionate to one another, *forgiving each other*, just as in Christ God forgave you.

—Ephesians 4:32, emphasis added

Submit to one another out of reverence for Christ.

—Ephesians 5:21, emphasis added

You, my brothers, were called to be free. But do not use your freedom to indulge the sinful nature; rather, *serve one another* in love.

—Galatians 5:13, emphasis added

Dear friends, let us *love one another*, for love comes from God. Everyone who *loves* has been born of God and knows God.

—1 John 4:7, emphasis added

NO TRAINING REQUIRED

God calls *every* Spirit-filled believer in Jesus Christ to minister to others. We should view counseling as a loving act done for free to help our fellow Christian brothers and sisters. God never meant for personal counseling to turn into a professional career requiring specialized training and on-the-job experience. We have already seen that those who receive training in counseling perform no better than those who do not. Even strictly biblical counseling, without psychology, does not require specialized programs, training and organizations. The Bible never mentions the title "counselor" as a separate and distinct ordained ministry in the church, yet many churches now have trained counselor positions on staff to do the work of the ministry that pastors and the body of Christ—the royal priesthood—once did. Laypeople like you and me do not need to belong to an elite group of trained counselors or church staff members to counsel effectively.

The Holy Spirit in us does not need our programs and centers, our memberships and affiliations, our training, our counseling experience or our "people person" gifts to help other people. He does just fine without our help—or more accurately, without our interference. As a pastor has said, "God doesn't want your ability. He wants your availability." God loves to use those Christians who don't think they've "got what it takes" to minister to others, for He gets all the glory.

144

No Gift Required

In fact, you will find no gift of counseling in the Bible. Of all of the spiritual gifts listed in the New Testament, counseling never appears. Even if counseling were a gift, why would we need to get specialized training for it? Some equate the gift of helps listed in 1 Corinthians 12:28 to the gift of counseling. But *Vine's Dictionary* defines the gift of helps as "rendering assistance, perhaps especially of 'help' ministered to the weak and needy... Anything that would be done for poor or weak or outcast brethren."[1] The gift of helps involves practical help, like giving money and clothing to the poor, more than spiritual help. The gift of counseling, however, is reserved for just one person... the person of the Holy Spirit (John 14:26).

God can use *any* Spirit-filled Christian—not just certain "gifted" Christians—to minister to others in their times of need. The fruit of the Spirit is love, joy, peace, patience, kindness, goodness, gentleness and self-control (Gal. 5:22–23). One would think that a Christian who displays these qualities would make a very effective counselor. Since the Bible commands each one of us to be filled with the Spirit (Eph. 5:18), it follows that each one of us can effectively minister to others in the body of Christ. If we accept that any believer in Christ can lead another to salvation and help them grow in sanctification, then we should also accept that any believer in Christ can minister to another in their time of need.

Intimacy in the Body of Christ

The body of Christ can minister to one another in many ways. If I become distraught, another believer can comfort me. If I become discouraged in my suffering, another believer can encourage me. If I have sin in my life, another believer can warn, reprimand and correct me. If I grow weak in the faith, another believer can uphold me. If I do not understand a verse, another believer can teach me. If I want to learn how to live a disciplined life for God, another believer can disciple me. If I feel unimportant or insignificant, another believer can build me up. If I want God to help me or bless my life in a particular way, another believer can pray for me. If I feel mistreated and used by other people, another believer can love me.

I can do these same things for other believers in their times of need. Our Christian friendships will grow more intimate, as "perfume and incense bring joy to the heart, and the pleasantness of one's friend springs from his earnest counsel" (Prov. 27:9).

Instead of paying a Christian counselor for help, I can just go to a friend or a pastor with whom I have a close and trustworthy relationship. That friend or pastor will more likely know my needs and genuinely care for me and help me through my situation than would a "specialist" I visit occasionally in a counseling office. A professional counselor will not hold me accountable and even discipline me spiritually for my actions as a true Christian friend or pastor would. I would rather go to a close confidant anytime I want for free than set a weekly appointment with a church counselor for a fee. Who would want a business relationship over a loving brother or sister in Christ? This type of pay-for-service relationship smacks of the world.

PAYING FOR SPIRITUAL THINGS

Nowhere in the Bible does a man of God charge others for praying and ministering the Word of God. Imagine if Paul, after speaking to the people of Troas into the early morning hours, concluded his twelve-hour sermon with, "All right, everyone, that's twelve hours of preaching and a man raised from the dead. I hope I've been of some assistance. Let's see . . . that will be ninety dollars each at the door. Thank you, and God bless you." This is ludicrous! Paul expressed his financial needs to the people concerning the rest of his missionary journey, but he never demanded payment from them. Paul demanding payment in that day would be like a church today demanding payment for a Sunday service or a prayer request. Therefore any Christian counselor who charges clients for counseling time does not act biblically. We would benefit more by receiving help from another brother or sister for free, for Jesus said to the twelve disciples, "Freely you have received, freely give" (Matt. 10:8).

While I can find no biblical examples of someone righteously charging for spiritual things, the Bible does mention a few who unrighteously wanted to buy spiritual things and sell them for a profit. Take for instance Simon the sorcerer, a popular magician of Paul's day. After witnessing the apostles lay hands on people to receive the Holy Spirit, Simon the sorcerer offered the apostles money to purchase the Holy Spirit, most likely to add the Holy Spirit's signs and wonders to his arsenal of magic and make more money. But Peter responded, "May your money perish with you, because you thought you could buy the gift of God with money!...Your heart is not right before God" (Acts 8:20–21).

We must avoid those counselors in the church who "sell the Holy Spirit" by charging people for spiritual help that should be free.

Ministering Effectively

The life of Christ provides us with the most biblical and effective method of counseling. Jesus counseled thousands of people during His earthly ministry by simply loving them and teaching them the Word of God. We can effectively minister to one another by depending solely on the flawless Word of God and the leading of the Holy Spirit. Love and compassion for the other person should motivate all of our ministering, as we see that person the way God does.

The Bible makes up the first ingredient for effective Christian ministering. When used correctly, the Word of God can produce powerful, supernatural results in the heart of another person: "For the word of God is living and active. Sharper than any double-edged sword, it penetrates even to dividing soul and spirit, joints and marrow; it judges the thoughts and attitudes of the heart" (Heb. 4:12). God's Word penetrates the hearts of those who read it and helps them understand how to live godly, righteous and fulfilling lives. Those doing the ministering must have a thorough working knowledge of biblical doctrine. We can easily take a verse out of context and live our lives ineffectively based on that verse. We should explain verses within the context of the entire Bible. It has been said that the best commentary on the Bible is the Bible.

The other ingredient for ministering effectively, the Holy Spirit, forms the reactive agent to the Word of God. After we read the Word of God, the Holy Spirit convicts us of our sin and guides us into the truth—the right things to say, think and do. The person of the Holy Spirit affects our wills and prompts us to do those things that please God. "When he comes, he will convict the world of guilt in regard to sin and righteousness and judgment...But when he, the Spirit of truth, comes, he will guide you into all truth" (John 16:8, 13). The Holy Spirit is our personal Counselor to guide us and lead us into lives of obedience to God. Both parties must depend on the Holy Spirit for effective results. The one ministering must yield to the Holy Spirit to know what to say, when to say it and how to say it. The one being ministered to must depend on the Holy Spirit to test the other's advice against God's word and to follow that advice. Both parties should take care in allowing the Holy Spirit to lead their discussions and decisions in order to keep from straying from God's will.

NO CONTRADICTIONS

The Bible and the Holy Spirit form the essential ingredients in producing effective ministering between Christians. Not only must both ingredients exist, but both must also complement each other. If the one ministering recommends that the other divorce her husband because she doesn't love him anymore, we know that person is not led by the Holy Spirit since the Bible forbids divorce for this reason. The one being ministered to should reject this advice. Or say, for instance, that a person feels "led" by the Holy Spirit to sleep with her boyfriend. Her feeling contradicts the Bible, since the Bible speaks of God's judgment on the sexually immoral. The one ministering should correct that person in this case.

The Bible and the Holy Spirit never contradict one another; they always coincide with one another. The God who inspired the Bible is the same God who lives in our hearts and directs our lives. The written words in the Bible simply confirm what we already know in our hearts as truth: "I will put my laws in their minds and write them on their hearts. I will be their God, and they will be my people" (Heb. 8:10).

In summary, then, the one ministering depends on the Holy Spirit and points the other to the appropriate verses in the Bible, not taking them out of context. The one being ministered to tests this advice in light of the Bible and the Holy Spirit's working in his or her heart, and then depends on the Holy Spirit to lead him or her in the right direction. Through mutual care, we hope to bring each other closer to Christ and closer to one another in love. The royal priesthood of believers functions beautifully when we minister to one another in this way.

FATHER KNOWS BEST

So what do we do if God's counsel strongly leads us in one direction, but another Christian's advice leads us in a different direction? We know both can't be right. Here we need to remember that the Wonderful Counselor's counsel takes precedence over any advice we receive from other Christians. As I learned from personal experience, Father knows best…

Shortly after becoming a Christian, I began to feel guilty about working as a psychotherapist. I slowly but surely realized that my treatments as a psychotherapist completely contradicted what the Bible says about how to live. Feeling uncomfortable about my situation for months, I finally sought the advice of an older Christian, herself a psychotherapist. In tears, I told her that I sensed God telling me to leave the field of psychology. She advised me, "You've come too far and you've worked too hard to leave now, because now is when you can start making money."

As a new Christian, I respected her and trusted her advice. I thought that since she had been a Christian longer than I had and she practiced psychology with no problem, I could just do the same. But I found myself fighting with God's will for me. It took months of God's Holy Spirit prompting me to leave before I finally obeyed His counsel in my heart and left the field of psychology for good. Through this experience I learned that people can never take the place of God in counseling me.

This woman did not depend on the Holy Spirit and the Bible to minister to me; instead she gave me subjective and self-serving advice. Of course she didn't want me to leave the field, for she was a part of it. Her self-interests interfered with providing me with godly advice. I made the mistake of not testing her advice with God's Word and with the Holy Spirit's leading. In my heart I knew God's will for me, but I trusted more in the seen than the unseen. The middle verse of the Bible sums up one of the foundational truths of the Christian life: "It is better to take refuge in the LORD than to trust in man" (Ps. 118:8).

GOD'S PRESCRIPTION FOR THE ROYAL PRIESTHOOD

What does God prescribe for the royal priesthood? Use God's Word and God's Spirit to love God's people by faith. The Bible says, "The only thing that counts is faith expressing itself through love" (Gal. 5:6). Who needs Christian psychology when God has given us such a beautiful support system in the body of Christ? Instead of taking the easy road of paying someone to be our friend for an hour, let's break down the walls of pride, mistrust and self-protection and just get real with one another. Let's step out of our self-sufficient comfort zones by faith and love our Christian brothers and sisters sincerely—from the heart. When you strip it all away, love truly is "the only thing that counts."

CHAPTER 13

CHOOSE
THIS DAY WHOM
YOU WILL SERVE

Let's take a moment to recall from chapter one psychology's three fundamental beliefs about the causes and cures of people's mental, emotional and behavioral problems:

- People are basically good, and through extensive introspection and self-effort they can improve themselves without God in order to achieve more pleasure in life.
- Our current problems result from environments and people from the past who have negatively influenced our inherently good unconscious, which controls our present behavior; we are victims of our past.
- To fix our current problems, we must gain insight into our unconscious to reveal and deal with past hurts using a trained therapist as our helper.

As we have seen thus far, the Bible paints a completely different picture about the causes and cures of our mental-emotional-behavioral problems, with differences in bold:

- People are basically **evil**, and through **the Bible, the Holy Spirit and other Christians** they can improve themselves **by**

having faith in God in order to achieve more **Christlikeness** in life.
- Our current problems result from **sin in our hearts** that has negatively influenced our inherently **evil minds,** which control our present behavior; we are **responsible for our sin.**
- To fix our current problems, we must **confess our sins to God** to **receive forgiveness and change our behavior,** allowing **the Holy Spirit** to be our Helper.

Let's also recall from chapter one the questions the client would typically want answered and the answers the therapist would give:

Client: Why am I unhappy?

Therapist: You are unhappy because of past environments or people who have hurt you in some way. You are a victim of your past.

Client: What is wrong with me?

Therapist: Your unconscious is influencing your present behavior without your knowledge or control.

Client: How can I solve my problems and be happier?

Therapist: You've come to the right place. I can help you analyze yourself and your past, and help you heal and be happier.[1]

Now let's answer those questions biblically (paraphrased):

Client: Why am I unhappy?

The Bible: You are unhappy because you have not been honest about you being the problem and not others. You are also unhappy because you are focused on yourself and seeking to please yourself instead of God.

Client: What is wrong with me?

The Bible: You have sin in your heart that is negatively influencing your behavior. You fail to realize that God knows your heart and He gives you everything you need to live a fulfilling life. Instead you have been placing your faith in yourself and others.

Client: How can I solve my problems and be happier?

The Bible: You can ask God for forgiveness for your failures. You can present your problems to Him through prayer and look to His Word for answers. You can trust Him to help you overcome your problems through His Spirit within you, instead of introspecting and trusting in your own abilities. You can focus on others' needs before your own in order to become more like Christ.

While the therapist's answers revolve around self, the Bible's answers revolve around God. We live to serve God and others, not ourselves. The answer to the age-old question "What is the meaning of life?" is to love God and love others, regardless of suffering, pain or discomfort that may result.

As we have looked closely at the differences between the self-worshiping lifestyle of psychology and the God-worshiping lifestyle of Christianity, you may have realized just how much the teachings of psychology have crept in and influenced your way of thinking. As you read this section, the Lord may have opened your spiritual eyes to any self-serving lifestyles. He may have revealed that you call Him Lord only out of convenience, entertainment or ritual, but not out of true commitment. You may have a lukewarm attitude toward Christ, like the church of Laodicea who used their time, talents and treasures for their own glory instead of for the glory of God (Rev. 3:14–22). God may have revealed to you any worldly ways of thinking, speaking and acting that sound more psychological than biblical. Perhaps in your acceptance of Christian psychology you have become a cultural Christian instead of a biblical Christian—more a friend of the world than a friend of God (James 4:4). Whatever you sense the Lord saying to you right now, listen to Him. Don't harden your heart, but humble yourself, admit your sins to Him and ask for His cleansing and filling. He stands ready to restore your fellowship with Him as you turn from your sins.

Elijah asked the Israelites on Mount Carmel, "How long will you waver between two opinions? If the LORD is God, follow him; but if Baal is God, follow him" (1 Kings 18:21). Don't waver between the opinion of God and the opinion of psychology. Choose to trust the

God who created you and reject the corruption of psychology. Choose to study the Bible and hide His Word in your heart, so that you may not sin against Him. Choose to take God at His Word and claim His promises for your own.

After Joshua settled the Israelites in the Promised Land, he exhorted the people:

> Now fear the LORD and serve him with all faithfulness. Throw away the gods your forefathers worshiped beyond the River and in Egypt, and serve the LORD. But if serving the LORD seems undesirable to you, then choose for yourselves this day whom you will serve, whether the gods your forefathers served beyond the River, or the gods of the Amorites, in whose land you are living. But as for me and my household, we will serve the LORD.
>
> —Joshua 24:14–15

Now is the time to put the self-serving life behind you and surrender your entire being to the Lord. Every moment of every day, in every situation we face, we must make the choice to serve ourselves or to serve God and others. You can't have it both ways. Either your self sits on the throne of your life and you proclaim your self as master, or Jesus sits on the throne of your life and you proclaim Him as your master. You must choose for yourself this day whom you will serve: self or God? Let's be like Joshua, who took a stand for his faith in the midst of an idolatrous culture: "But as for me and my household, we will serve the Lord."

PART IV

THE
OVERCOMING
LIFE

Now that we understand the futility of secular and Christian psychology, let's look practically at how to overcome life . . . without psychology. By God's grace, we really can live a holy, godly life—a life separated unto God that empowers us to love God, love others and fulfill our souls. The overcoming life is a sanctified life. Many Christians remain in the compromising lowlands of cultural Christianity and never experience the mountaintop blessings of a life separated unto God. They either believe living a holy life is impossible, or they label those who desire it as legalistic or self-righteous. Nevertheless, God desires that we live a life of faith and obedience to Christ that impacts the kingdom of God for eternity.

CHAPTER 14

DO YOU MEET THE QUALIFICATIONS OF THE OVERCOMING LIFE?

In this chapter we will discover the three qualifications for experiencing the overcoming life. Just as we have to put our trust in Christ to receive salvation, so also we have to meet certain criteria for us to experience the overcoming life. We won't have a chance to win the prize of the overcoming life unless we first qualify for the race.

WORK IN PROGRESS

Before looking at the three qualifications, let's get a good understanding of our current condition as Christians. We already know that Jesus forgives us of all of our sins—past, present and future. God now sees us as righteous and holy because of the blood of Jesus that covers our hearts. Jesus' righteousness covers our unrighteousness. We have become children of God and members of God's family.

But in between now and heaven we still live in our fleshly tents on this earth, with the same capacity to sin. Only now, God's indwelling Holy Spirit helps us overcome what once overcame us. Our sinful nature and external environment have no more power over us, for Christ broke that power at the cross and gave us His overcoming resurrection power in return. Learning how to consistently access this resurrection power takes time, but our God is a patient God.

God sees us as His work in progress. Next to the "Under New Management" sign that He posted when we received Christ, He posts another sign that reads "Under Construction." God has enlisted us in His spiritual boot camp to prepare us for our heavenly graduation. God the Father uses our Christian life to mold us into the image and likeness of His perfect, flawless Son, Jesus. He accomplishes this through the working of His Holy Spirit living inside us. God is the potter, and we are the clay that He molds and shapes to make us more like Jesus. One pastor puts it this way:

> At the moment of justification (receiving Jesus' forgiveness), you are given a position before God that is perfect, flawless and permanent based on Christ's sacrifice on the cross. In a practical sense, you will slowly begin to change and begin to catch up with your positional standing. When you die, He glorifies you with the glory of Christ. Then you eternally have the fullness of His (Christ's) image. [1]

God saved us to make us more like Christ in order to glorify Him. The Bible says concerning God's goal for us, "For those God foreknew he also predestined to be conformed to the likeness of his Son" (Rom. 8:29).

A TEAM EFFORT

This "work in progress" involves both God and us, cooperating together as a team. We can't try to become more like Christ by using our own energies and intellect. The Galatian church made that mistake. After receiving Christ into their hearts by faith for salvation, they tried to become more spiritual through outward acts and rituals. But their joy turned to misery as they depended on their own sufficiency to live the Christian life.

Only the Holy Spirit can give us the power and grace to become more like Christ. The Bible says, "And we, who with unveiled faces all reflect the Lord's glory, are being transformed into his likeness with ever-increasing glory, which comes from the Lord, who is the Spirit" (2 Cor. 3:18). The Holy Spirit acts like our internal spiritual engine to teach us God's Word, guide us into all truth, comfort us during trials, assure us of our salvation, give us power and strength when we need it and make us more like Christ. If the engine doesn't work, the car doesn't run. In the same way, we can't live the Christian life without the Holy Spirit!

The Holy Spirit does not help us grow spiritually without any cooperation on our part, however. We don't wake up in the morning and suddenly exclaim, "Wow, God laid a real growth boost on me last night!" God expects us to do our part in growing spiritually. Notice our part and God's part in the following verse: "Therefore, my dear friends, as you have always obeyed—not only in my presence, but now much more in my absence—continue to *work out your salvation* with fear and trembling, for *it is God who works in you* to will and to act according to his good purpose" (Phil. 2:12–13, emphasis added). If we set out to obey God's Word through faith in Him (we "work out"), God will empower us to overcome for His good purpose (God "works in").

Peter lists the things we can do to give the Holy Spirit free reign to make us more like Christ. After telling us that "His divine power has given us everything we need for life and godliness through our knowledge of him" (2 Pet. 1:3) in order to "participate in the divine nature and escape the corruption in the world caused by evil desires" (v. 4), Peter tells us how we can put that divine, overcoming power into action: "Make every effort to add to your faith goodness; and to goodness, knowledge; and to knowledge, self-control; and to self-control, perseverance; and to perseverance, godliness; and to godliness, brotherly kindness; and to brotherly kindness, love" (vv. 5–7). Our effort works with God's effort to make us more like Christ. The result? "For if you possess these qualities in increasing measure, they will keep you from being ineffective and unproductive in your knowledge of our Lord Jesus Christ...You will never fall" (vv. 8, 10). In other words, we will experience effective, productive and overcoming lives!

In God's Timing

You may overcome some sins immediately after receiving Christ into your life; others may take years. God has His own timetable in taking us through the refining process of overcoming our sins and becoming more like Christ. But you can find comfort that "he who began a good work in you will carry it on to completion until the day of Christ Jesus" (Phil. 1:6). Jesus will never give up on you! In this chapter we will understand how we can best do our part so that God can do His part in helping us overcome our sins and our circumstances.

QUALIFICATION #1: DIE TO SELF

To qualify for the overcoming life, we must first determine to die to ourselves. Contrary to psychology and our Western culture as a whole, our needs, desires, plans, pleasures, preferences, comforts, schedules, safety, reputation, security, money and future must die in order to truly live. To die to ourselves simply means to yield control and ownership of the people, plans and possessions of our lives to God. To die to ourselves means to obey God's Word, no matter what the cost. To die to ourselves means that our motivations become God-centered and others-centered, not self-centered. This is a high and holy calling. No wonder Jesus said, "Enter through the narrow gate. For wide is the gate and broad is the road that leads to destruction, and many enter through it. But small is the gate and narrow the road that leads to life, and only a few find it" (Matt. 7:13–14).

Author Roy Hession calls this death of our self-life *brokenness*. He says:

> The Lord Jesus cannot live in us fully and reveal Himself through us until the proud self within us is broken. This simply means that the hard unyielding self, which justifies itself, wants its own way, stands up for its rights, and seeks its own glory, at last bows its head to God's will, admits its wrong, gives up its own way to Jesus, surrenders its rights and discards its own glory—that the Lord Jesus might have all and be all.[2]

We die to *our purposes* so that God can live in and through us for *His purposes*. Dying to self forms the essential difference between the self-centered life of psychology and the Christ-centered life of

Christianity. Dying to ourselves is not easy. Even what we would call natural tendencies can have selfish roots. Hession lists a few of them:

> It is always self who gets irritable and envious and resentful and critical and worried. It is self who is hard and unyielding in its attitudes to others. It is self who is shy and self-conscious and reserved...Self-energy or self-complacency...is sin. Self-pity in trials or difficulties, self-seeking in business or Christian work, self-indulgence in one's spare time, sensitiveness, touchiness, resentment and self-defense when we are hurt or injured by others, self-consciousness, reserve, worry, fear, all spring from self and all are sin.[3]

These selfish actions stem from our sinful nature. In fact, the middle letter of the word *sin* is *I*. "I will," "I want" and "I deserve" all reek of selfishness. These "sins of self" hurt our marriages. These sins put Jesus on the cross.

Dying to self to identify with Christ

The apostle Paul wanted "to know Christ and the power of his resurrection and the fellowship of sharing in his sufferings, becoming like him in his death, and so, somehow, to attain to the resurrection from the dead" (Phil. 3:10–11). To experience the power of Christ's resurrection in his life, Paul first had to die to himself and experience Christlike sufferings. The same holds true for us today. It's not pretty, it's not easy, and it does not tickle our ears, but it is the only way to the overcoming life.

God did not create us to experience comfort and pleasure, as psychology would have us think; God created us to identify with Christ in His sufferings in order to grow closer to Him. Columbine martyr Cassie Bernall knew how to die to self in order to identify with Christ during the years before her death. Her mom recalls her pastor's words about Cassie's selfless life:

> Cassie struggled like everyone struggles, but she knew what she had to do to let Christ live in her. It's called dying to yourself, and it has to be done daily. It means learning to break out of the selfish life...It's not a negative thing, but a way of freeing yourself to live

161

life more fully. The world looks at Cassie's "yes" of April 20, but we need to look at the daily "yes" she said day after day, month after month, before getting that final answer...It's the same point Jesus was trying to make when He said that he who saves his life will lose it, but he who gives up his life will find it. Long before she died, Cassie had decided that instead of looking out for herself— instead of trying to get things to work her way, and wondering what life had to offer her—she was going to see what she could make of it. It's not a question of doing great deeds, but of being selfless in the small things.[4]

On a scrap paper marked "1998," Cassie wrote, "I try to stand up for my faith at school...It can be discouraging, but it can also be rewarding...I will die for my God. I will die for my faith. It's the least I can do for Christ dying for me."[5] Cassie lived a full life because she chose to die to herself every day in order to identify with Christ and let Him live through her. Her daily surrender to Christ culminated in the ultimate surrender of her life on April 20. We may not die for Christ as Cassie did, but we can choose to live for Him each day by dying to our self-life.

Christ, the supreme example of dying to self

Before His crucifixion, Jesus told His disciples, "I tell you the truth, unless a kernel of wheat falls to the ground and dies, it remains only a single seed. But if it dies, it produces many seeds. The man who loves his life will lose it, while the man who hates his life in this world will keep it for eternal life" (John 12:24–25). Jesus provided the supreme example of dying to self. Being God, He had all the power in the world to control His own life and destiny—to make Himself "happy." But He chose to lay His own will aside and humble Himself, taking the form of a servant. He always took the time to help others, even to the point of exhaustion. He gave up His rights to His enemies without resisting. He never defended Himself or explained Himself when falsely accused. He had no anger or resentment toward those who crucified Him, but instead said with compassion, "Father, forgive them, for they do not know what they are doing" (Luke 23:34). He forfeited His desires for those of His Father in heaven to become the Lamb of God, crucified in our place. Before His crucifixion, He pleaded with God the Father to change His circumstances, foreseeing the suffering and separation He would face. But He eventually yielded His own will to that of His Father, looking forward to the joy of reconciling mankind to God.

We desire to die to ourselves and yield our wills to God when we gaze upon the cross and consider the incredible love God has for us and the lengths He went to experience death so that we could have life. The Bible says, "For Christ's love compels us, because we are convinced that one died for all, and therefore all died. And he died for all, that those who live should no longer live for themselves but for him who died for them and was raised again" (2 Cor. 5:14–15). The Bible also says, "I have been crucified with Christ and I no longer live, but Christ lives in me. The life I live in the body, I live by faith in the Son of God, who loved me and gave himself for me" (Gal. 2:20). Our self-life died with Christ, and the Christ-life takes its place. Christ now becomes our life and our identity. Since Jesus died for us, we should "die" for Him by no longer living for ourselves, but for Him who bought our lives with His precious blood.

God's mysterious trade-in deal

"This kind of self-sacrifice seems impossible," you may say. Without Jesus in our hearts, it *is* impossible. We naturally tend to protect our own selfish interests and control the outcome of our lives. But the life of Jesus empowers us to do as He says and deny ourselves so that He can fill us with His peace and give us an abundant life—a life worth living. It's up to us to take the first step. We must tell ourselves, "I choose to die to myself today." We have to want His life more than our own livelihood. C. S. Lewis describes God's mysterious trade-in deal when we die to ourselves:

> Give up your self, and you will find your real self. Lose your life and you will save it. Submit to death, death of your ambitions and favourite wishes every day and death of your whole body in the end: submit with every fibre of your being, and you will find eternal life. Keep back nothing. Nothing that you have not given away will ever be really yours. Nothing in you that has not died

will ever be raised from the dead. Look for yourself, and you will find in the long run only hatred, loneliness, despair, rage, ruin, and decay. But look for Christ and you will find Him, and with Him everything else thrown in.[6]

You turn in your self to God, and He will give you the life of Christ in its place, along with everything else you desire as you seek His will. Then you will find what has eluded you for so long.

If after reading this section you realize that you have had some self-willed thoughts, attitudes and actions, don't get discouraged—we all have them every day. God already knows your heart. He stands waiting for you to come to Him and receive cleansing through Jesus' blood. Yes, God sees you as righteous because of your saving faith in Christ, but if you have unconfessed sin in your heart as a Christian, your practical, day-to-day relationship with God will suffer. You have "union" with God as His child, but no "communion" with God. Without communion or fellowship with God we can know nothing of the overcoming life. Take a moment in prayer to humble yourself like a child, confess any sins that come to your mind, ask for forgiveness from Jesus and thank Him for forgiving you, as His Word promises.

QUALIFICATION #2: TRUST IN GOD

Once we have done our part by humbling ourselves and emptying our hearts of the dirty, polluted water of self, we qualify for the second stage of the overcoming life: trust in God. We must trust in God to do His part and fill us up with the pure, living water of Jesus. Jesus said, "If anyone is thirsty, let him come to me and drink. Whoever believes in me . . . streams of living water will flow from within him" (John 7:37–38). This living water represents the life of Jesus Himself coming through us, unhindered by any self-centeredness or self-will.

God fills empty vessels

Imagine your heart as a cup or vessel. We can fill the vessel with pride, hypocrisy and selfish ambition, leaving no room left for God— only misery and discontent. Or we can empty the vessel with humility, transparency and surrender, allowing God to fill up the vessel with His living waters of peace and joy. The more we empty ourselves, the more

God can fill us up. The less we empty ourselves, the less God can fill us up. Dying to self involves emptying the vessel of our hearts for God. Hession explains the irony of dying to self: "People imagine that dying to self makes one miserable. But it is just the opposite. It is the refusal to die to self that makes one miserable. The more we know of death with Him, the more we shall know of His life in us, and so the more of real peace and joy."[7] We find fulfillment when God fills the vessel of our hearts to overflowing with His presence and love.

Feeding our faith

The living water of God's presence and love will flow once we empty ourselves, yield ourselves to God and place our faith and trust in Jesus. Faith is the key word here—the glue that holds our relationship with God together. In fact, the Bible says, "Everything that does not come from faith is sin" (Rom. 14:23); "Without faith it is impossible to please God" (Heb. 11:6). Each time we place our complete faith and trust in Jesus, we come under the power of the Holy Spirit, who then empowers us to live an overcoming Christian life.

If faith is the key to an overcoming life, then how do we get more of it? The Bible tells us that we feed our faith through the Word of God: "Faith comes from hearing the message, and the message is heard through the word of Christ" (Rom. 10:17). The more we read and obey the Word of God, the more faith we will have. Jesus said, "Sanctify them by the truth; your word is truth" (John 17:17). As we saturate our minds with God's Word, our faith will increase and Christ will rule in our hearts. Just as we need to feed our bodies daily with physical food to maintain our physical health, so also we need to feed our spirits daily with spiritual food to maintain our spiritual health.

Continual trust

Filling up on our favorite cereal and a good dose of God's Word in the morning prepares us for the daily battles that lie ahead of us. Throughout the day we have a moment-by-moment responsibility to "let the peace of Christ rule in [our] hearts" (Col. 3:15) by continually trusting in God. When we have the peace of Christ ruling in our hearts, we no longer act like slaves to our feelings and the circumstances around us. Instead, God shields and strengthens us with "the peace of God, which transcends all understanding" (Phil. 4:7).

QUALIFICATION #3: OBEY GOD

We must then obey God to meet the third and final qualification of the overcoming life. After trusting God to fill us with His Spirit, we must obey His Word in order to find victory. It is not enough to say we trust God and then fail to obey His Word. James says, "Faith without deeds is dead" (James 2:26). We can trust in God to help us live an overcoming life, but never apply that faith in the real world. Let's say your car stalls in the middle of an intersection. You sit in the driver's seat praying over and over, "Lord, please help me start this car!" But you never turn the key in the ignition. You just keep on praying. The car won't start if you don't act on your faith. If we don't put our faith into action by obeying God, we really don't have much faith in the first place! Action always accompanies true faith.

Thirsty for God

In this information age in which we live, we can store up all sorts of knowledge and doctrines of the Christian faith without applying that knowledge to real life. Some Christians can recite entire books of the Bible and yet not live them out. They live like unbelievers. Their faith is useless. James warns, "Do not merely listen to the word, and so deceive yourselves. Do what it says" (James 1:22). We can listen to the doctrines of the overcoming life and know all there is to know about it, but when a test comes, we fail miserably. Why? Because we haven't surrendered our wills to God. We must hunger and thirst for Christ as our overcoming life. Our souls (or wills) must thirst like David, who cried out to God, "As the deer pants for streams of water, so my soul pants for you, O God. My soul thirsts for God, for the living God" (Ps. 42:1–2).

God will reveal the overcoming life to us only *after* we become desperate, hungry and thirsty enough to obey Him. Once we obey God, we experience the supernatural overcoming life of God in our hearts. The living waters flow, and life becomes an exciting adventure in Christ!

USEFUL TO THE MASTER

When God's living waters flow through us, He can use us in mighty ways to accomplish His purposes. A pastor from the late nineteenth and early twentieth centuries understood this truth and preached these moving words: "The world has yet to see what God can do through a man totally yielded to Him." A man by the name of Dwight L. Moody heard these words, and they forever changed his life. D. L. Moody became one of the most influential and effective preachers of modern times. During his final days, someone asked D. L. Moody about his success as a preacher. He replied, "The world has yet to see what God can do through a man totally yielded to Him."

THE RESULT: GOOD FRUIT

So how do we know if the living waters of Christ are flowing through us and Christ is ruling in our hearts? We will know by the fruit, or outward manifestations, that our lives produce. If we die to ourselves, trust God and obey Him, we will show the fruit of the Spirit: "But the fruit of the Spirit is love, joy, peace, patience, kindness, goodness, faithfulness, gentleness and self-control" (Gal. 5:22–23). Wouldn't we all like to have these traits consistently? How our marriages would improve!

We can have these godly traits if we die to self, trust in God and obey God moment by moment. We simply need to ask God to fill us with His Spirit, and then trust that He will do as He promised: "If you then, though you are evil, know how to give good gifts to your children, how much more will your Father in heaven give the Holy Spirit to those who ask him!" (Luke 11:13). You can take a brief moment to submit to God and ask Him to fill you with His Holy Spirit right now, wherever you are. If you ask in faith, He will fulfill His promise to you as you obey Him.

THE ROTTEN FRUIT OF DISOBEDIENCE

On the flip side, how do we know if the living water is *not* flowing through us, but is "clogged" by our own self-centeredness and self-will? Again, we will know by the fruit that our lives produce—in this case, the rotten fruit of the sinful nature:

> The acts of the sinful nature are obvious: sexual immorality, impurity and debauchery, idolatry and witchcraft; hatred, discord, jealousy, fits of rage, selfish ambition, dissensions, factions and envy; drunkenness, orgies, and the like. I warn you, as I did before, that those who live like this will not inherit the kingdom of God.
>
> —Galatians 5:19–21

This fruit comes from disobeying God. Note that every fruit of the sinful nature involves some aspect of the self. When the self remains in control and does not yield to and trust in Jesus, bad fruit results. With bad fruit come bad relationships. How do we unclog our pipes? By emptying ourselves, trusting in God, saturating our minds in the Word of God and obeying it.

We can also "clog" the living water in us by attempting to live a godly life in our own strength, without yielding to God and trusting in His power to help us. If we strive to live a godly life on our own, we have not died to ourselves; if we have not died to ourselves, the Holy Spirit cannot take us over and fill us up with good fruit. This type of self-effort produces a legalistic attitude, impure thoughts, jealousy, guilt, worry, discouragement, a critical spirit, frustration, aimlessness, fear, unbelief, disobedience and other sinful behavior that displeases God.[8] Psychology and self-help tell us that we can improve the quality of our lives if we just read one more book, attend one more therapy session, try one more relaxation technique or apply one more time-management method. But without God's power, all of our efforts do nothing. God gives us the good fruit as we allow Him to water our roots and prune our branches.

BANANAS FOR JESUS

So what kind of fruit would you rather resemble? A brown, squishy, rotten banana, or a healthy, yellow banana? To resemble healthy bananas, we need to deny ourselves, trust in God and obey God on a continual basis—day by day, moment by moment. The Bible calls this continual trusting relationship with the Lord Jesus "abiding in Christ." Jesus said, "Abide in Me, and I in you. As the branch cannot bear fruit of itself, unless it abides in the vine, neither can you, unless you abide in Me. I am the vine, you are the branches. He who abides in Me, and I in him, bears much fruit; for without Me you can do nothing" (John 15:4–5, NKJV). As long as we abide in Christ, we "can do all things through Christ who strengthens [us]" (Phil. 4:13, NKJV). How many things are all things? Everything. The whole banana. Whatever comes our way, if we abide in Jesus, we will overcome it through Christ in us.

CHAPTER 15

OVERCOMING YOUR SINFUL NATURE

In the last chapter we learned about the three qualifications of the overcoming life: dying to self, trusting and abiding in Christ, and obeying God's Word. If you meet these qualifications, you are ready to win the prize in the race of faith (1 Cor. 9:24). You make yourself available for God to live through you and give you the good fruit of love, joy, peace, patience, kindness, goodness, faithfulness, gentleness and self-control—a fulfilling life. How can we keep the good fruit growing and avoid the bad fruit at all costs? In other words, how can we overcome the sinful nature that produces the bad fruit?

OVERCOMING POWER

We have the power to overcome our sinful nature through the Holy Spirit that dwells inside of us. Unfortunately, many Christians do not understand and use this overcoming power. Many still believe they have no power over sins like substance abuse, sexual immorality, adultery and homosexuality. Instead of controlling these sins, these sins control them, making them miserable and guilt-ridden. Because of our sinful nature, we say and do things we know we shouldn't, but yet feel powerless to change. We can be our own worst enemy.

The Bible, however, tells us that we have God's power in us to overcome these sins—to render our old, sinful nature dead and our new, divine nature alive. For example, a long-time friend told me, "I attended multiple twelve-step programs and saw counselors to help me with my drinking problem, but none of it worked. I still wanted to drink. Now I know that I just needed Jesus in my life. God is all I need. That's it!" He has had no desire for alcohol ever since he turned from other man-made methods and fully entrusted his life to Jesus. Through his faith, Jesus gave him the power to overcome his sin of debauchery.

Another Christian left her homosexual lifestyle after receiving Jesus into her life. Before Jesus, she spent years in therapy sessions with different therapists who essentially told her, "Just accept the fact that you are a lesbian. You can never change. It's just the way you are. The sooner you can accept it, the happier you will be." Confused, unhappy and searching for answers, she finally gave her life completely over to Jesus, who took away her sinful desire for other women. Now she overcomes a sin that used to enslave her. She has finally found peace.

"BE HOLY, BECAUSE I AM HOLY"

God commands the Christian to put to death the things of the sinful nature and instead to pursue righteousness and holiness. Although God already sees us as holy in Christ, God's Word tells us to walk worthy of our calling by living holy lives:

> Therefore, I urge you, brothers, in view of God's mercy, to *offer your bodies as living sacrifices, holy and pleasing to God*—this is your spiritual act of worship.
>
> —Romans 12:1, emphasis added

> God, *who has saved us and called us to a holy life*—not because of anything we have done but because of his own purpose and grace.
>
> —2 Timothy 1:8–9, emphasis added

> But just as he who called you is holy, so *be holy in all you do*; for

it is written: *"Be holy, because I am holy."*

—1 Peter 1:15–16

You ought to live holy and godly lives as you look forward to the day of God and speed its coming.

—2 Peter 3:11–12

Make every effort to live in peace with all men and to *be holy; without holiness no one will see the Lord.*

—Hebrews 12:14

In Old Testament times, God revealed His laws to Moses to show the Israelites His holy nature. Although God required the people to be holy, He gave them no power to carry this requirement out. As a result, the Israelites continually fell short of God's holy standards. Of course, God designed the Old Testament law with this in mind—to show us our need for a Savior. We had to realize how miserably short we fall from God's requirements of us. But in Christ, the Holy Spirit empowers us to be holy, just as God is holy. With Jesus, we now have the power to carry out God's requirements of us in life. We can now heed Peter's exhortation to "live holy and godly lives."

HOLINESS THROUGH THE SPIRIT

"Who, me, live a holy life?" Yes, you really can live a holy life through Christ! On the cross Jesus "condemned sin in sinful man, in order that the righteous requirements of the law might be fully met in us, who do not live according to the sinful nature but according to the Spirit" (Rom. 8:3–4). We can now fulfill God's law and His perfect will for our lives if we walk in the Spirit, abiding in Christ moment by moment. In fact, God says to His people, "I will give you a new heart and put a new spirit in you; I will remove from you your heart of stone and give you a heart of flesh. And I will put my Spirit in you and move you to follow my decrees and be careful to keep my laws" (Ezek. 36:26–27). Jesus summarized God's commandments as loving God and loving others (Matt. 22:37–40). If we walk in the Spirit, we will automatically love God and love others, thus fulfilling God's law. Thanks to God, we now have the power to live holy lives!

We should note that holiness does not mean perfection. As long as we live in our human flesh, we will sin. In fact, John says, "If we claim to be without sin, we deceive ourselves and the truth is not in us" (1 John 1:8). Rather, holiness simply means, "separated unto God." When we walk in the Spirit, we live holy, righteous lives separated unto God. But as James says, "We all stumble in many ways" (James 3:2). When we stumble (and we will), we fall back into our sinful nature and out of the fellowship of the Spirit. The quicker we get back up, dust ourselves off and walk in the Spirit again, the more we will grow. As we grow as Christians, we will walk in the Spirit more and fall back into our sinful nature less. Living a holy life becomes easier as we grow accustomed to walking in the Spirit, abiding in Christ.

BLESSINGS OR CURSES

God has given us the power to overcome our sinful nature, but we have to make a conscious decision to turn from those things that displease Him in order to unleash the Holy Spirit's power. The Bible calls this repentance: to change your thinking about your life, stop doing those things that displease God ("put them to death") and start doing those things that please Him. The Bible warns, "For if you live according to the sinful nature, you will die; but if by the Spirit you put to death the misdeeds of the body, you will live" (Rom. 8:13). God gives us a choice: We can reap blessings or curses in life based on our lifestyle (Deut. 30:19–20). We reap what we sow (Gal. 6:7). If we obey God's commandments, we will reap blessings. If we disobey God's commandments, we will reap curses.

SINFUL NATURE CRUCIFIED WITH CHRIST

To reap blessings then, we need to "put to death the misdeeds of the body." As Christians, we "have crucified the sinful nature with its passions and desires" (Gal. 5:24). We must consider everything related to our sinful nature as crucified with Christ. If it's crucified, it's no longer active in my life. It's dead. One of the greatest verses in the Bible to help us overcome our sinful nature warrants memorizing: "I have been crucified with Christ and I no longer live, but Christ lives in me. The life I live in the body, I live by faith in the Son of God, who loved me and gave himself for me" (Gal. 2:20). Not only has my old life of the sinful nature been crucified, but according to this verse, now the risen Christ lives in me, and I live by faith in Him.

NEW LIFE IN CHRIST

If we consider our sinful nature crucified and we abide in the living Christ by faith, we will overcome our sinful nature and enjoy our new lives in Christ: "Just as Christ was raised from the dead through the glory of the Father, we too may live a new life... For we know that our old self was crucified with him so that the body of sin might be done away with, *that we should no longer be slaves to sin*" (Rom. 6:4, 6, emphasis added). Because of Christ's resurrection life inside of us, we are no longer slaves to sin! We are now alive to God: "The death he died, he died to sin once for all; but the life he lives, he lives to God. In the same way, *count yourselves dead to sin but alive to God in Christ Jesus*" (vv. 10–11, emphasis added).

Thanks to Jesus, "[we] have been set free from sin and have become slaves to righteousness" (v. 18). Praise God—Jesus has set us free from sin! No longer do we have to submit to sin's power, for Christ has broken it forever. Instead we have become slaves to righteousness, as we gladly surrender our heart, mind, soul and strength to God in grateful appreciation for what He has done for us.

THE BLESSINGS OF OBEDIENCE

Once we put to death our sinful nature and live for God, we will reap the blessings in life that God has promised us in His Word. For example, the Bible tells us:

> Whoever would love life and see good days must keep his tongue from evil and his lips from deceitful speech. He must turn from evil and do good; he must seek peace and pursue it. For the eyes of the Lord are on the righteous and his ears are attentive to their prayer, but the face of the Lord is against those who do evil.
>
> —1 Peter 3:10–12

We can live for God and feed our spirit with good things by

praying, reading God's Word and spending time with other committed Christians. As we do these things regularly, God makes us more like Jesus, and we will "love life and see good days." While we have done nothing to deserve God's grace and favor, God does reward His children when they obey Him. Just as we give our children good things when they obey our wishes, so God bestows His blessings upon His children when they please Him. Psalms 103, 107, 112, 128 and 145 all describe just some of the blessings God gives us when we obey Him.

NO SIN IS TOO POWERFUL

God will never give us more than we can handle as we trust in Him—a comforting thought indeed. We will always have enough power from God to overcome the sins and temptations that come our way. The Bible says, "No temptation has seized you except what is common to man. And God is faithful; he will not let you be tempted beyond what you can bear. But when you are tempted, he will also provide a way out so that you can stand up under it" (1 Cor. 10:13). This verse contains a few good nuggets of knowledge:

- Others have been tempted in this way and have overcome, so we can do the same.
- God will never allow a temptation to come into our lives that is too powerful for us.
- God will always provide an escape route with every temptation He allows.

We cannot blame God, Satan or others for temptations. God makes it clear in this verse that we have complete control over how we deal with temptations. He wants us to count ourselves "dead to sin but alive to God in Christ Jesus" (Rom. 6:11).

CONTINUAL CLEANSING

As long as we live on this earth, the battle between our old, sinful nature and our new, divine nature will rage on. But if we make it a life-long practice to render our sinful nature dead and exercise faith in

Jesus, we will learn to overcome our sins and enjoy fellowship with God. When we do stumble in our struggle against our sinful nature, we will find that the peace of God leaves our hearts due to any number of reasons, such as anxiety, irritability, fear, discouragement and doubt. When this happens, we must submit ourselves to Jesus. We simply ask God for forgiveness through Jesus Christ and get back on our feet again, based on His wonderful promise: "If we confess our sins, he is faithful and just and will forgive us our sins and purify us from all unrighteousness" (1 John 1:9). We then continue to live and walk in the Spirit.

We may need to repeat this process of asking God to cleanse us from our sins and fill us with His Spirit twenty times a day. As we develop our relationship with God, we will not become sinless, but we will sin less and become more like Jesus. Our struggle with our sinful nature will finally end at the finish line of heaven. Until then, the writer of Hebrews encourages us with these words: "Let us throw off everything that hinders and the sin that so easily entangles, and let us run with perseverance the race marked out for us. Let us fix our eyes on Jesus, the author and perfecter of our faith" (Heb. 12:1–2).

Chapter 16

Overcoming the World

As we die to ourselves, walk in the Spirit and secure victory over our sinful nature, we will surely run into problems around us that are out of our control. But before we understand how to have victory over our circumstances, we must put the world system in which our circumstances take place in perspective. As Christians we must remember that our home is in heaven—not in this world. God considers us already seated in heaven: "And God raised us up with Christ and seated us with him in the heavenly realms in Christ Jesus" (Eph. 2:6). God has "rescued us from the dominion of darkness and brought us into the kingdom of the Son he loves" (Col. 1:13). God calls us citizens of heaven, and from the day of our adoption until the day that we enter heaven, we prove our citizenship by living for the kingdom of heaven and no longer for the kingdom of this world, in order to glorify God.

Worlds Apart

What exactly characterizes the kingdom of earth, or the world? God's Word tells us:

Do not love the world or anything in the world. If anyone loves the world, the love of the Father is not in him. For everything in the world—the cravings of sinful man, the lust of his eyes and the boasting of what he has and does—comes not from the Father but from the world. The world and its desires pass away, but the man who does the will of God lives forever.

—1 John 2:15–17

The lust of the flesh, the lust of the eyes and the pride of life make up the world in which we live. Turn on the television at any time, and you will see an abundance of sensual bed scenes, suspense and violence, powerful product advertising and people boasting of their possessions and accomplishments. In contrast, while the apostle Paul had a right to boast of his accomplishments in ministry, he chose instead to boast only in the cross of Christ that saved him: "May I never boast except in the cross of our Lord Jesus Christ, through which the world has been crucified to me, and I to the world" (Gal. 6:14). Adherents to the "look out for number one and do what's best for you" motto of psychology become selfish, boastful and arrogant as they become filled with the pride of life. These attitudes come from the world. God's Word warns us not to love this temporary, passing world; instead we are to love God and His eternal kingdom as we sit "in the heavenly realms in Christ Jesus."

A DOT IN THE TIMELINE OF ETERNITY

When we put it all into perspective, our earthly life looks like a tiny dot in the timeline of eternity. Once we get to heaven, we will live there forever and ever. That's a long time! Why waste our time living seventy or eighty years for this world and then get to eternity and have nothing to show for ourselves? Not preparing for eternity is like boarding a plane without luggage. When we reach our destination, we won't have anything to help us live there for we failed to prepare. Because of the brevity of life, the Bible says to "set your hearts on things above, where Christ is seated at the right hand of God. Set your minds on things above, not on earthly things. For you died, and your life is now hidden with Christ in God" (Col. 3:1–3). We can set our hearts and minds on things above by investing our time, talents and treasures in heaven.

INVESTING TIME IN HEAVEN

Carving out time each day to spend with Jesus will help us overcome the world's powerful influence. If we want to have a relationship with Jesus, we should spend time with Him. Have you ever heard of someone having a best friend whom they never talk to or know anything about? Jesus is our best friend, and we should talk to Him and get to know Him better each day. As we get to know Jesus, we will see Him more clearly and the world will seem to fade away. We become more holy and less like the world around us. When we get to heaven, we will have already built a strong foundation for our relationship with God.

INVESTING TALENTS IN HEAVEN

God has also given us talents and gifts that He wants us to use to glorify Him and serve others in the church body. If we can sing or play an instrument, we should play for the enjoyment of others. If we work well with children, we should teach God's Word to them. If we excel at our jobs, we should use any opportunity we get to give God the credit. Kurt Warner, Rams' quarterback and most valuable player in the 2000 Super Bowl, exclaimed to a worldwide television audience, "Thank You, Jesus!" when presented with the trophy. When we use our talents and gifts for the world, we become a slave to pleasing the world. But when we use them for God's glory, the world has no power over us. The things we do in Jesus' name wait for us in heaven and will clothe our heavenly bodies in bright splendor (Rev. 19:8).

INVESTING TREASURES IN HEAVEN

God provides us with money to meet our needs and to invest in the work of the kingdom of God. Our money comes from Him, and He owns it. Jesus knows how the love of money can lead our hearts away from Him and toward the world, so He gives us the preventative: invest in the kingdom of God. Jesus tells us:

> Do not store up for yourselves treasures on earth, where moth

and rust destroy, and where thieves break in and steal. But store up for yourselves treasures in heaven, where moth and rust do not destroy, and where thieves do not break in and steal. For where your treasure is, there your heart will be also.

—Matthew 6:19–21

We essentially make deposits into our heavenly bank accounts, which wait for us when we arrive in the form of rewards from Jesus. As we build up our heavenly treasures, our hearts will follow, and we will grow closer to God's ways and further away from the world's ways. If we live for God and His kingdom, all of our efforts—time, talents and treasures—will wait for us in eternity.

YOU CAN'T HAVE IT BOTH WAYS

We run into problems, however, when we try to live both for God and for the world. Jesus said, "No one can serve two masters. Either he will hate the one and love the other, or he will be devoted to the one and despise the other. You cannot serve both God and Money" (Matt. 6:24). We can't have it both ways—one foot in the world and one foot in heaven. As long as we place our affections on the things of this world, we will never overcome the circumstances around us.

As Director of Social Services in a skilled nursing home, I faced the choice of serving God or serving this world. I had witnessed staff treating residents inhumanely and not watching and assisting them when required. When the residents suffered injuries from falls, the owners told me to provide false information in the paperwork and to reassure the residents' families of our quality of care in order to protect the facility from possible litigation and loss of license. I firmly declined, knowing that God would take care of me if I lived for the kingdom of heaven. In the face of persecution, God helped me overcome my circumstances. My boss even threatened my job, but she never did let me go. I eventually left the job due to the unethical behavior there. Sacrificing living for the kingdom of heaven to move up in the kingdom of the world would have displeased God and made me feel horrible for the residents and their families. Having one foot in the world and one foot in heaven just doesn't work. God wants us to choose sides and not remain on the fence, for only then can we overcome the world.

Instead of overcoming the world, fence-sitting Christians put themselves in a terrible position where the world can easily overcome them. A friend of mine started out following Christ, but eventually went back into the things of the world while still professing her faith. She began to "party" with her old friends. She pursued a career while neglecting her family. She eventually cheated on her husband and then divorced him. She has become a completely different person, lost in the world. It all started with compromise—trying to live in the kingdom of the world and the kingdom of God at the same time. In searching for fulfillment in the kingdom of the world, she sacrificed her commitment to the kingdom of God and paid dearly. Someone has said, "The worldly Christian is the most miserable person on earth. He has too much of the world to be happy with Christianity and too much of Christianity to be happy with the world."

Dare to Be Different

As Christians, God calls us to stand out from the world as a unique people called by His name. To live a holy life means to set ourselves apart for God. Only then can we effectively overcome the circumstances around us. God's Word asks, "Do not be yoked together with unbelievers. For what do righteousness and wickedness have in common? Or what fellowship can light have with darkness?...What does a believer have in common with an unbeliever?" (2 Cor. 6:14–15). Instead, we must "come out from them and be separate, says the Lord. Touch no unclean thing, and I will receive you. I will be a Father to you, and you will be my sons and daughters, says the Lord Almighty" (vv. 17–18).

Does that mean we all pack up and head to the hills? Then we would have no world to overcome! God wants us among unbelievers; He just doesn't want us to be *like* them. A Christian should be "the salt of the earth" (Matt. 5:13) making the world thirsty for God and "the light of the world" (v. 14) pointing the world to the Savior, but at the same time should "keep oneself from being polluted by the world" (James 1:27).

As Christians, our viewpoints always diametrically oppose the world's viewpoints, since we belong to God and the world belongs to Satan (whether they know it or not). The field of psychology speaks from the world's viewpoint. As we have already seen, the viewpoints of psychology completely oppose those of biblical Christianity.

JUST LIKE THE WORLD

Although we should swim upstream and go against the flow of the world's viewpoints, some Christians take the easy road and float along with the current. For example, they adhere to certain psychological teachings like self-esteem, looking into the past to explain the present and taking care of yourself before others. Their beliefs slowly drift away from biblical Christianity as they allow the world to squeeze them into its mold. Before long they can become just like the world—materialistic, self-seeking consumers whose biggest question in life is, "What's in it for me?" Instead of living for Christ, they live for temporal things. Jesus said that since the pagans run after such things, we as followers of Christ should put these things in the proper perspective: below God in importance (Matt. 6:32). Christians who put worldly things above God will not overcome the world because to them, there is no world to overcome.

It's hard to tell the difference between a Christian and a nonbeliever these days. Who started the mistaken idea that to make Christianity attractive, we must think like the world, talk like the world and act like the world? It just doesn't work that way. When nonbelievers see Christians thinking and acting just like them, they say to themselves, "I'm no different from them, so I must be doing OK." On the other hand, when nonbelievers see Christians thinking and acting completely different—being salt and light to those walking in darkness—they become thirsty for Christ and eager to see the truth. The world will see their need for Christ when they witness every aspect of our daily lives lived out in the holy fear of God.

RENEW YOUR MIND

Concerning worldly, or cultural, Christians, the Bible warns, "You adulterous people, don't you know that friendship with the world is hatred toward God? Anyone who chooses to be a friend of the world becomes an enemy of God" (James 4:4). Instead, we should heed the apostle Paul's advice, which is worth memorizing: "Do not conform any longer to the pattern of this world, but be transformed by the renewing of your mind. Then you will be able to test and approve what God's will is—his good, pleasing and perfect will" (Rom. 12:2). Let's dare to be different!

If we want to experience the amazing and unique plan that God has for us, we must change our way of thinking from the viewpoint of the world to the viewpoint of God. If we renew our minds and think biblically, we can understand and follow God's good, acceptable and perfect plan for us. We will also possess the biblical knowledge needed to effectively deal with our circumstances around us.

GOD WILL PROVIDE

Before we can overcome our circumstances, we first need to see the world's viewpoint as our enemy and not our friend; then we begin to live for the kingdom of heaven instead of for the kingdom of earth. Perhaps you wonder, "If I live for the kingdom of heaven, what happens to my life here on earth?" Jesus tells us that He will reward our labors here on earth by providing for us:

> So do not worry, saying, "What shall we eat?" or "What shall we drink?" or "What shall we wear?" For the pagans run after all these things, and your heavenly Father knows that you need them. But seek first his kingdom and his righteousness, and all these things will be given to you as well. Therefore do not worry about tomorrow, for tomorrow will worry about itself.
> —Matthew 6:31–34

If we make God's kingdom our first priority, God will *always* provide us with the necessities of life. That's a promise!

CHAPTER 17

OVERCOMING YOUR CIRCUMSTANCES

If we live for God's kingdom, we are now prepared to overcome life's circumstances. As long as we live in this world, we will experience trials, heartbreak, disappointments, pain, sorrow and suffering. That's just life on this sin-ridden earth. Although we can't control our circumstances, we *can* control how we handle them. Instead of reacting to bad circumstances, we can view them through eyes of faith. Jesus Christ can help us overcome our circumstances and find victory, even in the midst of the worst trials.

PERSPECTIVE IS EVERYTHING

It all starts with our perspective. If we live for God's kingdom and God's glory in everything we do, then we have a heavenly perspective. We know we have life beyond the grave. On the other hand, if we died and just ceased to exist, we would have no such perspective. The apostle Paul wrote, "If only in this life we have hope in Christ, we are to be pitied more than all men" (1 Cor. 15:19). But indeed we do have the hope of heaven in Jesus Christ. Since He rose from the dead, so will we. We have the hope of paradise, just like the Garden of Eden, where we will find no more sadness, no more pain, no more suffering, no more stress and no more injustice.

Paul saw the value of looking heavenward: "I consider that our present sufferings are not worth comparing with the glory that will be revealed in us" (Rom. 8:18). He focused on the eternal: "For our light and momentary troubles are achieving for us an eternal glory that far outweighs them all. So we fix our eyes not on what is seen, but on what is unseen. For what is seen is temporary, but what is unseen is eternal" (2 Cor. 4:17–18). We can get through our circumstances by looking forward to the light at the end of the tunnel of life. That light is Jesus Christ, waiting with open arms to embrace us as we enter into our eternal glory. We will receive glorified (perfect and sinless) bodies after we die, just as Jesus received His glorified body after He rose from the dead. Then we will live with the Lord in paradise forever and ever. We truly have a blessed hope.

THE "ALL" GOD

Not only do we have a heavenly hope, but we can also rest in God's hand today. Our unchanging God is all-powerful, all-knowing and all-present. He has power over everything on earth, He knows about everything happening on earth, and He is present everywhere on the earth at once. What an awesome God we serve! Let this fact permeate your thinking. Absolutely nothing happens in your life apart from the power, knowledge and presence of God.

First, since God is all-powerful, He is always in control. He never takes a day off. The Bible says, "The LORD has established his throne in heaven, and his kingdom rules over all" (Ps. 103:19). All is nothing short of everything! After His resurrection, Jesus said to His disciples, "All authority in heaven and on earth has been given to me" (Matt. 28:18). We can rest in the fact that Jesus has power over *all* things that happen to us. He even has power over our unbelieving bosses and government officials: "God, the blessed and only Ruler, the King of kings and Lord of lords..." (1 Tim. 6:15). Remember this the next time you feel stressed out at your job. With God in control, you can rest in His loving plan for you.

Second, since God is all-knowing, nothing happens without God knowing about it. God never gets distracted when we experience a problem and says, "Oh boy, missed that one. Sorry, Lisa. Next time I'll be more attentive." On the contrary, God knows us better than we know ourselves. Jesus said, "Even the very hairs of your head are all numbered" (Matt. 10:30). Tell that one to your hairdresser!

King David understood God's intimacy with every detail of his life:

> O LORD, you have searched me and you know me. You know when I sit and when I rise; you perceive my thoughts from afar. You discern my going out and my lying down; you are familiar with all my ways. Before a word is on my tongue you know it completely, O LORD.
>
> —Psalm 139:1–4

Third, since God is all-present, He is with us *wherever* we are to guide us and strengthen us. King David continues:

> Where can I go from your Spirit? Where can I flee from your presence? If I go up to the heavens, you are there; if I make my bed in the depths, you are there. If I rise on the wings of the dawn, if I settle on the far side of the sea, even there your hand will guide me, your right hand will hold me fast.
>
> —Psalm 139:7–10

Even when we don't "feel" like Christians, God promises, "Never will I leave you; never will I forsake you" (Heb. 13:5).

The "All" God also never changes. The Bible proclaims, "Jesus Christ is the same yesterday and today and forever" (Heb. 13:8). While circumstances may change, we can always lean on the rock of Christ. God never has a bad day. His character is consistently holy, loving and dependable, making Him the best Father we could ever want when circumstances don't go our way.

GOD HAS A PLAN

With God's heaven and God's character also comes God's plan. Isn't it comforting to know that God has a plan for you and me? He has a plan fully customized to each person. No two people have the same plan. The conglomeration of God's plan for each person forms

God's master plan for the universe. Each of us plays a particular part in God's master plan.

When circumstances look grim and you raise your head to the sky and wonder, "What's going on? My life seems completely out of control, and I have no clue where I'm headed," remember, God has a plan. He knows what He is doing. Although we can't see the big picture, God can: "And we know that in *all things* God works for the good of those who love him, who have been called according to his purpose" (Rom. 8:28, emphasis added). We have been "predestined according to the plan of him who works out *everything* in conformity with the purpose of his will" (Eph. 1:11, emphasis added). All things, good and bad, added up, work together for our good. We must trust that God knows what He is doing when our part in the big picture looks grim.

GOD'S PLAN FOR JOSEPH

The life of Joseph gives us one of the best examples of how God sees the big picture when we may not. Joseph's brothers hated him for being their father's favorite son. One day their jealousy got the best of them. They threw Joseph down a well, fished him out awhile later and sold him to Egyptian slave traders. They didn't see him again for years. While in Egypt, Joseph was mistreated as a slave, falsely accused of adultery with Egyptian royalty and thrown into prison. But keeping faith in God during these trials, Joseph was eventually made ruler over all of Egypt when he correctly interpreted Pharaoh's dream that Egypt would suffer seven years of famine. Joseph directed the Egyptians to store up grain for the famine to come.

During the famine, guess who shows up for grain—Joseph's brothers! After some discipline from God, Joseph's brothers finally realize that the brother they sold into slavery has now become their master, the ruler over all Egypt. God planned for Joseph to provide for his family during this great famine. Joseph tells his brothers:

> And now, do not be distressed and do not be angry with yourselves for selling me here, because it was to save lives that God sent me ahead of you. For two years now there has been famine in the land,

and for the next five years there will not be plowing and reaping. But God sent me ahead of you to preserve for you a remnant on earth and to save your lives by a great deliverance. So then, it was not you who sent me here, but God. He made me father to Pharaoh, lord of his entire household and ruler of all Egypt.

—Genesis 45:5–8

Joseph persevered throughout his many trials by his faith that God had a wonderful plan in store for him and his family.

GOD'S PLAN IS PERFECT

Not only does God have a plan, but His plan is also perfect. Any plan for our lives that we could dream up will never compare with the perfect plan that God has for us, based on "his good, pleasing and perfect will" (Rom. 12:2). God tells Israel, "'For I know the plans I have for you,' declares the LORD, 'plans to prosper you and not to harm you, plans to give you hope and a future'" (Jer. 29:11).

Many times we tend to assume that the perfect plan would be to win the lottery, to have a successful business or ministry, or to live on a tropical island and surf for a living. While some people may experience these things, God cares more about our character than our comfort. He wants to make us more like Christ through life's difficulties, for "we know that suffering produces perseverance; perseverance, character; and character, hope. And hope does not disappoint us, because God has poured out his love into our hearts by the Holy Spirit, whom he has given us" (Rom. 5:3–4). This process draws us nearer to God. One pastor writes, "The valleys of life are part of God's plan and process for drawing you nearer to Him and helping you to experience His great love for you."[1]

The parents of Columbine martyr Rachel Scott have experienced a very low valley of life in the death of their daughter. "But in some ways," they say, "the losses we have endured have helped us experience a deeper level of trust in God and a more accepting faith that He knows exactly what He is doing."[2] They have drawn closer to God through their suffering. As He did for the Scotts, God can use bad circumstances as part of His perfect plan in order to draw us near to

Him and deepen our faith.

FOCUS ON CHRIST

When negative, unpleasant circumstances come our way, we can do a few practical things to overcome them. First, we should focus not on the circumstance itself, but on Christ. The story of Peter walking on the water gives us a beautiful illustration of this concept. When Peter saw Jesus walking on the water, he wanted to do the same:

> Then Peter got down out of the boat, walked on the water and came toward Jesus. But when he saw the wind, he was afraid and, beginning to sink, cried out, "Lord, save me!" Immediately Jesus reached out his hand and caught him. "You of little faith," he said, "why did you doubt?" And when they climbed into the boat, the wind died down.
>
> —Matthew 14:29–32

The minute Peter took his eyes off of Jesus and focused on the wind, he began to sink. When winds come our way we will begin to sink if we do not focus on Jesus and His power to help us overcome the impossible. What does it mean to focus on Jesus? It means to steadfastly trust Him with all your mind, heart, soul and strength. When that happens, we're bound to win.

PRAISE, PRAYER AND THANKSGIVING

We can more easily focus on Jesus during difficult circumstances by adopting an attitude of praise, prayer and thanksgiving. An amazing thing happens when we focus on God instead of our problems and our feelings—God gets bigger and bigger and our problems get smaller and smaller. Praise, prayer and thanksgiving help us rise above the situation and catapult our being into the presence of Almighty God. The Bible encourages us to "be joyful always; pray continually; give thanks in all circumstances, for this is God's will for you in Christ Jesus" (1 Thess. 5:16–18). We can praise God for who He is and what He has done in our lives. All throughout the Book of Psalms, King David praises God during his trials, always expecting the mighty hand of God to prevail.

We can also pray for the strength to get through the trial and for deliverance from it. The Bible encourages us to confidently ask God for help when we need it: "Let us then approach the throne of grace with confidence, so that we may receive mercy and find grace to help us in our time of need" (Heb. 4:16). The Lord draws near to us and hears us when we come to Him in humility and brokenness. King David knew this fact firsthand:

> The eyes of the LORD are on the righteous and his ears are attentive to their cry...The righteous cry out, and the LORD hears them; he delivers them from all their troubles. The LORD is close to the brokenhearted and saves those who are crushed in spirit. A righteous man may have many troubles, but the LORD delivers him from them all.
>
> —Psalm 34:15, 17–19

Finally, we can thank God for all things—past, present and future—knowing that God is in control and has a perfect plan. When we praise, pray and give thanks, we will find that the Holy Spirit comforts us and fills us with peace and renewed strength in the midst of our circumstances.

OVERCOME EVIL WITH GOOD

We can also overcome the negative circumstances in our lives by showing God's love to others. When others mistreat and persecute us for living godly lives, we no longer have to react to our hurt feelings. We no longer need to act nice on the outside while inside we really want to retaliate. Instead we can remember the heartfelt love and compassion that Jesus had for His enemies, even while being crucified. Jesus said, "Love your enemies, do good to those who hate you, bless those who curse you, pray for those who mistreat you" (Luke 6:27–28). We will find this an impossible task in our own strength, but very possible in God's strength.

God's love contains power, blasting its way through even the hardest of hearts. Love never fails (1 Cor. 13:8). No matter what negative circumstances come our way, we can overcome evil circumstances with good using the power of love: "Do not be overcome with evil, but overcome evil with good" (Rom. 12:21).

JESUS HAS OVERCOME

Jesus knew firsthand the difficulties that this life would bring. He sympathizes with our weaknesses (Heb. 4:15). He overcame, so He knows we can overcome as well if we abide in Him. Jesus said, "I have told you these things, so that in me you may have peace. In the world you will have trouble. But take heart! I have overcome the world" (John 16:33). If Jesus has overcome the world, we can too through faith: "For everyone born of God overcomes the world. This is the victory that has overcome the world, even our faith. Who is it that overcomes the world? Only he who believes that Jesus is the Son of God" (1 John 5:4–5).

MORE THAN CONQUERORS

Jesus is our hope in overcoming the circumstances of this world. We have everlasting life in Christ, and no circumstance can take this away from us. The apostle Paul rejoices in this fact: "Who shall separate us from the love of Christ? Shall trouble or hardship or persecution or famine or nakedness or danger or sword?...No, *in all these things we are more than conquerors through him who loved us*" (Rom. 8:35, 37, emphasis added). Nothing that happens to us will separate us from the love of Jesus Christ! In *all* things we are "more than conquerors" in Christ. Since Christ conquered death by His resurrection, we have conquered death through our faith in Him. If we have conquered death, surely we can conquer any other circumstance that comes our way.

CHAPTER 18

OVERCOMING
SATAN

With Jesus in our hearts, not only can we overcome our sinful nature, the world system and our circumstances, but we can also overcome Satan and his demons. I'm not talking about the funny-looking red guy with a cape and horns that you see in cartoons. A real angelic being, Satan uses his demons to work in and through people's lives for evil. The Bible states, "The whole world is under the control of the evil one" (1 John 5:19). The evil one, Satan, influences people to do, say, think and believe things completely contrary and opposed to the Word of God. It has been said that God loves you and has a wonderful plan for your life, while Satan hates you and has a terrible plan for your life. Satan will attempt to destroy our lives either directly or through other people. But God has given us all we need to overcome the enemy's attacks and live victoriously.

SATAN'S STRATEGY

At one time God considered Satan one of the most beautiful and powerful angels He ever created, but God cast him out of heaven when he tried to steal God's glory for himself. Ever since, Satan and the fallen angels that followed him have waged war against God and

195

His creation. Satan hates people, and he will do anything to ruin their lives both now and in eternity. Satan especially hates Christians, for they have left Satan's team for God's team and seek to worship the same God that Satan despises. Satan attacks Christians to draw them away from their relationship with God and the joyful, fulfilling life that God desires for them. Jesus says that Satan comes "only to steal and kill and destroy," but Jesus comes "that they may have life, and have it to the full" (John 10:10). Thus a battle rages every day in the spiritual realm between God's angels and Satan's demons, and the battle takes place in the lives of men and women on this earth.

OUR AUTHORITY AND PROTECTION

Thankfully, Jesus has given Christians authority over Satan and his demons. We have authority because Jesus has authority. When Jesus died on the cross, He disarmed Satan's ability to have power over the lives of those who put their faith in Christ: "And having disarmed the powers and authorities, he [Jesus] made a public spectacle of them, triumphing over them by the cross" (Col. 2:15). After His resurrection, Jesus said, "All authority in heaven and on earth has been given to me" (Matt. 28:18). When we received Jesus into our hearts, we also received His authority over Satan and His demons: "The one [God] who is in you is greater than the one [Satan] who is in the world" (1 John 4:4). If Christ is in you, Satan no longer has free reign over your life!

If Christ is in you, nothing can happen to you apart from God's knowledge and permission. The protective wings of a loving heavenly Father surround you. If Satan wants to interfere in your life, he must go through God first for permission, as he had to do with Job in the Old Testament. If God chooses to allow Satan to tempt you, God will only give you what you can bear (1 Cor. 10:13). Whatever God allows Satan to do in your life, know that your battles will strengthen your faith and ultimately glorify God.

SATAN'S WEAPONS

We should also remember that while God is all-powerful, all-present and all-knowing, Satan is not. Satan does not have more power than God (although he has much more power than us), he can't be everywhere at once (although he has a highly organized force of demons all over the world), and he doesn't know about everything happening on the earth (although he observes his targets and knows their vulnerabilities very well). But even though he does not possess the same characteristics as the God he envies so well, he does use an arsenal of weapons against believers: persecution from nonbelievers, division among believers, false believers, doubt, discouragement, fear, compromise, temptation, lies and so forth. Because God has allowed Satan limited control over the world system until Christ's bodily return, Satan can use the world as a stage for carrying out his wicked schemes.

Take, for example, temptation. The Bible says, "For everything in the world—the cravings of sinful man, the lust of his eyes and the boasting of what he has and does—comes not from the Father but from the world" (1 John 2:16). Ever since Adam and Eve, Satan has used the lust of the eyes (our senses and imagination), the cravings of the flesh (carrying out our sinful desires) and the pride of life (boasting, self-confidence) to tempt many a vulnerable soul into sin. Eve saw the fruit, ate it and became "wise." Satan still uses these same tactics today!

Satan Always Denies the Word of God

Satan attacks us first and foremost in our minds. He questions and denies the truth of the Word of God and then substitutes the truth with lies. Jesus said about Satan, "There is no truth in him. When he lies, he speaks his native language, for he is a liar and the father of lies" (John 8:44). Imagine that—a language of lying, and Satan is the linguistic expert.

Satan has succeeded in weakening and polluting the church with psychological doctrines that deny the Word of God. Using scientific-sounding terms, professional licenses and degrees, and strategic positioning of psychology as a helping and caring profession, Satan seeks to undermine the Christian's faith in the authority and sufficiency of God's Word through well-meaning Christian therapists.

While some Christian therapists are ignorant of the spiritual dangers of Christian psychology, Paul warns us of others who knowingly preach false gospels: "For such men are false apostles, deceitful workmen, masquerading as apostles of Christ. And no wonder, for Satan himself masquerades as an angel of light. It is not surprising, then, if his servants masquerade as servants of righteousness. Their end will be what their actions deserve" (2 Cor. 11:13–15). Satan "masquerades as an angel of light" to work through his servants who "masquerade as servants of righteousness." The light that appears sincere, innocent and helpful actually masks the darkness that wants to destroy our faith in the Word of God.

SATAN HITS THE STREETS

Satan's denial of God's Word manifests itself in a variety of ways in our lives. For instance, when our marriages get rocky the therapist tells us, "You deserve more than this. After all, your happiness is what really matters. If you aren't happy with him, you should do what's best for you and divorce him." We get home and Satan makes us think, "The therapist is right! I need to move on. If God loved me, He wouldn't want me to go through this!" A month later we're in the divorce courts, our families fall apart, we become angry and bitter, and we look to God and say, "Why, God? Why did You allow this to happen to me?" Using the therapist's advice, Satan has won the battle in destroying our relationship with our spouse and with God.

Of course, Satan never bothers to tell us the truth from God's Word that God hates divorce. He never bothers to tell us that God's love never fails. He never bothers to remind us of the vows we made before God: for better or for worse, for richer or for poorer, in sickness and in health, to love and to cherish, until death do we part. He never bothers to tell us how our children will suffer in a broken home. Satan lies to us first and laughs in our face later when our lives are falling apart.

Satan shows up on the scene when the eighteen-year-old girl who just received Jesus feels pressured to have sex with her unbelieving boyfriend. Her therapist counsels her, "Before you have sex, make sure you understand the risks of pregnancy and AIDS—and practice safe sex."

Although she feels uncomfortable becoming intimate with her boyfriend, her boyfriend insists, "C'mon! If you really loved me you would do this. After all, I've waited six months. Isn't that long enough? And it's prom night! You may never get this chance again. Don't blow it and ruin our night together."

After becoming pregnant, Satan makes her think, "I can't have a baby now! I had better get an abortion. I heard it's really common, quick and painless. Plus, my family would disown me if they found out." After the abortion the girl suffers from extreme guilt, and her boyfriend dumps her. Through the counsel of her therapist and the coaxing of her boyfriend, Satan has succeeded in ruining her life.

But Satan never told her the truth from God's Word that Christians should not date unbelievers. He never told her the truth that God designed sex for marriage and that God would judge the sexually immoral. He never told her the truth that life is precious in God's sight, even from conception, and that God has a wonderful plan and purpose for that unborn baby.

OUR DEFENSE: THE ARMOR OF GOD

These two examples didn't have to turn out this way. God has given us spiritual weapons to fight against Satan's attacks. "Why all the war analogies?" you might ask. Contrary to popular opinion, the Christian life is not a playground, but a battleground. Since "the whole world is under the control of the evil one" (1 John 5:19) and we now belong to God, we find ourselves in enemy territory. We have become "strangers" and "pilgrims" in this world, on our way to our true home in heaven. While we pass through this world, we must fight against Satan's attacks in order to live the abundant and effective lives God wants us to experience.

Using the weapons that God has given us, we can defeat Satan's efforts to make our lives miserable. The sixth chapter of Ephesians identifies these spiritual weapons: the sword of the Spirit, the girdle of truth, the breastplate of righteousness, the helmet of salvation, the shield of faith, and the shoes of peace (Eph. 6:13–18). We "put on" this armor of God daily through prayer, remembering what each weapon means. God's Word reminds us to use these weapons to defend ourselves against Satan and his demons, not against the people through whom they work (v. 12). God wants us to love people but hate the evil empowering them.

Our most effective weapon against Satan's lies is the sword of the Spirit, or the Word of God. Just as an experienced cashier can easily detect a counterfeit bill, someone well versed in God's Word can easily detect Satan's lies. Once we detect a lie from Satan, we can expose it with truth from the Word of God. Reading, meditating on and memorizing God's Word and then applying it to situations we face in life will help us outwit the enemy of our souls. If we don't read it, study it, pray over it, ponder it, digest it and apply it regularly, we won't know how to defend ourselves when Satan turns up the heat, takes aim and fires away. With a sharp sword of the Spirit, we can, like Paul, "demolish arguments and every pretension that sets itself up against the knowledge of God," and we can "take captive every thought to make it obedient to Christ" (2 Cor. 10:5).

Through prayer, we put on the girdle of truth as the basic foundation of our other armor. The girdle of truth, or the belt of truth, symbolizes our being held together by walking in the light and having fellowship with God on a continual basis. It represents our lives as being full of truth and integrity, not hypocrisy and double-living. If we try to defeat the enemy with sin in our lives, we have already been defeated.

We put on the breastplate of righteousness to remember that whatever accusations Satan throws our way, either in our consciences or from other people, God forgives and forgets our sins because of Christ's sacrifice on the cross. When the accusations come, we can recall the righteousness we have in Jesus: "God made him [Jesus] who had no sin to be sin for us, so that in him we might become the righteousness of God" (2 Cor. 5:21).

We put on the helmet of salvation to remind us of the hope we have in the return of Jesus Christ to earth. We have a hope that one day in the very near future, Jesus will snatch us up to heaven and spare us from the coming judgment on the world. We will soon live forever with Jesus in heaven. This hope helps us persevere when Satan's forces discourage us and tell us to quit.

We also take up our shield of faith to "extinguish all the flaming arrows of the evil one" (Eph. 6:16). The evil one, Satan, discourages us and makes us fear, doubt or worry about our lives. But we can defend ourselves by exercising faith in God. Satan's arrows frequently come through people closest to us, for he knows these arrows hurt the most. When we detect his schemes, we hold up our shield of faith and keep close to the Lord until he flees.

We step into our shoes of peace to remind us that we find victory through peace. We realize that we don't fight against people, but against the power behind people–Satan. Satan is no match for the gospel of peace. No evil power can overcome it. By being armed with the Word of God and the motivation to save souls for Him, we can overcome evil by making all our paths peaceful ones.

We put on each and every piece of armor by faithful prayer in the Holy Spirit. This prepares our minds for the battles that lie ahead of us. If we leave any area of our lives open and vulnerable to Satan's attacks, he will surely find and exploit it. We must be continually watchful and alert. If we wait until the battle begins before putting on the armor of God, it will be too late.

Our Battle Plan

We can sum up these weapons of our warfare in a simple battle plan that God has given us:

> Be self-controlled and alert. Your enemy the devil prowls around like a roaring lion looking for someone to devour. *Resist him, standing firm in the faith,* because you know that your brothers throughout the world are undergoing the same kind of sufferings.
> —1 Peter 5:8–9, emphasis added

> *Resist the devil,* and he will flee from you. *Come near to God* and

he will come near to you.

—James 4:7–8, emphasis added

It's really that simple: Resist the devil and draw near to God, using the weapons of warfare just discussed. The devil will never overcome us when we do these things. Praise God for that!

SATAN AT COLUMBINE HIGH

Recently, one man used the armor of God to overcome Satan's evil with God's good. Darrell Scott, father of Columbine High School martyr Rachel Scott, wrote a moving account of his daughter's life, death and faith surrounding the events of the horrific shooting on April 20, 1999. In *Rachel's Tears*, a recollection of the events of that day illustrates the reality of the existence of spiritual battles between good and evil:

> According to Richard's earliest account, he and Rachel were sitting outside when they saw Harris and Klebold approaching. Without warning, the two young men opened fire, severing Richard's spine and shooting Rachel twice in her legs and once in her torso.
>
> As Richard lay stunned and Rachel attempted to crawl to safety, the shooters began to walk away, only to return seconds later. At that point, Harris reportedly grabbed Rachel by her hair, held her head up, and asked her the question: "Do you believe in God?"
>
> "You know I do," replied Rachel.
>
> "Then go be with Him," responded Harris before shooting her in the head.[1]

Harris and Klebold premeditated the shooting, as their homemade videos before the shooting make clear:

> "What would Jesus do?" asks Klebold at one point in the tapes, making fun of the popular WWJD slogan that appears on more than a million bracelets and T-shirts. Yelling and making faces at the camera, Klebold asks a second question. "What would I do?" he screams before pointing an imaginary shotgun at the camera, taking aim, and making a shooting motion and corresponding

sound: "*Boosh!*"

In the same tape, made on March 15, Harris is heard saying, "Yeah, I love Jesus. I love Jesus. Shut the f*** up." Harris later chants, "Go Romans... Thank God they crucified that a******." Then the two troubled teenagers join together in chanting, "Go Romans! Go Romans! Yeah! Whooh!"[2]

Rachel's father Darrell had this to say about the spiritual implications of the shootings:

> It is true that there is a spiritual battle going on. It is true that there is a spirit in this world that is hostile to Christianity... I was appalled at the hatred and venom toward Christianity that I saw coming from the two boys who executed this tragic crime. As I watched their video diary, I was amazed at how many times they blasted the Christian faith. It appears that they had opened themselves up to spiritual influences that went beyond their control.[3]

A year earlier, Rachel Scott, a committed Christian, knew that her life would soon end. She filled her journals with symbolic references of the massacre that would claim her life. Rachel realized the powerful spiritual truth that "neither death nor life, neither angels nor demons, neither the present nor the future, nor any powers, neither height nor depth, nor anything else in all creation, will be able to separate us from the love of God that is in Christ Jesus our Lord" (Rom. 8:38–39). No demons or powers could separate her from the Lord she loved so much—not even death itself. Rachel took up the armor of God that day and overcame Satan through her immovable faith in Christ.

With *Rachel's Tears*, Darrell Scott, has used this tragedy that Satan meant for evil to tell others about Jesus Christ. Instead of continuing in despair and ceding the victory to Satan, Darrell has hope in Christ's return, faith in God's plan for his life and shoes of peace to carry an important message to the world. Using the armor of God, he overcame evil with good.

CHAPTER 19

SUFFERING WITH A PURPOSE

In our struggles to overcome our sinful nature, the world, our circumstances and Satan, we can find comfort in knowing that God has a divine purpose behind our suffering. In this chapter we will get a glimpse of God's design behind suffering in the life of the Christian. With this understanding, we can look forward to suffering with joyful expectation instead of dreaded fear.

GOD CALLS US TO SUFFER

Let's face it. Nobody likes suffering. You rarely hear a Christian claiming the promises of God that "everyone who wants to live a godly life in Christ Jesus will be persecuted" (2 Tim. 3:12), and that "we must go through many hardships to enter the kingdom of God" (Acts 14:22). Try finding those verses in a Bible promise book! Whether or not we hear it from the pulpit, God calls us to suffer for Him: "For it has been granted to you on behalf of Christ not only to believe on him, but also to suffer for him" (Phil. 1:29).

But thanks to psychology, Christians have come to abhor suffering and avoid it at all costs. We place more value on comfort and pleasure than on self-sacrifice and holiness. We have redefined the God of the

Bible as the god of our happiness. So when we see another Christian suffering, we automatically assume that person has disobeyed God. We forget that God willed for Jesus Christ to suffer and that Jesus never sinned: "Yet it was the LORD's will to crush him and cause him to suffer" (Isa. 53:10). We are certainly no better than Jesus. On the contrary, we should become concerned if we never experience any kind of suffering or persecution as a Christian. After all, as someone once said, "Satan doesn't kick a dead horse."

Jesus Christ suffered a bloody death at the hands of sinners—nailed to a cross for nine excruciating hours. No amount of our suffering will ever compare with the suffering Jesus experienced, for we "have not yet resisted [against sin] to the point of shedding [our] blood" (Heb. 12:4). Since God calls us to follow Christ's example, we should view suffering as a very necessary and rewarding part of the growing Christian's life.

GOD IS ON THE THRONE

We will inevitably suffer in this sinful, fallen world. Thankfully, our heavenly Father has complete control over our suffering. When a trial comes upon us, we can remember the chain of command in heaven that controls every detail of our trial. The Book of Job gives us great insight into the chain of command in heaven. Satan asks God to harm Job so that Job would curse God. God replied, "Everything he has is in your hands, but on the man himself do not lay a finger" (Job 1:12). First we see that Satan wanted God to harm Job directly, but God would never harm him, for it would go against God's character. We also see that Satan had no power over Job until God granted it to him. Satan reports to God in the heavenly chain of command. Isn't it comforting that God sits on the kingly throne of the universe? Finally, we see that God only allowed Satan to harm Job up to a certain point. He did not allow Satan to kill Job, but only to inflict suffering. God will never give us more than we can handle. He knows our breaking point better than we do. Later we will see why God allowed this suffering into Job's life.

With God on the throne of the universe, He calls the shots on this earth. God has a plan for the universe that involves both good and evil and that uses our free will to accomplish His purposes. We must trust that God's love, wisdom and power direct every decision He makes. God's character forms the foundation of our trust and faith. If He loved us enough to sacrifice His own Son, He loves us enough to know when to allow evil and when to intervene. One day, God will bind Satan when Jesus Christ returns to judge the earth and establish His reign of peace for one thousand years. But until then, God uses suffering in our lives to *discipline* us as His children, have us *depend* completely on Him, produce *dedication* in our Christian faith, prepare us for our future *dominion* over the nations and create *delight* in our souls for the spiritual blessings awaiting us in heaven.

SUFFERING TO INSTILL DISCIPLINE

God loves His sons and daughters, and He shows His love through discipline when we go astray: "My son, do not despise the LORD's discipline and do not resent his rebuke, because the LORD disciplines those he loves, as a father the son he delights in" (Prov. 3:11–12). Undergoing discipline proves our sonship and demonstrates the effectiveness of our faith in Him.

God's Goal: Holiness

When God sends His servants your way to warn you about your sin, you can bet God is disciplining you. When your job promotion falls through after acting a little too boastful and confident, you know God is keeping you humble. The Christian radio program cuts to your heart as God convicts you of an area of your life that displeases Him. God disciplines us out of love to draw us back into His sheepfold. Although painful at the time, it accomplishes God's purposes. God disciplines us "for our good, that we may share in his holiness. No discipline seems pleasant at the time, but painful. Later on, however, it produces a harvest of righteousness and peace for those who have been trained by it" (Heb. 12:10–11). Our heavenly Father disciplines us to draw us nearer to Him and farther away from the world. God desires holiness and righteousness in our lives more than our personal comfort.

Jonah's Discipline Lessons

Jonah, God's classic rebel child of the Old Testament, received some harsh discipline for his disobedience. God told him to go to Nineveh, but instead he headed the other direction, to Tarshish. After boarding the boat to Tarshish, the Lord gave him discipline lesson number one: the lesson of the mighty tempest. The other passengers found him in the lowest parts of the boat and asked him to pray to his God so that the tempest might subside. But the Bible doesn't mention that Jonah did anything. Bad move, Jonah!

Discipline lesson number two: the lesson of public shame and disgrace. The others cast lots to identify the one responsible for the tempest, and the lot fell on Jonah. Jonah must have thought, *Why doesn't God just leave me alone?* But God would have His way.

After Jonah finally admitted his responsibility for the tempest, God gave him discipline lesson number three, the biggest lesson of all: the lesson of the big fish. Instead of repenting, Jonah thought to himself, *I would rather die than preach to the people of Nineveh!* So at Jonah's request, the others threw him overboard and a great fish swallowed him. After three days and three nights of sloshing inside the belly of the great fish, Jonah finally repented and asked the Lord for forgiveness. Immediately the fish spit up Jonah onto dry land like a bad meal.

Jonah preached judgment to the people of Nineveh, and the people repented. But Jonah still had some more discipline coming his way. Jonah's anger toward God's mercies brought him discipline lesson number four: the lesson of the withered plant. Through this lesson God contrasted Jonah's stubborn, prideful heart with God's heart of mercy and compassion.

We can all relate at times to Jonah's stubborn independence and self-righteousness toward others walking in darkness. In what ways have you experienced God's discipline? Know that God will use your suffering to bring you into a closer walk with Himself.

SUFFERING TO FOSTER DEPENDENCE

God wants us to depend on Him for everything. As our gracious heavenly Father, He will reward our trust by providing all we need for life and godliness. In daily life we have a tendency to depend on our own resources. Whether we depend on the stock market, our bank account, our job security, our talents, our skills or our health, we find it much easier to live by sight than by faith. God uses suffering to break our self-sufficient, self-reliant wills and teach us to live by faith alone.

Following Paul's Example

Paul knew what it meant to depend on God alone. Describing a missionary trip to Asia he explains, "We were under great pressure, far beyond our ability to endure, so that we despaired even of life. Indeed, in our hearts we felt the sentence of death. But this happened that we might not rely on ourselves but on God, who raises the dead" (2 Cor. 1:8–9). Paul faced death. But he realized that with everything stripped away and death staring him in the face, his childlike trust in Jesus would help him through his despair. Through his suffering, Paul had no choice but to rely completely on God.

The apostle Paul certainly had his share of adventures. On another occasion he went into heaven and "heard inexpressible things" that he could not mention (2 Cor. 12:4). Imagine being taken into heaven for a moment and then returning to the daily grind. You would have quite a story to tell. Books, T-shirts, guest appearances on *Touched by an Angel* . . . You would find it very easy to get caught up in yourself and forget the glory of God. God knew this and so allowed Paul to experience great suffering to keep him humble: "To keep me from becoming conceited because of these surpassingly great revelations, there was given to me a thorn in my flesh, a messenger of Satan, to torment me" (v. 7). God uses suffering in our lives to keep us from becoming prideful and independent of His lordship.

Of course, Paul didn't appreciate this messenger of Satan causing him so much pain, and he pleaded with Jesus to take it away. But Jesus said to him, "My grace is sufficient for you, for my power is made perfect in weakness" (v. 9). Jesus basically said, "I am all you need to get through this. You don't need psychological treatment, you don't need support groups, and you don't need a vacation. You just need me." God's grace was sufficient for every problem Paul experienced.

"When I Am Weak, Then I Am Strong"

God in His mercy may choose to remove our suffering. But if He doesn't take it away, then He wants to use our weakness to show off His strength and glory. Why does our weakness show off His strength? Because God can do more with a humbled, surrendered person who knows he is nothing than he can with a prideful, self-sufficient person who thinks he is God's gift to the world. How can God's strength show in someone who always calls attention to himself? God will not share His glory with another person. The stronger we are, the weaker He is in us, and the weaker we are, the stronger He is in us. God made us from the dust of the earth to show off His power and glory in and through us. The Bible says, "But we have this treasure in jars of clay to show that this all-surpassing power is from God and not from us" (2 Cor. 4:7).

Paul knew this spiritual secret from experience. After he learned that Christ expressed Himself more fully in his weakness, he concludes, "Therefore I will boast all the more gladly about my weaknesses, so that Christ's power may rest on me. That is why, for Christ's sake, I delight in weaknesses, in insults, in hardships, in persecutions, in difficulties. For when I am weak, then I am strong" (2 Cor. 12:9–10). Paul didn't just accept his weaknesses—he boasted about them. Psychology would have a field day with Paul! Paul didn't whine about his weaknesses to a therapist, try to improve his low self-esteem or look for other abused apostles and form a support group. No, he took pleasure in his suffering, for then Christ's power would shine through him and impact his world.

I can attest to this truth in my own life. I bear the most good fruit and have the most joy when I pour out my life to everyone but myself... when my world crashes down on me all at once and I surrender control out of frustration, look up to God and just laugh... when God strips away everything in which I have put my trust and leaves me simply clinging to Him. When we feel weakest, God is strongest in us. On the other hand, when life gets easy, we begin to trust ourselves again, and the bad fruit begins to spread like gangrene in our hearts. It has been said about weakness that when we get to the end of ourselves, we get to the beginning of God.

The ultimate example of getting to the end of Himself through suffering, Jesus Christ, God incarnate, "made himself nothing, taking the very nature of a servant, being made in human likeness. And being found in appearance as a man, he humbled himself and became obedient to death—even death on a cross!" (Phil. 2:7–8). We learn the traits of dependence, humility and weakness as we experience suffering, helping us become more like Christ.

SUFFERING TO PRODUCE DEDICATION

God also uses suffering to stretch our faith and dedicate ourselves more fully to Him. God cares more how we finish the race of the Christian life than how we start it. He sees the final product. We start off as a lump of clay as a brand-new believer, but He refuses to leave us that way. He uses suffering to keep us near to Him so He can shape and mold us into the beautiful masterpiece that He desires. He takes us through the fiery trials to make us strong and immovable. We finish the race as a fine piece of pottery prepared for the glories of heaven.

A Means to Maturity

God wants us to see the genuineness of our faith by giving us tests along the way. How can we know the measure of our faith unless God tests us so we can see what we're made of? I call these tests "faith tests." God's faith tests usually start out easy and then become more difficult as we advance in our faith. Peter said, "These [trials] have come so that your faith—of greater worth than gold, which perishes even though refined by fire—may be proved genuine and may result in praise, glory and honor when Jesus Christ is revealed" (1 Pet. 1:7). He wants us to pass His faith tests with straight *As* so we can become strong and purified in our faith. These faith tests can only happen through trials and suffering. Therefore we should view suffering positively, as a means to grow in our Christian faith. Paul writes, "We also rejoice in our sufferings, because we know that suffering produces perseverance; perseverance, character; and character, hope" (Rom. 5:3–4). As we persevere in our suffering, we develop godly character and firm hope that stays with us the rest of our lives.

James also sees suffering as a means to build godly character and maturity: "Consider it pure joy, my brothers, whenever you face trials of many kinds, because you know that the testing of your faith develops perseverance. Perseverance must finish its work so that you may be mature and complete, not lacking anything" (James 1:2–4). Count it joy when you suffer? It sounds masochistic at first, but note that we don't count the suffering itself as joy, but the results it will produce—a mature and complete soul. Whenever we fall into trials, we know that God plans on stretching and maturing our faith. Faith is like a muscle. If not exercised regularly, it becomes flimsy and weak. But if faith gets stretched and worked out frequently, it becomes strong and healthy. As our heavenly trainer, God keeps us spiritually fit with the weights of trials and suffering. With the best trainer around, we can win the race to heaven marked out for us.

Job's Perseverance

Job knew what it meant to persevere in suffering. You could call him the Mr. Universe of faith. He managed to persevere through losing all his livestock, his servants and his sons and daughters. How did Job respond to his suffering? Falling to the ground in reverent worship, Job said, "Naked I came from my mother's womb, and naked shall I return there. The LORD gave, and the LORD has taken away; blessed be the name of the Lord" (Job 1:21, NKJV). Job had a deep trust in the Lord that went beyond his circumstances and focused on the character of God Himself. He even persevered through the physical pain of painful boils from the soles of his feet to the crown of his head, as well as the mental discouragement from his wife's demoralization and his three "friends" who accused him of sinning against God and who deplored him to repent. How did Job respond to all of this? "Shall we accept good from God, and not trouble?" (Job 2:10). Job understood that God had a right to allow good as well as evil into his life, for the simple reason that He is God.

God had only loving intentions toward Job. He tested Job's faith through suffering to bring him into an even deeper relationship of trust with Himself. Not only did God strengthen Job's faith, but He provided twice as many possessions than he had before these tests of faith. He also provided seven more sons and three more daughters. James speaks of the positive results of Job's perseverance:

> Brothers, as an example of patience in the face of suffering, take the prophets who spoke in the name of the Lord. As you know, we consider blessed those who have persevered. You have heard of Job's perseverance and have seen what the Lord finally brought about. The Lord is full of compassion and mercy.
>
> —James 5:10–11

You can't make wine from unsqueezed grapes. God cannot take us into a deeper, more abiding relationship with Himself until He squeezes the grapes in our lives. His squeezing hurts, but we will not mature in the Christian faith through any other way.

SUFFERING TO HAVE DOMINION

God also uses suffering to prepare us for our dominion over the earth during the reign of Christ. Hebrews 11, the "Hall of Faith," commends those Old Testament saints whose faith in the next life brought them through many trials and persecutions in this life. People like Abel, Enoch, Noah, Abraham, Isaac and Jacob pleased God with their faith and "admitted that they were aliens and strangers on earth" (Heb. 11:13). They were "longing for a better country—a heavenly one" (v. 16). Their strong faith in God resulted in many persecutions and hardships on this earth. The prophets of the Old Testament and other men of God suffered greatly at the hands of the world:

> Some faced jeers and flogging, while still others were chained and put in prison. They were stoned; they were sawed in two; they were put to death by the sword. They went about in sheep-skins and goatskins, destitute, persecuted and mistreated—the world was not worthy of them. They wandered in deserts and mountains, and in caves and holes in the ground. These were all commended for their faith.
>
> —Hebrews 11:36–39

Aliens on the Earth

If we have strong faith, we will feel just like the prophets of old—

213

aliens on this earth and longing for our heavenly home. Also like the prophets of old, we will suffer persecution and hardship if we choose to live righteously before others, stand for the truth, and uphold justice. It's not easy to swim upstream against the current of the world! Fortunately, God gives us the strength to live out our faith and will reward us for our struggles. When God sees us suffer for doing good, He promises in His Word that He will give us dominion and authority in the heavenly home for which we wait patiently. It's as if God says to us, "If you care about righteousness, truth and justice in this fallen earth, I can trust you to enforce righteousness, truth and justice in My kingdom."

Ruling With Christ

After Jesus Christ returns to earth to judge the wicked and establish His kingdom of peace, Christians "will be priests of God and of Christ and will reign with him for a thousand years" (Rev. 20:6). We will reign with Christ on a restored earth where righteousness is rewarded, truth is exposed and justice is upheld. In Revelation the four living creatures and the twenty-four elders who surround God's throne sing, "You have made them [Christians] to be a kingdom and priests to serve our God, and they will reign on the earth" (Rev. 5:10). Those who endure suffering for Christ now will reign with Him then: "If we endure, we will also reign with him" (2 Tim. 2:12). God will have the perfect job description for us in this kingdom of peace where Jesus Christ rules as the King of kings.

The overcoming life reaps blessings in God's kingdom as well as in this life. Jesus says to the church, "To him who overcomes, I will give the right to sit with me on my throne, just as I overcame and sat down with my Father on his throne" (Rev. 3:21). If we overcome, we will rule with Christ on His throne of glory! Jesus encourages us to overcome so that we can rule with Him over the nations in righteousness, truth and justice: "To him who overcomes and does my will to the end, I will give authority over the nations...just as I have received authority from my Father" (Rev. 2:26).

When you experience suffering for doing good, let those in the

"Hall of Faith" encourage you as you look forward to the time when Christ will set up His kingdom on earth. If we overcome, God will give us a place on His throne and dominion over the nations when Jesus reigns as King of the world. We will be princes in the royal court of the King!

SUFFERING TO CREATE DELIGHT

Finally, God uses suffering to create delight in our souls as we hope in heaven. The more we suffer in this world, the more we look forward to heaven. The more we look forward to heaven, the more joy we will have. Suffering weeds out the worldliness from our hearts and creates a delight for the things of God.

Joy in the Hope of Heaven

Paul the Apostle suffered greatly for Jesus' sake, yet he knew incredible joy. Paul wrote the book of Philippians from a dark, damp, rat-infested jail cell, yet the word *rejoice* comes up repeatedly in this book. Delighting in the sufferings of Christ, Paul writes, "Rejoice in the Lord always. I will say it again: Rejoice!" (Phil. 4:4). He rejoiced in the midst of inhumane living conditions as he learned the secret of contentment: "For I have learned to be content whatever the circumstances. I know what it is to be in need, and I know what it is to have plenty. I have learned the secret of being content in any and every situation, whether well fed or hungry, whether living in plenty or in want" (vv. 11–12). Where did Paul get this joy? How could he have so much hope and contentment in such a terrible place? Paul rejoiced because he anchored his hope in God's unchanging, eternal kingdom, "the city with foundations, whose architect and builder is God" (Heb. 11:10). No earthly experience can compare with heavenly joy.

Jesus and the apostles experienced joy in suffering for God's kingdom, for they looked forward to their heavenly homes. Every trial represented another deposit into their heavenly bank account, waiting for them when they arrived. They had reason to rejoice! Peter wrote:

> Dear friends, do not be surprised at the painful trial you are suffering, as though something strange were happening to you. But *rejoice* that you participate in the sufferings of Christ, so that you

215

may be *overjoyed* when his glory is revealed. If you are insulted because of the name of Christ, you are blessed, for the Spirit of glory and of God rests on you.

—1 Peter 4:12–14, emphasis added

When this world persecutes us for the name of Christ, it proves that heaven is our true home. When Christ returns, we will rejoice knowing that we have finally arrived. Christ is our hope of glory, giving us a glorified body to praise and worship God for all eternity.

Heavenly Crowns and Rewards

God also promises heavenly crowns to those who suffer for Him. Heavenly crowns give us another reason to rejoice when we suffer. James writes, "Blessed is the man who perseveres under trial, because when he has stood the test, he will receive the crown of life that God has promised to those who love Him" (James 1:12). We can persevere amidst our suffering with the hope that the Lord Jesus Himself will give us the crown of life when we get to heaven. We can endure the crown of thorns on earth knowing we will receive the imperishable crown of life in its place.

Jesus promises the crown of righteousness to those who long for the reality of heaven more than the pleasures and pursuits of this life. Paul said, "I have fought the good fight, I have finished the race, I have kept the faith. Now there is in store for me the crown of righteousness, which the Lord, the righteous Judge, will award to me on that day—and not only to me, but also to all who have longed for his appearing" (2 Tim. 4:7–8). When we suffer for Christ, we can rejoice in looking forward to His Second Coming to judge the wicked and set up an everlasting kingdom of peace and righteousness. Christ will award us the crown of righteousness if we long for the kingdom of righteousness that He will bring.

Jesus has other rewards for us in heaven besides the crown of life and the crown of righteousness. Jesus said, "Blessed are you when people insult you, persecute you and falsely say all kinds of evil against you because of me. Rejoice and be glad, because great is your reward in heaven, for in the same way they persecuted the prophets who were before you" (Matt. 5:11–12). Jesus promises that if we get persecuted because of our faith in Him, He will reward us greatly in heaven. We can smile and praise God in our heart when people insult us and discriminate against us for our faith, for we know that for every insult they intend for evil, God adds another reward for us in heaven. Whatever makes up these rewards, they will surely fulfill the desires of our hearts.

The Hope of Glory

Paul sums up the proper attitude toward suffering: "I consider that our present sufferings are not worth comparing with the glory that will be revealed in us" (Rom. 8:18). The majesty and ecstasy waiting for us in our heavenly home make any hardships we experience on this earth well worth it. With new bodies, no more sinful nature, a vast understanding of the universe, and perfect fellowship and oneness with God Himself, heaven will be more glorious than anything imaginable. Our hope of glory gives us good reason to "rejoice in the Lord always!"

We no longer have to view suffering as a miserable and terrible experience. God can use suffering in our lives to discipline us, have us depend on Him, increase our dedication to Him, prepare us for our future dominion and create delight in our hope of heaven. Instead of viewing suffering as an enemy, we can welcome it into our lives as a friend when we know God allows it for His purposes. Praise and thanks be to God for preparing us for an eternity with Him, through Christ in us, the hope of glory.

CHAPTER 20

TREATMENT THAT WORKS!

In Christ, we have the power to overcome our sinful nature, the world, our circumstances and Satan. God uses the suffering in our lives to strengthen our faith and conform us into Christ's likeness. In this chapter we will look at how to apply these general guidelines of the overcoming life to the specific mental health problems that plague our culture. According to the California Association of Marriage and Family Therapists, the most common reasons people see a therapist include (in no particular order):

- Feelings of depression, moodiness, loneliness, and isolation
- Emotional stress or anxiety
- Family conflict or tension
- Child behavior problems
- Sexual disturbances
- Divorce or separation
- Excessive alcohol or drug use
- Unusual eating patterns
- Unexplained fatigue
- Difficulty coping with changes
- Unexplained injuries to family members

- Fear, anger or guilt
- Grief or emotional pain[1]

For each problem, let's see what Jesus Christ, our faithful and true Counselor, prescribes to us. If we choose to obey Jesus' prescription, we will effectively handle the most common problems that drive people to the therapist office.

FEELINGS OF DEPRESSION

The LORD is close to the brokenhearted and saves those who are crushed in spirit.

—Psalm 34:18

Why are you downcast, O my soul? Why so disturbed within me? Put your hope in God, for I will yet praise him, my Savior and my God. My soul is downcast within me; therefore I will remember you.

—Psalm 42:5–6

You have made known to me the path of life; you will fill me with joy in your presence, with eternal pleasures at your right hand.

—Psalm 16:11

Over seventeen million people suffer from depression at any one time in the United States alone.[2] We all get depressed at one time or another. Sometimes God allows us to experience times of depression to tell us that we need to draw closer to Him. Concerning depression, one pastor writes, "Depression equals a deep need—a need that only God can fulfill...Depression results from feeling far away from God..."[3] We may also experience temporary depression due to the tragedies of life and the sins of others that grieve our spirit. God uses these valleys in our Christian life to draw us into a deeper relationship with Him and help us grow spiritually. The valleys also have a wonderful way of accentuating the mountain tops of the future.

Depression Because of Sin

We do, however, experience times of depression that God does not will. If we have sinned in some way either in our hearts or outwardly, we break our fellowship with God and may feel depressed as a result. God will cleanse us and restore our joy if we come to Him with our sins and confess them. After David committed adultery with Bathsheba, he became extremely depressed—so much so that he experienced physical repercussions: "When I kept silent, my bones wasted away through my groaning all day long. For day and night your hand was heavy upon me; my strength was sapped as in the heat of summer" (Ps. 32:3–4). Contrast this mood with his mental condition after he confessed: "Blessed is he who transgressions are forgiven, whose sins are covered... The LORD's unfailing love surrounds the man who trusts in him. Rejoice in the LORD and be glad, you righteous; sing, all you who are upright in heart!" (vv. 1, 10–11). There is nothing sweeter to the soul than tasting God's forgiveness.

Depression From Focusing on Ourselves

Depression also results from focusing on ourselves instead of God. It seems the more we analyze our feelings or circumstances, the more depressed we become. Depression can become a more acceptable form of self-pity and self-worship. When we take our mind's eyes off of God and onto ourselves, we lose our perspective in life. We begin to think, *This very moment holds my entire existence! I'll never get through this! I feel so miserable!* When we fall into this state, we should do what David did: Deliberately take our focus off of ourselves and redirect it toward God regardless of our feelings and circumstances, realize that the Lord is near, confess our sins, put our hope and trust in God, remember His character and blessings, praise Him for His help and love and enjoy His presence. When we praise God, we rise above the earth and take our places in heaven as we gaze on the Lord of all creation.

Gaining the Proper Perspective

One man in history who had a legitimate right to get depressed was Paul the Apostle. Paul was imprisoned, whipped, beaten with rods, stoned, shipwrecked, almost drowned at sea, sleepless, hungry, thirsty, without clothes, slandered, persecuted outside the church, persecuted inside the church and in danger everywhere he went.

Added to all this, he still had to earn a living. We think *we* have it bad! In the midst of these sufferings, Paul says something truly amazing. He describes himself as "sorrowful, yet always rejoicing" (2 Cor. 6:10). He had perspective in life. He lived for the line of eternity instead of for the dot of this life. He figured, "What does it matter if people hate me for Christ? A few more years, and I'll be with my Lord forever and ever." If we have our hearts and minds set on eternal things, waiting in watchful anticipation for the Lord's return, we would seldom get depressed over our feelings or circumstances.

Focusing on the Good

The Bible encourages us to focus on the good things when we become depressed. When David got depressed, he said, "Therefore I will remember you" (Ps. 42:6). Remembering the holy, loving character of God and all of His many blessings toward us displaces our depression with thankfulness. How little our problems become when compared to the many blessings He has bestowed upon us! Paul encourages us to think on good things: "Finally, brothers, whatever is true, whatever is noble, whatever is right, whatever is pure, whatever is lovely, whatever is admirable—if anything is excellent or praise-worthy—think about such things" (Phil. 4:8). Remembering the good things of the past and dwelling on the good things of the present will lift our spirit.

Serving Others

In addition to the mental and spiritual actions of confessing our sins, focusing on God, having an eternal perspective and dwelling on the good of the past and present, we can also overcome our depression through practical means. We can conquer depression by simply doing something for someone—this keeps your mind off of yourself. Jesus provided the ultimate example of looking beyond oneself during trials. In the midst of excruciating pain and agony, with hands and feet nailed to a wooden cross, Jesus did not get depressed over His condition, but instead He focused on the person crucified next to Him, a convicted criminal. The criminal pleaded, "'Jesus, remember me when you come into your kingdom.' Jesus answered him, 'I tell you the truth, today you will be with me in paradise'" (Luke 23:42–43). Jesus cared more about the criminal's salvation than His own suffering. Jesus also cared more about His family's pain in watching Him die than He cared about His own pain: "[Jesus] said to his mother, 'Dear woman, here is your son,' and to the disciple [John], 'Here is your mother'" (John 19:26–27). What awesome love! Jesus showed so much love for others that it drowned out any possibility of self-pity or depression in His mind.

A man hiking in the Sierras on a beautiful day found himself suddenly caught in the middle of a snowstorm. He grew tired and wanted to lie down and fall asleep, but he knew he would never wake up if he stopped walking. Beginning to freeze, he felt his body dying. Finally, he collapsed. He couldn't go any further. Just then he felt something next to him under the snow—a person that still had a pulse. Somehow he managed to muster up the strength to raise the other man to his feet and carry him. Freezing and fatigued, he eventually stumbled onto a cabin. He opened the door to a warm fire and gracious host who cared for them. The man who could barely save his own life had the strength to save another's because he lost sight of himself.

Seeking Fellowship

We can also conquer depression by spending time with other encouraging Christians. In our postmodern, self-sufficient culture, we have isolated ourselves from others. An isolated Christian is a depressed Christian. Without loving fellowship, we eventually lose our fire and passion for God and become discouraged and depressed. A log on the fire with the other logs burn brightly, but when you take one log out and set it aside, it burns out and becomes cold. To keep the fire stoked, just call up a loving and faithful friend and absorb their positive outlook and commitment to serving the Lord. They will encourage you, and you will find that "as iron sharpens iron, so one man sharpens another" (Prov. 27:17). Suddenly your mind returns to worshiping God; your countenance changes, and you begin to feel better. Christian fellowship provides an amazing cure to depression. Just make sure your friend isn't more depressed than you!

Depression can visit us, but it doesn't have to move in. When we get depressed, we need to redirect our focus from ourselves to God and others, remembering that "weeping may remain for a night, but rejoicing comes in the morning" (Ps. 30:5).

FEELINGS OF MOODINESS

Be joyful always; pray continually; give thanks in all circumstances, for this is God's will for you in Christ Jesus.

—1 Thessalonians 5:16–18

Moodiness is just an emotional reaction to circumstances and feelings. If things are going well, I'm in a great mood. If things are not going well, I'm in a bad mood. If I feel healthy, I'm in a great mood. If I feel terrible, I'm in a bad mood. The Lord gives us a simple prescription to handle any circumstance or feeling, whether good or bad:

Take one dose of prayer.
Take one dose of giving thanks.
Take one dose of rejoicing.
Repeat until moodiness subsides.

Jesus does not intend that we be ignorant of our situation. Rather, we realize that God allows our situation for His purposes. As we discipline ourselves to pray to, thank and praise God for all things, our moodiness will subside because we have risen above our circumstances and feelings. Our circumstances and feelings become slaves to us, not vice-versa. Thanking God for all things frequently flies in the face of common sense and human reasoning, but God's thoughts and ways are higher than ours (Isa. 55:8–9).

FEELINGS OF LONELINESS

Never will I leave you; never will I forsake you.

—Hebrews 13:5

Before becoming Christians, all of us suffered from feelings of loneliness and emptiness. We sensed a gaping hole in our soul that desperately needed filling, so we tried to fill it with everything but God. After that didn't work, we realized we really needed God, so we asked Him to forgive us and come into our hearts. From that point to the present, Jesus has been our comfort and our peace. Some days, however, we just don't feel like Christians. Other days we feel like our prayers never get past the ceiling. But God makes us a promise, and He will never change His mind: "I will never leave you." We must believe Him when our feelings say otherwise.

FEELINGS OF ISOLATION

And let us consider how we may spur one another on toward love and good deeds. Let us not give up meeting together, as some are in the habit of doing, but let us encourage one another—and all the more as you see the Day approaching.

—Hebrews 10:24–25

Carry each other's burdens, and in this way you will fulfill the law of Christ.

—Galatians 6:2

The church is not a building, but the collection of people from around the world who have put their trust in Christ. To live the Christian life to the fullest, we should meet with others in the church on a regular basis—not just on Sunday mornings. As the royal priesthood, we meet together to love, encourage and help one another as Jesus has done for us. Loving God and loving others make up the two greatest commandments of the Bible. If we isolate ourselves we do not love others, but ourselves. We will become self-focused and discouraged, and the world will pull us right back into its ways. Fellowship with other Bible-living Christians keeps our lives full of excitement, meaning and purpose. God blesses our meeting together, "for where two or three come together in my name, there am I with them" (Matt. 18:20).

EMOTIONAL STRESS OR ANXIETY

Do not be anxious about anything, but in everything, by prayer and petition, with thanksgiving, present your requests to God. And the peace of God, which transcends all understanding, will guard your hearts and your minds in Christ Jesus.

—Philippians 4:6–7

When you pass through the waters, I will be with you; and when you pass through the rivers, they will not sweep over you.

—Isaiah 43:2

Cast all your anxiety on him because he cares for you.

—1 Peter 5:7

He who did not spare his own Son, but gave him up for us all— how will he not also, along with him, graciously give us all things?

—Romans 8:32

We all experience anxiety and nervousness at times. Getting nervous in certain situations doesn't mean we have a psychological disorder; it simply means we have not fully surrendered to and trusted in God. But as we grow as Christians, we learn to trust God more in each and every situation, resting in His sovereignty and care.

When we feel anxious about something, we have not surrendered that area of our lives to God's care. If we stop worrying about our lives, focus completely on God and pray about our situation, His peace will come to us as we trust Him. If we pray but still feel anxious, we did not trust God to answer our prayer—we prayed in the energies of the sinful nature instead of the Holy Spirit. Why does God deserve our trust? Because of who He is and what He has done. Our Lord is holy, righteous, just and good. As our heavenly Father, His mercy endures forever. He is always with us, knows all things and controls everything. He loves us. If Christ died for us, why wouldn't He take care of us now?

Family Conflict or Tension

Wives, submit to your husbands as to the Lord . . . Husbands, love your wives, just as Christ loved the church and gave himself up for her . . . Each one of you also must love his wife as he loves himself, and the wife must respect her husband . . . Children, obey your parents in the Lord, for this is right. Honor your father and mother . . . that it may go well with you and that you may enjoy

long life on the earth…Fathers, do not exasperate your children;
instead, bring them up in the training and instruction of the Lord.
—Ephesians 5:22, 25, 33, 6:1–4

A cord of three strands is not quickly broken.
—Ecclesiastes 4:12

I am convinced that if husbands would love their wives sacrificially, wives would respond to this love by respecting and submitting to their husbands. Guys, it starts with you. During our engagement, our pastor told us an illustration about a bridge that represented our marriage. Supporting cables above the bridge run from the center of the bridge to each end, forming a triangle (similar to the analogy of Ecclesiastes 4:12). The center represents God, while the ends represent us. If either one of us leaves the supports of God, the bridge collapses. But if both of us stay supported by God, the bridge functions beautifully. Jesus must be the center of a strong marriage. By the center I don't mean just going to church on Sundays or praying before dinner, but the husband and wife having a daily, abiding and obedient relationship with Christ.

The husband should take the initiative as the spiritual leader of the family. The husband's and wife's commitments to Christ and submission to one another will influence their children, as they bring them up "in the training and instruction of the Lord." This lifestyle will divorce-proof our marriages and gun-proof our schools.

CHILD BEHAVIOR PROBLEMS

These commandments that I give you today are to be upon your hearts. Impress them on your children. Talk about them when you sit at home and when you walk along the road, when you lie down and when you get up.
—Deuteronomy 6:6–7

Fathers, do not embitter your children, or they will become discouraged.
—Colossians 3:21

Folly is bound up in the heart of a child, but the rod of discipline will drive it far from him.

—Proverbs 22:15

The rod of correction imparts wisdom, but a child left to himself disgraces his mother.

—Proverbs 29:15

Discipline your son, and he will give you peace; he will bring delight to your soul.

—Proverbs 29:17

God wants us to diligently teach our children the Bible and to discipline them when they go astray. These two ingredients help develop healthy, loving relationships between parents and children. In order to teach the Bible, we have to know it, and before we know it, we have to read it! Deuteronomy 6:7 gives us the cure for the school-shooting epidemic: "Talk about them when you sit at home and when you walk along the road, when you lie down and when you get up." In modern-day vernacular, this verse would read, "Talk about God's Word in the morning, during the day, in the evening and before you go to bed."

Sadly, many parents in America do not diligently teach their children the ways of God or discipline them when they disobey. Instead we allow the schools and the media to form our children's morality and critical thought, and we withhold punishment for fear of being accused of child abuse. Psychology has taught us that our misbehaving child may have an attention deficit hyperactivity disorder or some other psychological phenomenon that requires "expert" help.

Many of our children's problems result from just being children. A child's behavior shows the natural folly within their hearts. Disciplining them will go much further in developing their character and preparing them for real life than labeling them with a disorder and treating them like psychological experiments.

SEXUAL DISTURBANCES

You have heard that it was said, "Do not commit adultery." But I tell you that anyone who looks at a woman lustfully has already committed adultery with her in his heart.

—Matthew 5:27–28

Marriage should be honored by all, and the marriage bed kept pure, for God will judge the adulterer and all the sexually immoral.

—Hebrews 13:4

Do not deprive each other except by mutual consent and for a time, so that you may devote yourselves to prayer. Then come together again so that Satan will not tempt you because of your lack of self-control.

—1 Corinthians 7:5

Many people do not realize that adultery occurs in the heart before the act ever unfolds. The act of adultery progresses in stages. It starts with a look, then enters the imagination. From the mind it ventures to the feet, and from the feet it ventures to the deed. From the deed comes death. God takes adultery very seriously. The subject appears repeatedly throughout the Bible. Jesus even cited adultery as the only valid cause for divorce because He knows how much pain it causes the other spouse. To avoid the trap of adultery, stop the process at the look stage and prevent the imagination from taking control. God's Word tells married couples to periodically come together and not deprive one another for too long in order to effectively resist sexual temptation.

Fornicators, or those who have sex outside of marriage, are equally at fault with God. God created sexual intercourse as a beautiful and pleasurable act of love, but He has given this act of love as a gift to those who have made a marriage commitment to each other for life. Relationships that involve sex outside of marriage will have problems and will eventually fail, no matter how much the couple tries to make it work. Anything outside God's design for sex will give us less than what God intended for us.

DIVORCE OR SEPARATION

"For this reason a man will leave his father and mother and be united to his wife, and the two will become one flesh..." So they are no longer two, but one. Therefore what God has joined together, let man not separate.

—Matthew 19:5–6

"I hate divorce," says the Lord God of Israel.

—Malachi 2:16

I say to you, whoever divorces his wife, except for sexual immorality, and marries another, commits adultery; and whoever marries her who is divorced commits adultery.

—Matthew 19:9, NKJV

When God joins together two people to become one flesh, He wants it to stay that way. When a couple gets married, they should immediately erase the word *divorce* from their vocabulary. They shouldn't even consider it an option. They should realize that every marriage will have its share of problems and conflicts. The covenant made before God ends with "'til death do we part," not "'til I'm no longer happy do we part" or "'til someone better comes along do we part." The Bible calls Christians the bride of Christ. Christ has forgiven His bride and continues to forgive His bride. We need to choose to forgive our spouse as Christ has forgiven us—even if it hurts—because love bears all things, believes all things, hopes all things and endures all things. Love never fails.

God hates divorce because of the pain it causes everyone involved. A friend of mine recalled his experience with psychology as tears filled his eyes. His wife took him to a psychotherapist, and soon after she divorced him. The pain and sadness in his face said it all. Surveys have shown that most people who get divorced later wish they never had because of the pain that followed.

EXCESSIVE ALCOHOL OR DRUG USE; UNUSUAL EATING PATTERNS

Do you not know that your bodies are members of Christ himself?... Do you not know that your body is a temple of the Holy Spirit, who is in you, whom you have received from God? You are

230

not your own; you were bought at a price. Therefore honor God
with your body.

—1 Corinthians 6:15, 19–20

Do not get drunk on wine, which leads to debauchery. Instead,
be filled with the Spirit.

—Ephesians 5:18

Excessive alcohol consumption inhibits our ability to think clearly
and opens us up to spiritual attack and compromise. As Christians,
we are dead to sin and alive to God. We no longer have to say *yes* to
the sinful desires that once controlled us. God purchased us not with
money, but with the blood of His Son. Instead of getting drunk, using
drugs or overeating, God wants us to be filled with His Spirit and
focused on Him, so we can please Him and stay on track with His
plan for our lives. We should avoid anything that pulls us away from
our relationship with God. The Bible gives some graphic illustrations
of the lifestyle of a drunkard in Proverbs 23:29–35.

UNEXPLAINED FATIGUE

Come to me, all you who are weary and burdened, and I will give
you rest. Take my yoke upon you and learn from me, for I am
gentle and humble in heart, and you will find rest for your souls.
For my yoke is easy and my burden is light.

—Matthew 11:28–30

But those who hope in the LORD will renew their strength. They
will soar on wings like eagles; they will run and not grow weary,
they will walk and not be faint.

—Isaiah 40:31

In the struggle to keep up with the lightning-fast pace of today's
high-tech culture, millions of Americans suffer from fatigue and burn-
out. We book our schedules solid and spend our weekends just
catching up. We return from our vacations exhausted and in need of a
vacation from our vacation. Where can we fill up again and find the
strength to continue? At the feet of Jesus Christ. He gives us rest, but
we must make the time to spend with Him and receive His rest every

day. He will fulfill His promise to renew our strength if we depend only on Him, and not our self-sufficiency. It takes discipline to slow down, empty ourselves and wait upon God. But when we do His grace comes to us and strengthens us. Periodically waiting upon God does wonders in preventing fatigue.

Difficulty Coping With Changes

Do not worry about your life, what you will eat or drink; or about your body, what you will wear. Is not life more important than food, and the body more important than clothes? . . . Therefore do not worry about tomorrow, for tomorrow will worry about itself. Each day has enough trouble of its own.

—Matthew 6:25, 34

Jesus Christ is the same yesterday and today and forever.

—Hebrews 13:8

God has a plan for you, and it's a good one! Although circumstances beyond our control sometimes turn our lives upside down, we can cling to Jesus, knowing He never changes. He always waits with outstretched arms to receive us, hold us and comfort us. The Jesus you met when you became a Christian is the same Jesus that wants to comfort you now. With our heavenly Father, we don't have to worry about how we will pay the next electric bill after being laid off from a job—He has promised to provide all of our needs, even through the difficult transitions of life. The world system can get overwhelming, but through Jesus we can overcome it.

Unexplained Injuries to Family Members

And we know that in all things God works for the good of those who love him, who have been called according to his purpose.

—Romans 8:28

The LORD has established his throne in heaven, and his kingdom rules over all.

—Psalm 103:19

Since God sits on the throne of the universe, nothing on earth happens without His knowledge and permission. We cannot see the entire picture, but God can. We can trust that because God is love, He works all things together for good for those who have put their trust in Him. As we learned from Cassie Bernall's story, her parents' faith and trust in God have deepened since the shootings that took their daughter's life. Many young people have come to a saving faith in Jesus Christ because of Cassie's courageous martyrdom. In the Bible and in real life, God uses evil for ultimate good. For those who have not yet put their trust in Christ, God sometimes uses tragedy to show them the brevity of life and the reality of death. Some people who have survived tragedies have trusted Christ for their salvation afterwards.

Fear

For God has not given us a spirit of fear, but of power and of love and of a sound mind.

—2 Timothy 1:7, NKJV

Fear of man will prove to be a snare, but whoever trusts in the Lord is kept safe.

—Proverbs 29:25

There is no fear in love. But perfect love drives out fear, because fear has to do with punishment. The one who fears is not made perfect in love.

—1 John 4:18

So we say with confidence, "The Lord is my helper; I will not be afraid. What can man do to me?"

—Hebrews 13:6

Are not two sparrows sold for a penny? Yet not one of them will fall to the ground apart from the will of your Father. And even the very hairs of your head are all numbered. So don't be afraid; you are worth more than many sparrows.

—Matthew 10:29–31

If God is for us, who can be against us?

—Romans 8:31

The Holy Spirit gives us power, love and a sound mind—the very things fear steals from us. When we fear man, our actions say to God, "This person is more powerful than You." So we please man instead of God and regret it in the end. Fear stems from self-preservation and self-love. But perfect love casts out all fear, because a person who loves perfectly has no concern for self at all. Fear also creates confusion and reactionary thinking instead of order and peace (1 Cor. 14:33).

Other people can do nothing to us apart from God's will and knowledge. God is *for* us. He fights our battles. To conquer fear, my husband always says, "If you honor God, God will honor you."

ANGER

Love . . . is not easily angered.

—1 Corinthians 13:5

Those who belong to Christ Jesus have crucified the sinful nature with its passions and desires. Since we live by the Spirit, let us keep in step with the Spirit. Let us not become conceited, provoking and envying each other.

—Galatians 5:24–26

Everyone should be quick to listen, slow to speak and slow to become angry, for man's anger does not bring about the righteous life that God desires.

—James 1:19–20

"In your anger do not sin": Do not let the sun go down while you are still angry, and do not give the devil a foothold.

—Ephesians 4:26–27

Anger in itself is not sinful, but how we handle that anger. If we handle our anger in love, we can use it constructively. If we handle our anger in wrath, it can turn destructive and harmful. The expression "you are what you eat" applies to the spiritual realm as well. If we do things to feed the sinful nature, we will show anger and hostility. If we do things to feed the Spirit, we will "walk in the Spirit" and show love and peace. To combat wrathful anger, we should feed the Spirit by reading God's Word, praying, praising and giving thanks.

We should resolve anger before the sun goes down each day. If we don't deal with our anger quickly, it can lead to unforgiveness, bitterness, resentment and even more anger down the road. Satan can have a field day with a person like this.

Cassie Bernall's mother, Misty, certainly has a right to be angry. But she says this about wrathful anger:

> [Wrathful] anger is a destructive emotion. It eats away at whatever peace you have, and in the end it causes nothing but greater pain than you began with. It also makes it that much harder for others to console you, when you're busy nursing resentment. It's not as if I don't have those seeds in me—I know I do—but I'm not going to let other people water them.[4]

Some therapists would tell us that venting our anger on a pillow or punching bag will help improve our anger problems. But research has shown that those who vent their anger develop habits and actually get worse![5] Or, we can pretend that the anger does not exist and just repress it until we explode like a time bomb. Both extremes don't work. "In your anger do not sin" means we can feel the anger, but should express it in a self-controlled and loving way.

GUILT

> There is therefore now no condemnation to those who are in Christ Jesus, who do not walk according to the flesh, but according to the Spirit.
>
> —Romans 8:1, NKJV

> Godly sorrow brings repentance that leads to salvation and leaves no regret, but worldly sorrow brings death.
>
> —2 Corinthians 7:10

Psychology would have us believe that guilt is unhealthy—something we should avoid at all costs. But God uses feelings of guilt to bring us to a point of confession and repentance so that we can again enjoy fellowship with Him. Instead of ignoring guilt or trying to get rid of it, we should deal with it biblically.

A Christian can experience two types of guilt: one that drives us away from God and one that drives us toward Him. The one that drives us away from God comes not from God, but from Satan. Satan enjoys whispering condemning comments into our ears like: "God will never forgive you for this one." "It's too late to turn back to God now, after all you've done." "You call yourself a Christian? You sure don't act like one." This "worldly sorrow" produces discouragement and hopelessness. We can defeat this worldly sorrow by using the sword of the Spirit, the Word of God. There is no condemnation in Christ, because He has paid for our sins in full. God sees us perfect in Christ, just as if we had never sinned.

The second type of guilt drives us toward God. God uses "godly sorrow," a good type of guilt, to bring us back to Him if we have strayed off the path of following Christ. God reaches out to us in love and prompts our hearts to return to Him. If we sense this godly sorrow in our hearts, we need to respond by making a U-turn on the road to nowhere and returning to a committed relationship with God.

Grief or Emotional Pain

> Even though I walk through the valley of the shadow of death, I will fear no evil, for you are with me; your rod and your staff, they comfort me.
>
> —Psalm 23:4

> Precious in the sight of the Lord is the death of His saints.
>
> —Psalm 116:15

> Death has been swallowed up in victory. "Where, O death, is your victory? Where, O death, is your sting?"... But thanks be to God! He gives us the victory through our Lord Jesus Christ.
>
> —1 Corinthians 15:54–55, 57

Jesus knows the sorrow and grief of seeing a loved one die. Jesus wept when his friend Lazarus died (John 11:35). When Christians die, they go immediately into the presence of God (2 Cor. 5:8). Numerous medical accounts of Christians on their death beds with peaceful, content looks on their faces give convincing evidence of this truth. Christians feel no sting of death, but unbelievers experience God's painful wrath when they die (John 3:18; Luke 16:22–24; Rev. 20:11–15).

Sometimes our grief and emotional pain result from someone else's wrong. We have a choice to respond with hatred and bitterness, or with love and forgiveness. Darrell Scott chose forgiveness:

> Our understanding of God's heart left us only one choice, the decision to forgive. It was the choice of Jesus as He hung on a cross dying. He said in Matthew 5:43–44: "You have heard that it was said, 'Love your neighbor and hate your enemy.' But I tell you: Love your enemies and pray for those who persecute you."
>
> Forgiveness is not just for the offender. It is also for the one who is offended. If we do not forgive, we end up in perpetual anger and bitterness and eventually offend others with our words or actions. If we forgive, we experience a "letting go" or cleansing process that frees us from the offender.
>
> There is a great misunderstanding about forgiveness. Forgiveness is not pardon. Forgiveness is an attitude, while pardon is an action. Had they lived, we would not have pardoned these boys for what they did. In fact, I (Darrell) would have killed them to prevent the slaughter that occurred if I had been given the chance. I believe most people would have done the same. If they had lived, we would have testified against them and demanded that justice be done. However, our hearts toward them could not have harbored unforgiveness. Unforgiveness blocks God's ability to flow through us to help others...
>
> God wants us to overcome evil with good. Such a thing is beyond human ability, but it is possible when we acknowledge our weakness and submit to God's grace.[6]

OTHER ISSUES

While the Bible provides guidance for some of the most common problems of life, it does not address many other situations that we may experience. We don't open our Bibles and find answers to questions like: "Should I take this job?" "Should I enroll my child in public or private school?" "Can I be physically intimate with my boyfriend without having sex?" Just as a compass tells us the general direction to go and not exactly how to get there, so also the Bible gives us guidelines for living but doesn't address every single possible situation we will face. When a situation isn't directly addressed in Scripture, we need to answer the 4 H's applied to the issue at hand:[7]

- Is it **helpful**, beneficial or constructive for me? Does it cause me to grow spiritually or help others grow? (1 Cor. 6:12; 10:23).
- Is it a **habit**? Is it an addictive behavior? Does it hold me in its power? Do I feel I need this to be happy and fulfilled? Does it control my thoughts or actions? (1 Cor. 6:12).
- Is it **hurtful** for another? A weaker Christian? In doing it, would I hurt someone else or cause them to be tempted to go against their conscience (what they think is right)? Is it hurtful for a non-Christian? Could my behavior cause a non-Christian to ignore the gospel or disregard Christ? (1 Cor. 8:13; 10:24–11:1).
- Is it **honoring** to God? Glorifying God means to exalt God, to please Him by seeking His interests above our own interests. In doing it, would I bring glory to God or dishonor Him? (1 Cor. 10:31).

Answering these questions and following the leading and guidance of the Holy Spirit will help us handle the "gray areas" of the Christian life. Let's apply the 4 H's to the question, "Can I be physically intimate with my boyfriend without having sex?"

- Is it **helpful** for me? Physical intimacy is not helpful spiritually—in fact, I could be tempted to go "all the way" and disobey God... NO.
- Is it a **habit**? Physical intimacy can develop into a habit whereby I feel I need it to be happy and fulfilled. I could become controlled by it... YES.
- Is it **hurtful** for another? Physical intimacy may hurt my boyfriend's relationship with God as well... YES.
- Is it **honoring** to God? Definitely not. Physical intimacy before marriage would not honor God. It will dishonor Him if we give in to our sinful nature... NO.

The answer here is obvious: No, I should not be physically intimate with my boyfriend, even if we're not having sex. The Holy Spirit should confirm this answer in our hearts.

OBEDIENCE IS THE KEY

In handling the real-life problems presented in this chapter, we must remember that *obedience is the key*. Knowing the biblical principles in our minds doesn't help if we continue to live a life of pleasing self. We must put God's Word into action. We must, as Daniel did, "purpose in our heart" to obey Him in everything we do. We must make the Bible a practical conviction, not just an intellectual stimulant. As James says, "Do not merely listen to the word, and so deceive yourselves. Do what it says" (James 1:22). Later he says, "The man who looks intently into the perfect law that gives freedom, and continues to do this, not forgetting what he has heard, but doing it—he will be blessed in what he does" (v. 25) We must *intently* apply the Bible to our lives on a *continual* basis for God to bless everything we do.

God has a lot to say to us in the Bible about how we should handle our mental, emotional and behavioral problems. Jesus is a practical God. He knows what it means to be human. He sympathizes with our weaknesses and so has given us a practical Book to help us with life's problems. Not only does He give us the principles, but He also gives us the power to carry them out. Our God is a living God!

CHAPTER 21

VICTORY
IN
JESUS

Hallelujah! We have victory in Jesus. Jesus has given us victory over our sinful nature, victory over the world, victory over our circumstances and victory over Satan. God has revealed Himself through His Holy Bible, manifested Himself through His Holy Spirit and glorified Himself through His holy people. Truly, "his divine power has given us everything we need for life and godliness through our knowledge of him who called us by his own glory and goodness" (2 Pet. 1:3). Through His Word and His Holy Spirit, God has given us everything we need for life (our relationship with others) and godliness (our relationship with God). Whatever the question, Jesus is the answer. Oh, that the body of Christ could internalize this marvelous reality!

JESUS IS THE SOLUTION

We can sum up the preceding chapters in one sentence: We are the problem, and Jesus is the solution. When you strip away all the complexities of life, you quickly realize that the problem is you! You could escape all of your problems and move halfway around the world with a new spouse, a new house, a new job and new friends. But before long, your problems return! Why? Because you're still the same old you! The circumstances have changed, but you have remained the same. To overcome, we must continually turn away from our sinful selves and look to Jesus, the author and finisher of our faith. Corrie ten Boom, World War II holocaust survivor, said, "Look within and be depressed. Look without and be distressed. Look to Jesus and be at rest." Jesus is our healer, our source, our identity, our purpose, our goal and our life.

Imagine closing the door to your "prayer closet" and seeking God's holy presence. The Lord says to you, "Come to Me, my child, and throw yourself upon My throne of grace, just as you are." Wretched, naked and needy, you fall down at the feet of the Lord Jesus and plead for mercy. The Lord looks upon you with love and compassion. He binds up your broken heart and heals your painful wounds. You thank Him and praise Him with inexpressible joy. You draw upon His inexhaustible resources and walk away filled to overflowing. You continue in the race of your faith with perseverance, determination and strength until you meet Jesus face to face. You have just experienced the abundant, overcoming life that God promises.

My husband, Ryan, enjoys writing poems. Before I decided to write this book, Ryan wrote a poem describing his first encounter with the abundant life that Christ offers. I want to share it with you because it paints a beautiful picture of how you can receive God's grace for living.

The Abundant Life

By turning our eyes upon Jesus
    And kneeling low at His feet;
By quieting our souls
    And seeking His peaceful face;
By breaking and emptying ourselves
    And humbling our hearts;
By confessing each sin
    And hating its presence;
By pleading with God for His mercy
    And praising Him for His faithfulness;
By being in awe of His holiness

> And comforted by His loveliness;
> By kissing His feet
>   And wiping them with our tears;
> By falling in love with Him
>   And choosing to die with Him;
> By pleading with Him to live His life in us
>   And being with others who we are with God;
> By receiving the power that raised Christ from the dead
>   We will live the abundant life.

BIBLE BENEFITS

Instead of heeding the man-made wisdom of psychology, we can receive godly wisdom by fearing the Lord and reading His Word: "The fear of the LORD is the beginning of wisdom, and knowledge of the Holy One is understanding" (Prov. 9:10). No chapter of the Bible better describes the benefits of reading God's Word and obtaining "knowledge of the Holy One" than Psalm 119. Here are just a few benefits of reading and obeying God's Word, according to Psalm 119:

- You will be blessed in all you do (vv. 1–2).
- Praising and rejoicing will be on your lips as you learn His ways (vv. 7, 14, 54, 108, 164, 171, 172).
- You will keep from sinning against God (v. 11).
- You will find delight in God's counsel (v. 24).
- Your soul will be strengthened (v. 28).
- You will keep yourself from deceitful ways (v. 29).
- You will feel a sense of freedom as you understand God's boundaries for your life (vv. 32, 45).
- Your priorities in life will fall in line with God's will for you (v. 36).
- God will preserve, protect and defend your life (vv. 37, 93, 154).
- You will find comfort in suffering (vv. 50, 52).
- God will show you grace as you seek His face (v. 58).
- You will overflow with thanksgiving for His righteous laws (v. 62).
- God will teach you knowledge and good judgment (v. 66).
- You will understand who God is and what He has done (v. 68).
- You will receive discipline from God as He reveals His Word to

you (vv. 71, 75).
- Your heart will be cleansed, purified, and blameless (v. 80).
- You will have renewed hope (v. 81).
- You will gain eternal, unchanging knowledge of God (vv. 89, 152, 160).
- You will gain wisdom (v. 98).
- God's Word will satisfy your soul like no other earthly thing (v. 103).
- You will find God's guidance and direction in the decisions of life (v. 105).
- You will experience joy in knowing and obeying God's laws (v. 111).
- Your life will be focused on the single purpose of knowing and obeying God (v. 113).
- You will fear and stand in awe of God (v. 120).
- You will love God and truth (vv. 127, 163).
- You will hate and avoid evil and falsehood (vv. 104, 128, 163).
- You will receive the ability to discern between good and evil, right and wrong (v. 125).
- You will gain an understanding of life (v. 130).
- You will seek righteousness and truth (vv. 137, 142, 160).
- You will draw near to Him (v. 151).
- You will have peace and security in life (v. 165).
- You will receive help in time of need (v. 173).

How precious is the Word of God, and how valuable it is for this life and the next! Remember these benefits the next time you consider putting off reading the Bible for some other earthly pursuit.

GOD INSIDE

The same God whose brilliant afterglow shone on the veiled face of Moses resides in our hearts. Imagine... the Creator of the universe, living inside of us! Such a reality is too wonderful to fully comprehend. You are just one person on this massive earth of over six billion people. The earth is just one planet in the vast solar system that revolves around the sun. Our solar system is just a tiny part of the

Milky Way Galaxy. The Milky Way Galaxy is just one of the many galaxies of the universe. The universe continues to expand, with no end or bounds in sight. God can span the universe with His hand (Isa. 40:12). Yet, this same God lives inside of us puny little human beings!

This same God gives us the power to overcome life's difficulties and live holy lives pleasing to Him. This same God knows every thought, every desire, every word and every action. This same God wants an intimate, living relationship with us every second of the day. This same God desires that we have an abundant, overflowing life by denying ourselves, taking up our cross and abiding in Him moment by moment. This same God desires to fill us with His living waters of comfort and love and peace.

THE ROYAL PRIESTHOOD IN ACTION

In contemplating the overcoming life, I can't help but wonder of the different outcome of Karen and Keith's therapy session in Chapter 1, had both of them been Christians and handled their problems biblically. Instead of going to a therapist, Karen and Keith would have approached a spiritually mature Christian friend for help (let's call her Elizabeth). With the "royal priesthood" of believers operating effectively, it might have sounded something like this:

Elizabeth: Hi, guys! Come on in. Would you like something to drink?

Karen: No thanks, Elizabeth. Thanks for having us over. We've been arguing a lot lately. I thought you could give us some good biblical advice.

Elizabeth: So what's going on?

Karen: Well, I spent all afternoon last Sunday preparing a full-course meal for Keith's parents. Keith sat on the couch watching football while I slaved over the stove and his parents talked my ear off. Keith's mom watched my every move. She was always quick to point out faults in my cooking techniques. When she wasn't criticizing my cooking, she would wait until she thought I wasn't looking and wipe her finger across the top of every cabinet and countertop she could find. Then, if that wasn't

245

enough to push me over the edge, Keith's dad reprimanded me for taking away the kids' dessert when they wouldn't eat their dinner.

Keith: *[To Karen]* C'mon, Karen, they were just being kids!

Karen: *[To Keith]* Kids need discipline, and I don't appreciate your parents telling me how to raise my kids! I am sick and tired of Keith's parents never accepting me and treating me with respect. I'll never be good enough for them.

Keith: *[To Karen]* How can you be good enough when you never see them? It took two years for you to finally have them over for dinner. But you can see your parents every weekend. *[To Elizabeth]* She's never around! I work all week to put food on the table, and when the weekend comes I expect some quality time together. But off she goes with the two kids to grandma's house, to "shop 'til they drop" as they always say. Then the credit card bills come rolling in, and who has to pay them? Me! In fact, we're maxed out on nothing short of nine credit cards right now. I see her bills more than I see her. And it's not like the bills are for things we need. No, she always has to have the latest everything—clothes, shoes, jewelry—and it piles up in the closet. Then she buys our kids everything they ask for. But when it comes around to me, it's socks and underwear, socks and underwear.

Elizabeth: *[After contemplating]* Keith, how is your relationship with God going?

Keith: Good…I guess. I've been attending church pretty regularly.

Elizabeth: No, I mean are you spending time with God in prayer and reading the Bible on a consistent basis?

Keith: I've been so busy lately. I haven't really had a chance to do that kind of thing.

Elizabeth: The reason I ask is because when your relationship with God suffers, it affects all of your other relationships, including your relationship with Karen. The Lord is your source of love and good fruit. When you don't spend time with Him and abide in Him, your spiritual life dries up. You can't live effectively without abiding in Christ. Spiritual problems show up first in the home. Try to think of marriage as a bicycle wheel. God is the center of the wheel, and the two of you are the spokes. The closer you get to God, the closer you automatically get to each other. When you guys fight like this, it's a sure sign that something has gone wrong spiritually.

Keith: So what are we doing wrong?

Elizabeth: Let's read the Book of Ephesians, chapter five. Starting in verse 25, it talks about how you should love your wife as Christ loved the church and gave himself up for her to make her holy. Part of loving your wife is by being the spiritual leader of the house and teaching her the Bible to present her holy and blameless to God. Do you do this?

Keith: Not as much as I should.

Elizabeth: Loving your wife also means protecting her from ridicule and harm. First Corinthians 13:7 says, "Love bears all things." When your parents don't treat her with respect and accept her as an equal in the family, you need to protect Karen and stand up to them in love. You need to show them that you and Karen are a team—that you have become one flesh.

Keith: But it just doesn't seem like we're one flesh, when Karen spends all of her time at her mom's house.

Elizabeth: I can see why you would think that way. When two people get married, God's design for that marriage is for the man to leave his father and mother and be united—or cleave—to his wife, so that the two become one flesh. The two key words are "leave" and "cleave." God wants us to leave the intimate relationship we had with our father and mother, and cleave to our spouse. He wants all other earthly relationships to be of secondary importance to the relationship we have with our spouse. Does that make sense, Karen?

247

Karen: Well, yes ... But does that mean I never see my parents again?

Elizabeth: Oh, of course not. God just wants us to keep our priorities straight. He wants us to put our relationship with Him first; our relationship with our spouse second; our relationship with our children third; and our relationship with others, like friends and co-workers, last. If we follow God's design, He will bless us. *[Karen nods in understanding.]*

Keith: So you're saying that if I have to decide between pleasing my parents and pleasing my wife, I should always please my wife, no matter what?

Elizabeth: Assuming whatever it is that pleases your wife also pleases God, then yes, that's exactly right!

Keith: Shopping pleases my wife—does that please God?

Elizabeth: That would depend on how Karen views shopping in relation to God. Karen, if I were to ask you to complete the sentence "To live is _(blank)_ ", what would the blank be? If, for you to live is shopping, then shopping has become an idol in your heart that is competing with God.

Karen: But I love shopping—it makes me feel good. Doesn't God want me to do things that I enjoy?

Elizabeth: God's will is not always about feeling good and experiencing pleasure. He does give us the desires of our hearts, but only as we seek Him first above everything else. If you love something in life more than God, then you are disobeying Him and sinning against Him. God wants your heart, Karen. He wants you to love Him with everything you've got inside. He wants you to turn your finances over to His care, and seek His will in every financial decision.

Karen: *[Looking at Keith]* Well, if Keith had his way, we would live like paupers!

Elizabeth: Just seek the Lord in prayer together. Ask for God's leading and guidance, and the Holy Spirit will direct both of you. Karen, even if you disagree with Keith's opinions,

248

remember that Keith is the head over the family. Keith's responsibility to God is to love you like Christ loved the church, and *your* responsibility to God is to submit to Keith in the same way that you submit to Christ, even if you disagree with him. *[Picks up her Bible]*... Ephesians 5:22 says, "Wives, submit to your husbands as to the Lord. For the husband is the head of the wife as Christ is the head of the church...Now as the church submits to Christ, so also wives should submit to their husbands in everything."

Karen: Oh, *that* verse. "Submit!"... Sounds so barbaric.

Elizabeth: *[Gently]* Well, it's what God commands us to do, and we reap what we sow. If you challenge Keith's leadership all the time, you'll reap strife and division in your home. But if you and Keith submit to one another out of reverence for Christ, your home will be filled with peace and unity. It just comes down to humility and surrender with one another. When you both decide to obey God, you'll begin to see your marriage improve. It won't happen overnight, but it will happen. You guys have to decide whether you're going to live your way or God's way. That decision will determine the quality of your marriage. It's up to you.

Notes

Introduction

1. San Diego North County Chapter, 1999–2000 (San Diego, CA: California Association of Marriage and Family Therapists, 2000), 3.

Part I: Can Psychology Help You?

1. Eva S. Moskowitz, *In Therapy We Trust* (Baltimore, MD: Johns Hopkins University Press, 2001), 6.

Chapter 1: Meet Karen and Keith

1. Tana Dineen, *Manufacturing Victims* (Westmount, Quebec, Canada: Robert Davies Multimedia, 1996), 21 (emphasis added).
2. Cited in Moskowitz, *In Therapy We Trust*, 6.
3. Ed Bulkley, *Why Christians Can't Trust Psychology* (Eugene, OR: Harvest House, 1993), 90.
4. Moskowitz, *In Therapy We Trust*, 5–6.
5. Martin and Deidre Bobgan, *The End of "Christian Psychology"* (Santa Barbara, CA: EastGate Publishers, 1997), 13.
6. Adapted from Gary L. Almy, *How Christian Is Christian Counseling?* (Wheaton, IL: Crossway Books, 2000), 82.
7. Dineen, *Manufacturing Victims*, 245–248.
8. Moskowitz, *In Therapy We Trust*, 8.

Chapter 2: Can You Trust Psychology As a Science?

1. Cited in Bobgan, *The End of "Christian Psychology,"* 27.
2. Jay S. Efran, Michael D. Lukens and Robert D. Lukens, *Language, Structure, and Change* (New York: W.W. Norton, n.d.), chapter 1.
3. Ibid.
4. Ibid.
5. Cited in Bobgan, *The End of "Christian Psychology,"* 24.
6. Cited in Martin and Deidre Bobgan, *PsychoHeresy* (Santa Barbara, CA: EastGate Publishers, 1987), 97.
7. R. Christopher Barden, National Association for Consumer Protection in Mental Health Practices Press Release, 1093 East Duffer Lane, North Salt Lake, Utah 84054. 888-947-6281.
8. Cited in Bobgan, *PsychoHeresy*, 201.

CHAPTER 3: DOES PSYCHOLOGY DELIVER ON ITS PROMISES?

1. American Psychiatric Association Commission on Psychotherapies, *Psychotherapy Research: Methodological and Efficacy Issues* (Washington, DC: American Psychiatric Association, 1982), 228.
2. E. Fuller Torrey, *The Death of Psychiatry* (Radnor, PA: Chilton Book Company, 1974), 47.
3. Efran and Lukens, *Language, Structure, and Change*, chapter 1.
4. Dineen, *Manufacturing Victims*, 160.
5. Ibid., 158.
6. Jeffrey A. Kottler, *On Being a Therapist* (San Francisco: Jossey-Bass, 1993), 186–187.
7. Ibid.,
8. E. Fuller Torrey, *Freudian Fraud: The Malignant Effect of Freud's Theory on American Thought and Culture* (New York: HarperCollins, 1993), 128.
9. Cited in Dineen, *Manufacturing Victims*, 219.
10. Cited in Bulkley, *Why Christians Can't Trust Psychology*, 94.
11. Ibid., 74.
12. Cited in Bobgan, *PsychoHeresy*, 173.
13. Dineen, *Manufacturing Victims*, 220–221.
14. County of San Diego Sample Ballot and Voter Information Pamphlet, November 7, 2000 General Election, Registrar of Voters, 5 (emphasis added).
15. Bobgan, *PsychoHeresy*, 168.
16. Moskowitz, *In Therapy We Trust*, 279.
17. Cited in John F. MacArthur, *Our Sufficiency in Christ* (Wheaton, IL: Crossway Books, 1991), 63–64.

CHAPTER 4: ANSWERING THE WHY OF LIFE

1. Peter R. Breggin and David Cohen, *Your Drug May Be Your Problem* (Cambridge, MA: Perseus, 1999), 5.
2. Henry H. Halley, *Halley's Bible Handbook* (Grand Rapids, MI: Zondervan, 1965), 18–19.
3. Henry M. Morris and Henry M. Morris III, *Many Infallible Proofs* (Green Forest, AR: Master Books, 1996), 206.
4. Norman L. Geisler and William E. Nix, *A General Introduction to the Bible* (Chicago, IL: Moody Press, 1986).
5. Cited in Morris, *Many Infallible Proofs*, 312.
6. Morris, *Many Infallible Proofs*, 250–251.

7. Ed Hindson and Howard Eyrich, *Totally Sufficient* (Eugene, OR: Harvest House, 1997), 181.

CHAPTER 5: TWO OPPOSING FAITHS

1. Paul C. Vitz, *Psychology as Religion*, Second Edition (Grand Rapids, MI: William B. Eerdmans, 1994), xii–xiii.
2. Moskowitz, *In Therapy We Trust*, 280.
3. Cited in Bobgan, *PsychoHeresy*, 43.
4. Cited in Bobgan, *The End of "Christian Psychology,"* 108.
5. Moskowitz, *In Therapy We Trust*, 7.
6. David L. Kirk, "Lack of Self-Esteem Is Not the Root of All Ills," *Santa Barbara News-Press* (January 15, 1990), cited at Biblical Discernment Ministries, www.rapidnet.com/~jbeard.bdm.
7. Cited in Dineen, *Manufacturing Victims*, 226.
8. Cited in Martin and Deidre Bobgan, *PsychoHeresy Awareness Letter* (May–June 2001): 7. Published in Santa Barbara, CA, by PsychoHeresy Awareness Ministries.
9. Moskowitz, *In Therapy We Trust*, 3, 8.
10. Cited in Vitz, *Psychology as Religion*, 16–17.
11. Cited in Bobgan, *PsychoHeresy*, 60.
12. Cited in Don Matzat, *Christ Esteem* (Eugene, OR: Harvest House, 1990), 81.
13. Cited in Vitz, *Psychology as Religion*, 128.
14. Cited in Bobgan, *PsychoHeresy*, 19.

CHAPTER 6: WHO IS AT FAULT?

1. Cited in Moskowitz, *In Therapy We Trust*, 7.
2. Misty Bernall, *She Said Yes* (Nashville, TN: Word, 1999), 63.
3. Ibid., 39.
4. Ibid., 83–84 (emphasis added).
5. Ibid., 82, 84–85, 92–93.
6. Ibid., 131–132 (emphasis added).

CHAPTER 7: WHICH FIGUREHEAD DO YOU FOLLOW?

1. Bob Hoekstra, *The Psychologizing of the Faith* (Costa Mesa, CA: The Word for Today), 13.
2. Hindson and Eyrich, *Totally Sufficient*, 261.

CHAPTER 8: WHERE IS YOUR FOCUS?

1. Jean C. McKinney, *Selfishness: The Source of All Sin* (Colorado

Springs, CO: Cool Springs, 1997), 88–96.

2. Mary Riemersma, ed., *The California Therapist* (November/December 2000): 4.

3. McKinney, *Selfishness: The Source of All Sin*, Preface.

4. Bernall, *She Said Yes*, 99 (emphasis added).

PART III: PSYCHOLOGY IN THE CHURCH

1. Greg Laurie, *Preparing for a Strong Marriage* (Ephesians 5), Teaching Tape M938 (Riverside, CA: Harvest Ministries, 1999).

CHAPTER 9: MY DISORDER MADE ME DO IT

1. Diagnostic and Statistical Manual of Mental Disorders, Fourth Edition (Washington, DC: American Psychiatric Association, 1994), Table of Contents.

2. Ibid., 26–27.

3. Dineen, *Manufacturing Victims*, 217–218.

4. Ibid., 218.

5. Bobgan, *PsychoHeresy*, 141.

6. Dineen, *Manufacturing Victims*, 282.

7. Cited in Bulkley, *Why Christians Can't Trust Psychology*, 111.

8. Cited in Bobgan, *PsychoHeresy*, 139–140.

9. Cited in MacArthur, *Our Sufficiency in Christ*, 64.

10. Cited in Almy, *How Christian Is Christian Counseling?*, 291.

CHAPTER 10: SHOULD I TAKE PSYCHIATRIC MEDICATION?

1. Cited in Dineen, *Manufacturing Victims*, 241.

2. Moskowitz, *In Therapy We Trust*, 6.

3. Joseph Glenmullen, *Prozac Backlash* (New York: Simon & Schuster, 2000), 196–197.

4. Breggin and Cohen, *Your Drug May Be Your Problem*, 112.

5. Ibid., 7, 35.

6. Glenmullen, *Prozac Backlash*, 198.

7. Breggin and Cohen, *Your Drug May Be Your Problem*, 5.

8. Almy, *How Christian Is Christian Counseling?*, 294.

9. Cited in Glenmullen, *Prozac Backlash*, 203.

10. Glenmullen, *Prozac Backlash*, 201.

11. Breggin and Cohen, *Your Drug May Be Your Problem*, 33–34.

12. Ibid., 34.

13. Ibid., 8.

14. Ibid., 37.

15. Ibid., 193.

16. Ibid., 49–50.

17. Ibid., 27.

18. Cited in Bobgan, *PsychoHeresy Awareness Letter* (September–October 2000): 4–5.

19. Breggin and Cohen, *Your Drug May Be Your Problem*, 60.

20. Ibid., 38.

21. Ibid., 98.

22. Ibid., 58.

23. *Depression* brochure, American Drug Stores, Inc., 1999.

24. Glenmullen, *Prozac Backlash*, 17.

25. Ibid., 20.

26. Bobgan, *PsychoHeresy Awareness Letter* (November–December 2000): 5.

27. Bobgan, *PsychoHeresy Awareness Letter* (September–October 2000): 5.

28. Breggin and Cohen, *Your Drug May Be Your Problem*, 105.

29. Bobgan, *PsychoHeresy Awareness Letter* (January–February 2001): 5.

30. Glenmullen, *Prozac Backlash*, 24.

31. Breggin and Cohen, *Your Drug May Be Your Problem*, 37.

32. *ADHD* brochure, American Drug Stores, Inc., 2000.

33. Bobgan, *PsychoHeresy Awareness Letter* (November–December 2000): 5.

34. Breggin and Cohen, *Your Drug May Be Your Problem*, 48, 66.

35. "Debarking" is a surgical procedure performed on dogs to eliminate loud barking.

36. Ibid., 38, 179.

37. Ibid., 4.

38. Ibid., 90.

39. Glenmullen, *Prozac Backlash*, 198.

40. Breggin and Cohen, *Your Drug May Be Your Problem*, 31.

41. Ken Nichols, *Overcoming the Overwhelming* (Atlanta, GA: Walk Thru the Bible Ministries, 1997), 11.

42. Bulkley, *Why Christians Can't Trust Psychology*, 136.

43. Breggin and Cohen, *Your Drug May Be Your Problem*, 191.

44. Ibid., 12.

45. MacArthur, *Our Sufficiency in Christ*, 97–98.

CHAPTER 11: WHAT ABOUT "CHRISTIAN" PSYCHOLOGY?

1. MacArthur, *Our Sufficiency in Christ*, 20.

2. Ibid., 57.
3. Vitz, *Psychology as Religion*, xiii.
4. Cited in Bulkley, *Why Christians Can't Trust Psychology*, 182, 184.
5. Jim Owen, *Christian Psychology's War on God's Word* (Santa Barbara, CA: EastGate Publishers, 1993), 20.
6. Cited in Gil Rugh, *Psychology: The Trojan Horse* (n.p.: Indian Hills Community Church, 1995), 12.
7. Cited in Bobgan, *PsychoHeresy Awareness Letter* (July–August 2001): 1.
8. Martin and Deidre Bobgan, *12 Steps to Destruction* (Santa Barbara, CA: EastGate Publishers, 1991), 218–219.
9. Ibid., 100–101.
10. Ibid., 98.
11. Ibid.
12. Cited in Bobgan, *PsychoHeresy Awareness Letter* (July–August 2001): 2.
13. Moskowitz, *In Therapy We Trust*, 253.
14. Cited in Bulkley, *Why Christians Can't Trust Psychology*, 239.
15. Ibid.
16. Cited in Bobgan, *PsychoHeresy*, 56.
17. Laurie, *Preparing for a Strong Marriage* (Ephesians 5), Teaching Tape M938.
18. MacArthur, *Our Sufficiency in Christ*, 20.
19. Cited in Almy, *How Christian Is Christian Counseling?*, 198.
20. Moskowitz, *In Therapy We Trust*, 247–248.
21. Cited in Bobgan, *PsychoHeresy Awareness Letter* (May–June 2001): 7.
22. Bobgan, *PsychoHeresy Awareness Letter* (November–December 2000): 1.
23. Almy, *How Christian Is Christian Counseling?*, 56.

Chapter 12: A Royal Priesthood

1. W. E. Vine, Merrill F. Unger, William White, Jr., *Vine's Complete Expository Dictionary of Old Testament and New Testament Words* (Nashville, TN: Thomas Nelson, 1996), 301.

Chapter 13: Choose This Day Whom You Will Serve

1. Adapted from Almy, *How Christian Is Christian Counseling?*, 82.

Chapter 14: Do You Meet the Qualifications of the Overcoming Life?

1. Danny Bond, *Overcoming Sin & Enjoying God* (Costa Mesa, CA: The Word for Today, 1996), 12 (parentheses added).
2. Roy Hession, *The Calvary Road* (Fort Washington, PA: Christian Literature Crusade, 1995), 22.
3. Ibid., 22, 29.
4. Bernall, *She Said Yes*, 119–120.
5. Ibid., 122.
6. C. S. Lewis, *Mere Christianity* (New York: Simon & Schuster, 1980), 191.
7. Hession, *The Calvary Road*, 28.
8. Bill Bright, *Have You Made the Wonderful Discovery of the Spirit-Filled Life?* (Orlando, FL: New Life Publications, 1996), 7.

Chapter 17: Overcoming Your Circumstances

1. Ray Bentley, *Dealing With Discouragement and Depression* (San Diego, CA: In the Word Books, 1999), 29.
2. Beth Nimmo and Darrell Scott, *Rachel's Tears* (Nashville, TN: Thomas Nelson, 2000), xxi.

Chapter 18: Overcoming Satan

1. Ibid., 91–92.
2. Ibid., 88.
3. Ibid., 100.

Chapter 20: Treatment That Works!

1. *San Diego North County Chapter 1999–2000 Directory* (San Diego, CA: California Association of Marriage and Family Therapists, 2000), 3.
2. Bentley, *Dealing With Discouragement and Depression*, 9.
3. Ibid., 16, 19.
4. Bernall, *She Said Yes*, 129.
5. Bobgan, *PsychoHeresy*, 69–70.
6. Nimmo and Scott, *Rachel's Tears*, xxii–xxiii.
7. Excerpted from Steve Bristol, "Shades of Gray," *Interacta Life Applications* (Orlando, FL: WSN Press, Campus Crusade for Christ, Inc., 1994), 3.

For speaking engagements please contact:

Ryan and Lisa Bazler
P.O. Box 864
Cardiff, CA 92007
Email: secondpeter13@yahoo.com